UNITED NATIONS AND WORLD PEACE

UNITED NATIONS AND WORLD PEACE

NITIN SHARMA
Department of Gandhian and Peace Studies,
Panjab University, Chandigarh

Foreword by

PROF. MANOHAR LAL SHARMA
Former Chairman, Deptt. of Gandhian and Peace Studies,
Panjab University, Chandigarh

REGAL PUBLICATIONS
New Delhi-110027

UNITED NATIONS AND WORLD PEACE

ISBN 978-81-8484-371-2

Typeset by
S.S. COMPOSERS
3190, Mohindra Park, Shakur Basti, Delhi-110034.

Printed in India at
MAYUR ENTERPRISES
WZ Plot No. 3, Gujjar Market, Tihar Village, New Delhi-110018.

Published by
REGAL PUBLICATIONS
F-159, Rajouri Garden, New Delhi-110027.
Phone: +91-11-45546396
E-mail: regalbookspub@yahoo.com

Contents

Prof. Manohar Lal Sharma
Recipient of Gandhi-Vinoba Peace Award (2008) & Pt. Nekiram Bhiwani Gaurav Samman (2012)
Former Chairman, Deptt. of Gandhian & Peace Studies, Panjab University, Chandigarh-160014

Mobile: 09417889900
email: doctormlsharma@yahoo.com

Foreword

After each of the major wars during the last over 60 years an attempt has been made to find a way of preventing future war. After the two World Wars, progressive thinkers and leaders of many countries decided to establish a system of collective security for the whole world which was still licking its wounds. So United Nations Organisation was established to maintain Peace and to save the succeeding generations from the scourge of war. Global Peace and security have been among the core missions of United Nations. At its founding in 1945, hopes were high that United Nations could serve, as a global high command to keep the peace in a post-Colonial, post-Fascist World. United Nations, thus, was expected to be a forum for amicable solutions to world conflicts.

The first serious effort to establish an international organisation for peace was made after the First World War by the then President of USA, Woodrow Wilson and as a result, the League of Nations was created. The failure of League of Nations eventually triggered the Second World War of 1939-45. It was another US President Franklin Roosevelt, who was the main inspiration behind the formation of the United Nations.

Although peace-making was really intended to be the UN's primary goal, but it has been observed by many that it has become a lost art. The UN was intended to save succeeding generations from the scourge of war; its hopes have in this respect been belied. More than 150 wars have been fought after the foundation of United Nations all over the world. The Middle East theatre of war has become so tense and witnessed in recent times two different wars in 1991 and in 1998. It is estimated that during the period from 2000 to 2050, 40.5 per cent of the population will die due to war among the nations. More dangerous than ever before, the nuclear arms are spread all over the world. In disputes between a big power and a small one, it has tended to dispense power politics rather than justice while in Third World conflicts it has kept on with good offices, mediation or peace-keeping operations instead of finding appropriate and just solutions. After the end of cold-war, the unilateral move of US-led coalition attacked Iraq without any authorisation from the UN. Also the unresolved Palestine problem, in which, according to some scholars, UN has created more wars than it has prevented. The regional organisations like NATO, Baghdad Pact, Warsaw Pact also undermined the peace making operations of UN.

Mahatma Gandhi had mastered the art and science of going to the root causes of human problems and therefore, his prescription always differed radically from the commonly accepted ones. This is very much true of his approach to the problem under consideration, that of World Peace. When we talk or think of World Peace, we normally imagine armistice negotiations, a disarmament talk or friendship treaties only, but Gandhi had a wide perspective as he emphasized on the use of 'Soul Force'. Our soul, thus, represents the entire Universe and its development makes us one with all living-beings. The basic factor in Gandhi's world view is the individual who has a soul, a will or consciousness. The individual expresses itself at various levels of human existence—local, national and international.

The force or violence based International politics, according to Gandhi, is power oriented. Power leads to competition. Competition creates in turn violence. This was noticed in the Cold War era of the world. Thus, international politics or national politics is centered on the use of force which creates only force all over the world. Gandhi on the other hand suggested that law could be adopted as the means for achieving perfect peace. Peace without love and love without peace is a kind of violence. Therefore, as he aimed, the concept of love should work replacing the use of force concept which would create the cycle of love all over and everywhere.

Theoretically United Nations seems to us an international body with core mandate of world peace by solving conflicts amicably, but in reality, for many, the picture may be a different one. In the past, the United Nations exacerbated many conflicts by blaming the Super-Powers. No major power submits any issue affecting its basic interest. In super power disputes such as the Cuba Crisis and Super-Power operations in Vietnam, the UN has been kept out. With the end of Cold-war there have been changes to the threat that the international community faces. We have instability through regional, ethnic, religious and cultural disputes. Moreover, with growing unilateral tendencies of sole Super Power: USA, after the end of Cold War, used United Nations as its proxy for furtherance of its national interests and with growing role of regional military pact like NATO undermining United Nations role as maintaining World Peace.

In view of the above facts the work in hand has covered various aspects. The study examines Gandhi's approach to manage conflicts in order to attain World Peace and also examines its viability or feasibility. It also tries to analyse the loopholes/lapses on the part of the UNO and also suggests the measures in Gandhian perspective to strengthen it for the promotion and maintenance of World Peace.

Similarly, the work also examines what were/are the challenges and constraints before United Nations in respect of its peace initiatives with main focus on the mentioned peace initiatives. Besides, the author has tried his best to examine the success and failures of UNO regarding peace initiatives..

To me the work is a fine and commendable piece of work which is quite relevant and significant work done by the researcher. It is a good addition to the subjects like International Relations and Organization and Gandhian and Peace Studies. I hope it will get a quite good response from the general readers, teachers, students and even the scholars in this field.

Chandigarh-160 014

(MANOHAR LAL SHARMA)

Acknowledgements

Today with humility, misty eyes and folded hands when I am thanking Almighty in these blissful moments, I am also expressing my innermost into words. Research is an arduous task, which involves consistent and dedicated mind with regards to the strenuous and hard labour put into it. This would only be made possible with the benediction and grace of Almighty.

It is a moment of gratification and pride to look back with a sense of contentment at the long travelled path, to be able to recapture some of the fine moments, to be able to thank the infinite number of people, some who were with me from beginning, some who joined me at some stage during the journey, whose kindness, love and blessings have brought me to this day. I wish to thank each of them by all my heart.

On the successful completion of my Ph.D. thesis, I consider it my distinct honour and privilege to express my deepest sense of gratitude and indebtedness to my venerable supervisor, Dr. Manohar Lal Sharma, Professor and Chairman, Department of Gandhian Studies, Panjab University, Chandigarh for his unstinted help, continuous encouragement and invaluable guidance, constructive criticism, precious suggestions and benevolent attention and tireless efforts without which it would not have been possible for me to execute this project successfully.

I am thankful to Professor J.N. Sharma and Dr. Ashu Pasricha for their kind cooperation during my research work. I also owe immense gratitude to Dr. Manish Sharma, whose advice, words of inspiration and immense knowledge enabled me to accomplish this study.

I owe to the moral support, sacrifices, support and encouragement they have showered on me. A stock of loving appreciation is reserved for my parents Sh. Prem Singh Sharma and Smt. Krishna Sharma, elder brother Pradeep Sharma, bhabhi Vanita and Neeraj Sharma and my sisters for their extreme affection and love that will always remain close to my heart.

My thanks are due to my friends and relatives for helping me in the arduous task of moving around for collecting the necessary material and complete my research work.

I am extremely thankful to University Grant Commission (UGC), New Delhi, for the award of J.R.F. and S.R.F. which enabled me to carry out my work comfortably. Besides, I am also grateful to the Librarian, A.C. Joshi Library, Panjab University, Chandigarh for helping me in procuring the relevant material for my study. Facilities provided by The British Library, Chandigarh, State Library, Chandigarh, National Gandhi Museum, New Delhi and The American Library, New Delhi are acknowledged with thanks. I am also very thankful to the staff of Gandhi Bhawan and Department of Gandhian Studies for their kind cooperation.

NITIN SHARMA

Preface

Although peace has a chequered history and there have been significant movements for peace throughout the recorded history of the world, yet much more emphasis is needed for the study of world peace. Peace has several meanings. Definitions of Peace range from the absence of war among nations to non-violent resolutions of strife within our communities, and to the serenity that follows resolution of internal conflicts. However, seeking greater clarity of discourse, many peace educators have defined peace as either Negative or Positive—with Negative Peace meaning only the absence of war and positive peace incorporating the promotion of social justice issues as well. Positive peace also means the satisfaction of basic human needs, such as food, shelter, health and education. It means guaranteed justice, enjoyment of all the basic human rights and fundamental freedoms. It includes an implicit set of normative assumption about the nature of justice and priorities for a better world order. Peace and Non-violence are two sides of a medal. Non-violence, according to Gandhi, is not merely a personal virtue. It is also a social virtue to be cultivated like other virtues.

After each of the major wars during the last over 50 years an attempt has been made to find a way of preventing future war. After the two World Wars, progressive thinkers and leaders of many countries determined to establish a system of collective security for the whole world which was still licking its wounds So United Nations Organisation was established to maintain Peace and to save the succeeding generations from the scourge of war. Global Peace and Security are among the core missions of United Nations. At its founding in 1945, hopes were high that United Nations could serve, as a global high command to keep the peace in a post-Colonial, post-Fascist world. United Nations thus, was to be a forum for amicable solutions to world conflicts.

Similar views were also expressed by Mahatma Gandhi, the Apostle of Peace, who advocated the settlement of conflicts by peaceful and amicable means and he pleaded that violence must be shunned. His philosophy finds echo in the charter of United Nations and other conventions which emphasize on abhorrence of use of physical force and the settlement of disputes be done away by peaceful means.

The first serious effort to establish an international organisation for peace was made after the First World War by the then President of USA, Woodrow Wilson and as a result, the League of Nations was created. The Failure of League of Nations eventually triggered the Second World War of 1939-45. It was another US President, Franklin Roosevelt, who was the main inspiration behind the formation of the United Nations.

If one analyses the UN's initiatives in direction of World Peace it has been observed that in a way it has not achieved its goal. But this does not mean that UN is a total failure in this direction. Right from its inception, UN did a commendable job in various conflicts such as Korean crisis, Congo, Lebanon crisis, etc. As per its commitment towards the World Peace, UN has established and running peace-keeping operations around the world.

Although peace-making was really intended to be the UN's primary goal, but it has been observed by many that it has become a lost art. The UN was intended to save succeeding generations from the scourge of war but hopes have in this respect been belied. More than 150 wars have been fought after the foundation of United Nations all over the world. The Middle-East theatre of war has become so tense and witnessed in recent times two different wars in 1991 and in 1998. It is estimated that during the period from 2000 to 2050, 40.5 per cent of the population will die due to war among the nations. More dangerous than ever before, the nuclear arms are spread all over the world. In disputes between a big power and a small one, it has tended to dispense power politics rather than justice while in Third World conflicts it has kept on with good offices, mediation or peace-keeping operations instead of finding appropriate and just solutions. After the end of cold-war, the unilateral move of US-led coalition attacked Iraq without any authorisation from the UN. Also the unresolved Palestine problem, in which, according to some scholars, UN has created more wars than it has prevented. The regional organisations like NATO, Baghdad Pact, Warsaw Pact also undermined the peace-making operations of UN.

Mahatma Gandhi had mastered the art and science of going to the root causes of human problems and therefore, his prescription always differed radically from the commonly accepted ones. This is very much true of his approach to the problem under consideration, that of World Peace. When we talk or think of World Peace, we normally imagine armistice negotiations, disarmament talks or friendship treaties. But Gandhi did not believe in this approach. Gandhi emphasized on the use of 'Soul Force'. Our soul, thus, represents the entire Universe and its development makes us one with all living-beings. The basic factor in Gandhi's world view is the individual who has a soul, a will or consciousness. The individual expresses itself at various levels of human existence—local, national and international.

The force or violence-based International politics, according to Gandhi, is power-oriented. Power leads to competition. Competition creates in turn violence. This was noticed in the Cold War era of the world. Thus, international politics or national politics is centered on the use of force which creates only force all over the world. Gandhi on the other hand suggested that law could be adopted as the means for achieving perfect peace. Peace without love and love without peace is violence. Therefore, as he aimed, the concept of love should work replacing the use of force concept which would create the cycle of love all over.

However, as a matter of fact the springs of disorder and violence are not to be found at the international level alone. According to Gandhi, violence permeates every sphere of life. Hence, a stable world order cannot be brought about by merely eschewing violence in international relations. The individual can achieve it by reordering his life through self-discipline, education and training and the nations of the world can achieve their objectives by restructuring their political and socio-economic structures along non-violent lines. To quote Gandhi, "...... the moral principle on which civilization rests are truth and love. If people everywhere respond to them truthfully, the world will be brought closer together and the darkness which we see around us may be dispelled."

Although the United Nations Organisation was set-up to maintain peace and to save succeeding generations from the scourge of war, yet the fact is that armed conflicts, weapons of mass destructions, unilateral move by great powers continue to undermine the position of United Nations and a grave threat to World Peace is very much visible. Envisioned as the Peace-keeper of the post-war world, the United Nations, it has been observed by many that it has been unable in most cases either to forestall war or to end a war once it was began. The major problems which threaten world stability are: ever growing arsenals of arms, eco-social justice conflicts which bring violence and destruction and despair to widespread region—all figure on the agenda of the United Nations' bodies.

Theoretically United Nations seems to us an international body with core mandate of world peace by solving conflicts amicably, but in reality, for many, the picture may be a different one. In the past the United Nations exacerbated many conflicts by blaming the Super-Powers. No major power submits any issue affecting its basic interest. In super power disputes such as the Cuba Crisis and Super-Power operations in

Vietnam, the UN has been kept out. With the end of Cold War there have been changes to the threat that the international community faces. We have instability through regional, ethnic, religious and cultural disputes. Moreover, with growing unilateral tendencies of sole Super Power: USA, after the end of Cold War, used United Nations as its proxy for furtherance of its national interests and with growing role of regional military pact like NATO undermining United Nations role as maintaining World Peace.

In view of the above facts the following objectives were kept in mind to examine and analyse the work in hand:

- To study and examine Gandhi's approach to manage conflicts in order to attain World Peace.
- To find out: could Gandhian approach be viable or feasible for World Peace?
- To analyse the loopholes/lapses on the part of the UNO (if any) and to suggest the measures in Gandhian Perspective to strengthen it for the promotion and maintenance of World Peace.
- To study and examine what were/are the challenges and constraints before United Nations in respect of its peace initiatives with main focus on the mentioned peace initiatives.
- How far United Nations has been successful in its peace operations?
- To analyse the factors which are responsible for the failure of UN in its peace initiatives, if any.
- To analyse: should the UN adopt a traditional approach to peace-making or a more comprehensive strategy incorporating conflict management, peace-keeping and conflict prevention in consonance with the present scenario.
- To examine and analyse: is there any proper say of member-states other than Super Powers in peace decision/Initiatives taken by United Nations?

NITIN SHARMA

World Peace: A Conceptual Introduction

World Peace is an ideal of freedom, peace, and happiness among and within all nations and/or people. World peace is an idea of planetary non-violence by which nations willingly cooperate, either voluntarily or by virtue of a system of governance that prevents warfare. The term is sometimes used to refer to a cessation of all hostility among all individuals. For example, World Peace could be an end to wars, fighting between any two people, fighting between people and animals, fighting between people and any living element and/or crossing boundaries via education. While world peace is theoretically possible, some believe that human nature inherently prevents it. This belief stems from the idea that humans are naturally violent, or that rational agents will choose to commit violent acts in certain circumstances. Others however believe that war is not an innate part of human nature, and that this myth in fact prevents people from reaching for world peace.[1]

CONCEPTIONS OF PEACE

The concept of peace is as old as human knowledge of society. The quest for peace has been a central motive in the life of man. From the first moment of his entrance in the worldly scene, mankind has been searching for an ideal society where men can lead a happier, worthier and more rewarding life. Peace continues to be a powerful wish, desire and a passion with millions as well as a conviction deeply felt and aspired too. All nations long for it. Leaders negotiate for it yet it remain most elusive than ever. The culture of peace is a fabric that has been woven for generations of all societies, though. Its practices are not necessarily dominated by that specific title. All over the world it has its defenders, some working in obscurity others in the spotlight of public life.

The concept of peace in our modern civilization is the facade a war, dominated by the calculations of realpolitik. This English word originates from the French concept which denotes 'agreement'—agreeing to stop a conflict or war. According to The Universal Dictionary of the English Language, the first notion of 'peace' is 'cessation of freedom from strife, warfare', and the second notion of it is 'treaty of peace between hostile nations'. In the Third notion, it is understood as, 'freedom from strife, controversy or agitation or freedom from civil disorder and disturbances. After these notions come 'tranquility, concord, mental calm, serenity of mind'.

Hindu, Jain and Buddhist traditions treat peace as peace of mind, peace of the inner self, interpersonal peace and non-violence, the moral injunction of not committing violence against nature (the biosphere) and also against micro-organisms, the Chinese and Japanese traditions focus on the culture space that is harmony and order in personal, social and global organization as well as in nature itself. Presently, we look at the problem of peace through the spectrum of beauty, creativeness and art. We regard beauty and art as the most powerful mediums in the process of mutual understanding of different nations and their peaceful co-existence.[2]

Johan Galtung, a celebrated peace researcher, in his article 'Violence, Peace and Peace Research', has stated that peace is absence of violence. This of course is not a definition of peace since it is a clear cause of what he calls obscurum per obscurcur. What is intended is only to suggest that the terms "peace" and "violence" be liked together in such a manner that peace can be regarded as absence of violence.[3]

There is no agreed upon definition of what 'peace' in reality means. This is evident from the other fact that, broadly speaking, peace has been defined in two different ways: One, to equate peace with the absence of non-peace. Definitions of peace in terms of a condition opposite of war are what Rapoport calls "definitions by exclusion."[4] For example, peace has been viewed as "respite from war", 'quiet from suits or disorder,'[5] 'rest form commotion, etc.' The range of definitions associated with the word "peace" does not give us any precise idea of what peace practically means. Peace has the potential to mean many things. The definitions of peace can vary with religious, social, cultural or of the study of things. However, two dominant interpretations of peace exists as Negative Peace; and Positive Peace. Galtung's negative and positive peace framework is the most widely used today. Negative peace refers to the absence of direct violence. Positive peace refers to the absence of indirect and structural violence, and is the concept that most peace and conflict researchers adopt.[6]

Several conceptions, models, or modes of peace have been suggested in which peace research might prosper.[7]

- The first is that peace is a natural social condition, whereas war is not. The premise is simple for peace researchers: to present enough information so that a rational group of decision-makers will seek to avoid war and conflict.
- Second, the view that violence is sinful or unskillful, and that non-violence is skillful or virtuous and should be cultivated. This view is held by a variety of religious traditions worldwide: Quakers, Mennonites and other Peace churches within Christianity; Jains, the Satyagraha tradition in Hinduism, Buddhism, and other portions of Indian religion and philosophy; as well as certain schools of Islam.
- Third is pacifism: the view that peace is a prime force in human behaviour.
- A further approach is that there are multiple modes of peace.[8]

There have been many offerings on these various forms of peace. These range from the well known works of Kant, Locke, Rousseau, Paine, on various liberal international and constitutional and plans for peace. Variations and additions have been developed more recently by scholars such as Raymond Aron, Edward Azar, John Burton, Martin Ceadal, Wolfgang Dietrich, Kevin Dooley, Johan Galtung, Michael Howard, Vivienne Jabri, Jean-Paul Lederach, Roger Mac Ginty, Hugh Miall, David Mitrany, Oliver Ramsbotham, Anatol Rapoport, Mikkel Vedby Rasmussen, Oliver Richmond, S.P. Udayakumar, Tom Woodhouse, others mentioned above and many more. Democratic Peace, liberal peace, sustainable peace, civil peace, trans-rational peace(s) and other concepts are regularly used in such work.

Negative Peace

The meaning of the peace that are usually given are mostly in the negative sense. As peace denotes bombs not falling on Bergrades, it denotes artillery and missiles are not falling, Hindus and Muslims are not rioting, bloods not driving by the cries spraying bullets through doors and windows so on and so forth. The negative peace will be discussed under three headings which are as give below:

- Absence of violence;
- Absence of antagonistic conflicts; and
- Absence of war

To start with, two compatible definitions of peace:

- Peace is the absence/reduction of violence of all kinds.
- Peace is non-violent and creative conflict transformation.

The underlying assumption in both the definitions are:

- Peace is to reduce or absence of violence by peaceful means.
- Peace is the study of the conditions of peace work.

First definition by John Galtung[9] is violence-oriented; peace being its negation, i e. if one wants to known what the peace is, he should know what the violence is? The second definition is conflict-oriented; peace is the context for conflicts to unfold non-violently and creatively. To know about peace we have to know about conflicts and how conflicts can be transformed, both non-violently and creatively. Both definitions focus on human-beings in a social settings. Therefore, Peace is the reduction of violence in non-violent way then peace and violence belinked together in such a manner that peace seems to be mere absence of violence.

Peace as Absence of Violence

Peace is often regarded as 'Absentia Belli" mean the absence of any organized violence. Like John Galtung concept of "Negative peace as absence of violence." Reardon insists that "Peace is the absence of violence in all its forms, physical, social, psychological and structural."[10] This definition is negative in a sense that it fails in providing any affirmative picture of peace or its ingredients. Reasons behind this popular version of negative concept of peace may be that peace studies tend to focus on violence as a unit of analysis rather than peace as a unit of analysis and these is a strong tendency to define peace simply as a 'Non-violence.'

The Encyclopedia of social science defines negative peace as the "absence of any organized violence between such major human groups or nations but also between social and ethical groups because of the magnitude that can be reached by internal wars."[11]

Peace as Absence of Conflicts

Absence of violence should not be confused with absence of conflicts. There may be conflicts in society but without any violence or there should be no violence but no other forms of interaction either. Can there be loving, cooperative and just peaceful society with a society of damage, slavery, injustice but without any violence? Conflicts will be there in such society through violence may be missing. Violence may occur without conflicts and conflicts can be solved non-voluntary. Is peace means absence of conflicts?[12]

Galtung is of the view that, "there is no substitute for creative conflict resolutions in breach for peace."[13] Unsolved conflicts may lead to frustration, which may again lead to aggression and ultimately to violence. Some define conflict as "a state of mutual antagonism or hostility between two or more parties."[14]

The popular meaning of conflict is quarrel between two persons or groups. It is a physical fight or verbal duel preceded by disagreement and followed by indifference and enmity. Kennth Boulding says, "conflicts exists when any potential positions of two behaviour units are mutually incompatible."[15] He further defines conflict as a situation of a competition in which the parties are aware of the incompatibility of potential future positions and in which each party wishes to occupy a position that is incompatible with wishes of the other.[16]

John Galtung suggests that a conflict moves among the triangle's three corners where comes A refers to conflicts attitude, B to conflict behaviour and C the conflict or contradiction itself (the incompatibility), A conflict sequence can begin in any of these comes. Galtung emphasis on 'C' as a more frequent starting point.[17]

FIGURE 1.1

The Conflict Triangle

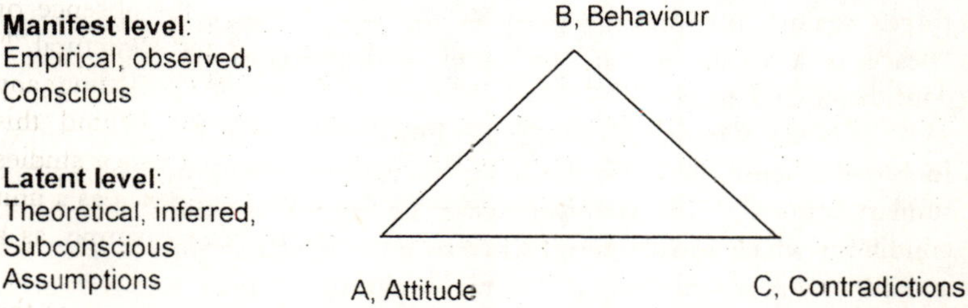

Manifest level:
Empirical, observed,
Conscious

Latent level:
Theoretical, inferred,
Subconscious
Assumptions

B, Behaviour

A, Attitude

C, Contradictions

It will be difficult to conceive of an ongoing society where conflicts are absent. The society without conflicts is a dead society. Conflicts are realty of human existence and therefore a means to understand behaviour of human-beings.

Peace as the Absence of War

Peace should not be judged by negative yardstick of absence of war or explicit violence, or control over armaments and banning of all nuclear arms and neither should we derive satisfaction from the fact that a Third World War has not taken place. A peaceful world should provide and create condition where individuals can lead fuller and richer lives, that is, a balanced development of human personality in its social, cultural, political and economic aspects. Predominance of one aspect (economic as at present) would not be conducive to peace amongst the individuals, small groups, nation-states, and to the world community at large. It should provide for a rapport between the individual and the social order and permit peaceful social-economic changes consistent with changing times and aspirations of the people. The imitation and leadership should remain with individuals and small groups. In such an order, conflicts at the individual, small groups, nationals, and international levels will be reduced to insignificant dimensions. In those rare cases where conflicts may still arise, they can be resolved speedily by peaceful methods.[18]

In the era of cold war, war has been as a form of politics a way, in which states sought to resolve certain issues in inter nation relations. Outcome of this is states' willingness to amass military power for defence and deterrence and to project it in support of their defence and foreign policy. So many writers especially of the west asserted anything that "peace is absence of war." Clausewitz said that "war is an act of force intended to compel our opponents to fulfil our will and a continuation of political intercourse with a mixture of other means."[19] Webster dictionary defines war as "state of usually open and declare armed hostile conflict between states or nations.[20] According to New English dictionary, "war is a hostile contention by means of armed forces, carried on between nations or states, the employment of armed forces against an opposing party in the state."[21] Spinoza argued that "peace is a virtue, a state of mind, a disposition for benevolence, confidence and justice."[22]

Quincy Wright defines war in a broader as well as in narrow sense. In broader sense, he defines war as: "A violent contact of distinct but similar entities."[23] In narrower sense he means by war, "The legal conditions which equally permits two or more hostile groups to carry on a conflict by armed forces."[24] Over a period of time war has been considered as legitimate instrument of state policy.

O' Kane defined peace as an vacuous, passive, simplistic and unresponsive escape mechanism too of fever resorted to in the past without success. Mere absence of war can't lead us towards peaceful states. It is a myopic version of peace. We can't ignore the feeling of mistrust and suspicion that the winners and leaders of a war harbor towards each other. The suppression of mutual hostile feelings is not taken into account by those who define peace so simply. Their stance is as long as people are not actively engaged into overt, mutual, violent, physical and destructive activity, peace keep in existing.

They define the term 'peace' to the state of affairs that are not truly peaceful. John Galtung is of the view that "No war" is a negative version of peace. Which is simply saying, "let us not destroy each other." Negative version of peace is paired with positive version of peace. Peace as absence of "violence, war and conflicts", articulated within itself a structural theory of peace, i.e. positive peace. He further said, "Peace is the absence of violence shall be retained valid."

Positive Peace

Two concepts of peace may be empirically related even though they are logically independent. According to the encyclopedia of social science, "positive peace is a pattern of cooperation and integration between major human groups. Absence of violence of combined with a pattern of cooperation."[25] Positive peace is associated with ideology, particularly as defined by John Galtung. He is the main exponent of the positive concept of peace.

Negative Versus Positive Peace

Negative peace simply denotes the absence of war. It is a condition in which no active, organized military violence is taking place. The noted 20th century French intellectual Raymond Aron was thinking of negative peace when he defined peace as a condition of "more or less lasting suspension of rivalry between political unit."[26] Aron's is the most common understanding of peace in the context of international relations, and it epitomizes the (neo-) realist view of matters of war and peace. This view suggests that peace is found whenever war or other direct forms of organized state violence are absent. For this perspective then, the peace proclamations of pharaonic Egypt, the Philanthropa, were actually statements of a negative peace, expressions of benevolence from a stronger party toward those who were weaker. The Pax of Roman times really indicated nothing more than the absence of overt interstate violence, typically a condition of non-resistance or even acquiescence enforced by legal arrangements and the military might of Roman legions. The negative peace of the Pax Romana was created and maintained through social and political repression of the people who lived under Roman Law.

An alternative view to this realist" (or Realpolitik) perspective is one that emphasizes the importance of positive peace. Positive peace is more than the mere absence of war or even the absence of interstate violence it refers to a social condition in which exploitation is minimized or eliminated, and in which there is neither overt violence nor the more subtle phenomenon of underlying structural violence.

The Role of Structural Violence

One commonly understood meaning of violence is that it is physical and readily apparent through observable bodily injury and/or the infliction of pain. But as Galtung, notes, it is important to recognize the existence of another form of violence, one that is more indirect and insidious than observable physical violence. This structural violence is typically built into the very structure of social, cultural and economic institutions. For example, both ancient Egypt and imperial Rome practiced slavery and were highly despotic, although they were technically in states of negative peace for long periods of time.

Structural violence is present when there is no concrete individual actor and the violence results from the structure and is perceived as unequal power, deprivation and unequal life chances."[27] Violence is built into the structure and shows up as unequal power and consequently as unequal life chances. Structural violence refers to inegalitarian and discriminating social structures which also indirectly inflict violence upon individuals or groups in a systematic and organized way. Slavery was an example of structural violence in the past and discrimination on the basis of race, ethnicity or gender is an example of structural violence in our time. A society in which such social structural exist is not at peace even though it may not be at war.

Structural violence = Unactualized human potentials social injustice inequality = No peace.

So the positive concept of "peace would lead us to consider not only absence of direct violence and structural violence, but presence of a non-violent type of egalitarian, non-exploitative and non-suppressive cooperation between units, nations as well as individuals."[28]

Positive Peace = Equality = Social Justice = Realized Human Potentials = Absence of Structural Violence.

Roads to Peace: the Eight-fold Path[29]

There are two types of therapies or remedies, i.e.: curative and preventive aiming at negative and positive peace respectively. And four types (with the two sub-types) of violence have been identifies. This gives us eight combinations, the 'eight-fold path'. Each combination, for instance, 'cultural power, positive peace', confronts us with a question: what can be done?

There is no place to start and certainly no place to end policies for peace. The best is to work on all eight cells at the same time. Better some moves ahead on all than a single thrust on one, hoping that the others will take care of themselves or can be easily handled afterwards. Experience with single-factor peace theories has generally been negative. Kant hoped for republics and democracy, liberals for free trade and democracy, Marxists for social production and guided democracy, mondialists for a strong UN. Peace did not follow in their wake.

Most proposals aim at the world as a system of countries with states inside them: the inter-country system usually called the inter-state system. With slight modifications they also apply to inter-gender, inter-generation, inter-class and inter-nation (ethnic) systems; all relevant today.

People working for world peace, whether in the state system or the non-state system of organizations, will recognize something; few will recognize all the points made or necessarily agree. That debate is essential if peace movement is to grow and become at least as influential as the anti-slavery and anti-colonialist movements were intheir time. Being against war is a good moral position, but the questions of *alternatives to war* and the conditions for *abolition of war* will not disappear. They have to be addressed.

Dimensions of Peace

The Political Dimension

Democracy is a great idea, but it has been badly understood in relation to inter-state affairs. If a democracy works well within a country it will, in principle, produce a relatively content population that, on the average and over time, gets much of its wishes satisfied, within the limits of the feasible. Again, in principle this should lead to a peace surplus inside the country, with democracy functioning as a non-violent arbiter between parts of the population vying with each other for power and privilege. But there is no guarantee that this intra-state peace surplus will translate into peaceful activity in the inter-state system. The democracy has to be global, in the inter-state system, in the world system. But that system is today conservative-feudal, not liberal-democratic.

That opens for two approaches: making the inter-state system more democratic, and making the intra-state system even more peaceful, with democratic means. Both are laudable goals and approaches: there is no need to justify a more democratic country with the (at best unproven, at worst blatantly wrong) assumption that infra-peace translates automatically into inter-peace. If that were the case, the leading democracies in the world today would not also have been slaving, colonialist, and highly belligerent in general—except for the smaller democracies, which probably are peaceful more because they are small than because they are democratic. This also works the other way: a democratic inter-state system does not automatically guarantee that all component parts will become democracies overnight.

The most direct approach is to democratize the inter-state system. One country/one vote is a formula that could be applied to the Bretton

Woods institutions, reducing the money power of the richest countries in the world. This would probably also reduce the credit available. The question is whether the World Bank record makes that eventuality so deplorable. Obviously, the formula rules out Big Power veto—that has to go.

Military Dimension

The argument made here is not to abolish the military but to give it new tasks. That institutions had very bad habits in the past, such as attacking other countries and nations, and other classes usually at the behest of the ruling elites, killing and devastating through external and internal wars. But there have also been virtues: good organization, courage, willingness to sacrifice. The bad habits have to go; not necessarily the military, and certainly not the virtues.

Let us give the military new tasks, substituting defensive defense with defensive means (short-range conventional military, para-military and non-military defense) for aggressive external warfare. Pure defense provokes nobody and causes no fear, yet makes it clear that attacks will be strongly resisted.

Peace-keeping forces can be used to prevent aggressiveness, even in places where there has been no open display of violence (but good reasons to assume that something may happen). One idea may be to station such forces preventively in the 30-odd small countries without military forces, to forestall the possibility of some Big Brother demanding to be a 'protector' in crisis.

But this is not enough. There has to be further development along non-violent lines, delegitimizing arms, non-violent skills, reducing the conventional and para-military components, at the same time building up non-military defense, turning to civilian peace-keeping and to international peace brigades in hot areas. We are at the threshold of such important endeavours; they must be developed much further. The military are hereby invited!

There is also a negative side to all of this. The long-term goal is the abolition of war as an institution, like the abolition of slavery and colonialism as institutions—an entirely realistic goal, but demanding difficult and absolutely necessary. Of course, there will still the violence around, some still organized collectively as wars. But it will not be institutionalized, and not internalized, nor legitimate. What upholds war? Many factors, three of them being patriarchy (rule by the male gender of the human species), the state system with its monopoly on violence, and the super-state or superpower system with the ultimate monopoly of the hegemons. Males more than females tend toward violence; and those who possess arms tend to think and act according to the old adage that to the person with a hammer the world looks like a nail. Incidentally, this is not necessarily so because such a person is violent, but because he has the use of military power as both profession and monopoly and simply wants to be relevant.

To fight patriarchy means fighting patriarchal cultures and structures and arriving at a motor equitable power-sharing between the genders. The danger is that, in the process of the struggle women may take on some of the male values they are fighting.

The struggle against the tendency of states to seek recourse to military power goes by way alternatives that are more compelling. And the struggle against hegemonic tendencies in the world society of societies goes by way of democratization of that society, creating alliances of non-hegemonic countries within or across their 'spheres of interest', and through decision-making of the one country/one vote variety.

The Economic Dimension

The problem here is not only economic practice, but also economic theory with its carefully nurse neglect of the side-effects of economic activity the externalities. Some of them are positive, like the *challenge* derived from taking on complex problems for which there are no immediate, routine solutions. And some of them are negative, like *ecological degradation,* not to mention *human degradation.* They are not reflected in economic theory, or at most as side and after-thoughts. Economists focus on quantities and prices of products, goods, and services offered on the market without reflecting whether they might also be bads and disservices. Such variables are referred to as *internalities,* internal to the paradigm. One example is 'terms of exchange', the quantity of one product needed to get in exchange a constant quantity of another product, like how much oil for one tractor. Another approach would be to compare the working hours needed.

Exploitation means that one party gets much more out of a deal than the other—measured by the sum of internalities and externalities. The terms of exchange may be bad and getting worse: in addition, one party gets all the challenge, leaving the routine work to the other, who also gets ecological and human degradation in the bargain. As this is a fairly adequate description of the trade between rich (not all in the North) and poor (not all in the South) countries in the world today, we are dealing with a key case of structural violence. This condition often leads to direct violence intended to change or to maintain the structure, and is solidly protected by the cultural violence provided by mainstream theory. A heavy triangle of violence.[33]

The Cultural Dimension

Why do people kill? Partly because they are brought up that way—not directly to kill, but to see killing as legitimate under some conditions. That brings us to culture, that great legitimizes of violence, but also of peace. Where do we find the key carriers of violence? The easy answer would be 'religion and ideology', since people are known to kill in the name of either. However, not ill religions or ideologies are violent; some are even outspoken in their advocacy of non-violence. Or, to use the formulation preferred here: religions and ideologies can come in hard and soft varieties, the harder varieties tending to focus on some abstract, transcending goal and the softer ones on empathy, even compassion. Examples of the former world be the triumph of it transcendent God, for instance in the occidental version of a male deity 'in the heavens'; of some political over the world (capitalism, socialism, democracy, fascism); of some 'great' nation. Examples of softer or gentler goals would be an immanent God, as 'that-of-everyone' satisfaction of concrete basic needs in concrete human-beings; regard for all life.

Obviously, the greatest occidental religions and ideologies, Islam and Christianity, liberalism and Marxism (the latter will probably have some kind of comeback) have streaks of both, so we should speak of hard and soft 'aspects' rather than hard and soft religions and ideologies, or even of hard and soft varieties. In addition, all four are also *singularist,* claiming to be the single, valid carrier of truth, and *universalist,* claiming validity all over the world and for all future time.

Such faiths become particularly dangerous when they define a *chosen people* (gender, generation, race, class, nation) with the right and duty to spread and defend the faith. The occidental faiths (and not only those) have elements of this, the archetype being the Judaic of a Chosen People with a Promised Land. All such notions should be challenged, replete as they are with violence and war. And violence itself should be challenged directly. In the pragmatic West that is perhaps best done by pointing out how *violence breeds violence,* probably one of the safer propositions of social science. And the best form of challenge is dialogue. Christianity comes in hard and soft varieties; the dialogue between the two varieties within a faith may be more meaningful to the believers than ecumenical dialogues across faiths. One approach need not exclude the other, however.

Therefore, the best approach is probably a positive one. The four systems criticized above are carriers of a faith maximum, with answers to (almost) everything. To demand the same belief from everybody is like prescribing the same size shoes for all. And yet, a world civilization needs some faith minimum.

WORLD PEACE THEORIES

Many theories as to how world peace could be achieved have been proposed. Several of these are listed below. World peace is achievable when there is no longer conflict over resources. For example, oil is one such resource and conflict over the supply of oil is well known. Therefore, developing technology that utilizes reusable fuel sources may be one way to achieve world peace. The definition of "peace" can vary with religion, culture, or subject of study.

Peace is a state of balance and understanding in yourself and between others, where respect is gained by the acceptance of differences, tolerance persists, conflicts are resolved through dialog, people's rights are respected and their voices are heard, and everyone is at their highest point of serenity without social tension.

Game Theory

The Peace War Game is a game theory approach to peace and conflict studies. An iterated game originally played in academic groups and by computer simulation for years to study possible strategies of co-operation and aggression.[31] As peace-makers became richer over time, it became clear that making war had greater costs than initially anticipated. The only strategy that acquired wealth more rapidly was a "Genghis Khan", a constant aggressor making war continually to gain resources. This led to the development of the "provokable nice guy" strategy, a peace-maker until attacked, improved upon merely to win by occasional forgiveness even when attacked. Multiple players continue to gain wealth cooperating with each other while bleeding the constant aggressor. Such actions led in essence to the development of the Hanseatic League for trade and mutual defense following centuries of Viking depredation.[32]

Democratic Peace Theory

The democratic peace theory holds that democracies will never go to war with one another. Proponents of the controversial democratic peace theory claim that strong empirical evidence exists that democracies never or rarely wage war against each other.[33] (the only exceptions being the Cold Wars, the Turbot War and Operation Fork). Jack Levy (1988) made an oft-quoted assertion that the theory is "as close as anything we have to an empirical law in international relations."

An increasing number of nations have become democratic since the Industrial Revolution. A world peace may thus become possible if this trend continues and if the democratic peace theory is correct.

Active Peace Theory

Borrowing from the teachings of Johan Galtung, Norwegian co-founder of the field of Peace Research, on 'Positive Peace',[34] and on the writings of Maine Quaker Gray Cox, a consortium of researchers and disputants in the experimental John Woolman College initiative have arrived at a theory of Active Peace. This theory posits that Peace is part of a triad, which also includes justice and wholeness (or well-being), consonant with scriptural scholarly interpretations of the meaning of the early Hebrew word S-L-M or 'Shalom', called by some the Bible's word for salvation, justice, and peace. Furthermore, the consortium have integrated Galtung's teaching of the meanings of the terms peace-making, peace-keeping, and peace-building, to also fit into a triadic formulation. Vermont Quaker John V. Wilmerding, Jr., founder of John Woolman College, posits five stages of growth applicable to individuals, communities, and societies, whereby one transcends first the 'surface' awareness that most people have of these kinds of issues, emerging successively into acquiescence, pacifism, passive resistance, active resistance, and finally into Active Peace, dedicating themselves to peace-making, peace-keeping, and/or peace-building.[35]

Many Peaces

Following Wolfgang Dietrich, Wolfgang Sützl[36] and the Innsbruck School of Peace Studies, some peace thinkers have abandoned any single and all-encompassing definition of peace. Rather, they promote the idea of Many Peaces. They argue that since no singular, correct definition of peace can exist, peace should be perceived as a plurality. This post-modern understanding of peace(s) was based on the philosophy of Jean Francois Lyotard. It served as a fundament for the more recent concept of trans-rational peace(s) and elicitive conflict transformation.

Trans-rational Peaces

In 2008, Wolfgang Dietrich enlarged his earlier approach of the Many Peaces to the so called "five families" of peace interpretations: the energetic, moral, modern, post-modern and trans-rational approach.[37] Trans-rationality unites the rational and mechanistic understanding of modern peace in a relational and culture-based manner with spiritual narratives and energetic interpretations.[38] The systemic understanding of trans-rational peaces advocates a client-centred method of conflict transformation, the so-called elicitive approach.[39]

Various Political Ideologies

World peace is sometimes claimed to be the inevitable result of a certain political ideology. According to former US President George W. Bush: "The march of democracy will lead to world peace."[40] Leon Trotsky, a Marxist theorist, assumed that the world revolution would lead to a communist world peace.[41]

Capitalism Peace Theory

In her "capitalism peace theory," Ayn Rand holds that the major wars of history were started by the more controlled economies of the time against the freer ones and that capitalism gave mankind the longest period of peace in history—a period during which there were no wars, involving the entire civilized world—from the end of the Napoleonic wars in 1815 to the outbreak of World War I in 1914.

It must be remembered that the political systems of the nineteenth century were not pure capitalism, but mixed economies. The element of capitalism, however, was dominant; it was as close to a century of capitalism as mankind has come. But the element of statism kept growing throughout the nineteenth century, and by the time it blasted the world in 1914, the governments involved were dominated by statist policies.[42]

However, this theory ignores the brutal colonial wars waged by the western nations against countries outside Europe; as well as the German and Italian Wars of Unification, the Franco-Prussian war, and other conflicts in Europe. It also posits a lack of war as the barometer for peace, when in reality class antagonisms were ever present.

One could argue that the argument is based on a non-sequitur fallacy since it may not have been *capitalism* that was the cause but rather the little state authority, which would make it an argument for anarchism in general, ranging from anarcho-capitalism to anarcho-communism, and not necessarily capitalism.

Cobdenism

There are proponents[43] of cobdenism who claim that by removing tariffs and creating international free trade, wars would become impossible, because free trade prevents a nation from becoming self-sufficient, which is a requirement for long wars. An example is, if one country produces firearms and another produces ammunition, the two could not fight each other, because the former would be unable to procure ammunition and the latter would be unable to obtain weapons.

Critics argue that free trade does not prevent a nation from establishing some sort of emergency plan to become temporarily self-sufficient in case of war or that a nation could simply acquire what it needs from a different nation. A good example of this, is World War I. Both Britain and Germany managed to become partially self-sufficient during the war. This is particularly important, due to the fact Germany had no plan for creating a War Economy.

More generally, other proponents argue that free trade—while not making wars impossible—will make wars, and restrictions on trade caused by wars, very costly for international companies with production, research, and sales in many different nations. Thus, a powerful lobby—not present if there are only national companies—will argue against wars.

Mutual Assured Destruction

Mutual assured destruction (sometimes known as MAD) is a doctrine of military strategy in which a full-scale use of nuclear weapons by two opposing sides would effectively result in the destruction of both the attacker and the defender.[44] Proponents of the policy of mutual assured destruction during the Cold War attributed this to the increase in the lethality of war to the point where it no longer offers the possibility of a net gain for either side, thereby making wars pointless.

Globalization

Some see a trend in national politics by which city-states and nation-states have unified, and suggest that the international arena will eventually follow suit. Many countries such as China, Italy, the United States, Germany, India, and Britain have unified into single nation-states, with others like the European Union following suit, suggesting that further globalization will bring about a unified world order.

Isolationism and Non-interventionism

Proponents of isolationism and non-interventionism claim that a world made up of many nations can peacefully coexist as long as they each establish a stronger focus on domestic affairs and do not try to impose their will on other nations.

Non-interventionism should not be confused with isolationism. Isolationism, like non-interventionism advises avoiding interference into other nation's internal affairs, but also emphasizes protectionism and restriction of international trade and travel. Non-interventionism, on the other hand, advocates combining free trade (like Cobdenism) with political and military non-interference.

Nations like Japan are perhaps the best known for establishing isolationist policies in the past. The Japanese Edo, Tokugawa, initiated the Edo Period, an isolationist period where Japan cut itself off from the world as a whole. This is a well-known isolation period and well documented in many areas.

Self-organized Peace

World peace has been depicted[45] as a consequence of local, self-determined behaviours that inhibit the institutionalization of power and ensuing violence. The solution is not so much based on an agreed agenda, or an investment in higher authority whether divine or political, but rather a self-organized network of mutually supportive mechanisms, resulting in a viable politico-economic social fabric. The principle technique for inducing convergence is thought experiment, namely, Backcasting, enabling anyone to participate no matter what cultural background, religious doctrine, political affiliation or age demographic. Similar collaborative mechanisms are emerging from the Internet around open-source projects, including Wikipedia, Need Peace, and the evolution of social media.

Economic Norms Theory

Economic Norms Theory links economic conditions with institutions of governance and conflict, distinguishing personal clientelist economies from impersonal market-oriented ones, identifying the latter with permanent peace within and between nations.[46]

Through most of human history societies have been based on personal relations: individuals in groups know each other and exchange favors. Today in most lower-income societies hierarchies of groups distribute wealth based on personal relationships among group leaders, a process often linked with clientelism and corruption. Michael Mousseau argues that in this kind of socio-economy conflict is always present, latent or overt, because individuals depend on their groups for physical and economic security and are thus loyal to their groups rather than their states, and because groups are in a constant state of conflict over access to state coffers. Through processes of bounded rationality, people are conditioned towards strong in-group identities and are easily swayed to fear outsiders, psychological predispositions that make possible sectarian violence, genocide, and terrorism.[47]

Market-oriented socio-economies are integrated not with personal ties but the impersonal force of the market where most individuals are economically dependent on trusting strangers in contracts enforced by the state. This creates loyalty to a state that enforces the rule of law and contracts impartially and reliably and provides equal protection in the freedom to contract – that is, liberal democracy. Wars cannot happen within or between nations with market-integrated economies because war requires the harming of others, and in these kinds of economies everyone is always economically better off when others in the market are also better-off, not worse-off. Rather than fight, citizens in market-oriented socio-economies care deeply about everyone's rights and welfare, so they demand economic growth at home and economic cooperation and human rights abroad. In fact, nations with market-oriented socio-economies tend to agree on global issues[48] and not a single fatality has occurred in any dispute between them.[49]

Economic norms theory should not be confused with classical liberal theory. The latter assumes that markets are natural and that freer markets promote wealth.[50] In contrast, Economic norms theory shows how market-contracting is a learned norm, and state spending, regulation, and redistribution are necessary to ensure that most everyone can participate in the "social market" economy, which is in everyone's interests.

RELIGIOUS VIEWS

Many religions and religious leaders have expressed a desire for an end to violence and/or world peace.

Bahá'í Faith

With specific regard to the pursuit of world peace, Bahá'u'lláh of the *Bahá'í Faith* prescribed a world-embracing *collective security* arrangement as necessary for the establishment of a lasting peace. The Universal *House of Justice* wrote about the process in *The Promise of World Peace*.[51]

The Bahá'í Faith arose from Islam in the 1800s based on the teachings of Baha'u'lláh and is now a distinct worldwide faith. The faith's followers believe that God has sent nine great prophets to mankind through whom the Holy Spirit has revealed the "Word of God." This has given rise to the major world religions. Although these religions arose from the teachings of the prophets of one God, Bahá'í's do not believe they are all the same.[52] The differences in the teachings of each prophet are due to the needs of the society they came to help and what mankind was ready to have revealed to it. Bahá'í beliefs promote gender and race equality, freedom of expression and assembly, world peace and world government. They believe that a single world government led by Bahá'ís will be established at some point in the future. The faith does not attempt to preserve the past but does embrace the findings of science. Bahá'ís believe that every person has an immortal soul which can not die but is freed to travel through the spirit world after death.[53]

The Bahá'í community thus provides a model of a global society equipped to meet the challenges and opportunities inherent in establishing a new world order where peace is an achievable reality rather than a utopian ideal. As such, its experience is worthy to study by individuals or organizations seriously investigating the issues of the world peace.

Shinto

Shinto is an ancient Japanese religion, closely tied to nature, which recognizes the existance of various "Kami" nature dieties. The first two deities, Izanagi and Izanami, gave birth to the Japanese islands and their children became the deities of the various Japanese clans. One of their daughters, Amaterasu (Sun Goddess), is the ancestress of the Imperial Family and is regarded as the chief deity. All the Kami are benign and serve only to sustain and protect. They are not seen as separate from humanity due to sin because humanity is "Kami's Child." Followers of Shinto desire peace and believe all human life is sacred. They revere "musuhi", the Kami's creative and harmonizing powers, and aspire to have "makoto", sincerity or true heart. Morality is based upon that which is of benefit to the group. There are "Four Affirmations" in Shinto:

- Tradition and family: the family is the main mechanism by which traditions are preserved.
- Love of nature: nature is sacred and natural objects are to be worshipped as sacred spirits.
- Physical cleanliness: they must take baths, wash their hands, and rinse their mouth often.
- "Matsuri": festival which honors the spirits.

Confucianism and Neo-Confucianism

K'ung Fu Tzu (Confucius) was born in 551 BCE in the state of Lu in China. He traveled throughout China giving advice to its rulers and teaching. His teachings and writings dealt with individual morality and ethics, and the proper exercise of political power. He stressed the following values:

- Li: ritual, propriety, etiquette, etc.
- Hsiao: love among family members
- Yi: righteousness
- Xin: honesty and trustworthiness
- Jen: benevolence towards others; the highest Confucian virtue
- Chung: loyalty to the state, etc.

With the advent of the Neo-Confucian thinkers in the Sung Dynasty (960-1279) there came a reintegration of Confucian themes into a metaphysically more profound understanding of the universe.[54] "The Great Harmony" of Chang Tsai (Chang Heng-Ch'u, 1020-1077) was an intellectual achievement with consolidated Confucian ethics and principles of governing into a harmonious unity comprehend the universe. Having constructed a rationalistic and naturalistic theory on the basis of the universal presence of the principle of vital individuation, ch'i, Chang could claim a metaphysical grounding for a universally comprehensive ethical value of benevolence, jen.[55]

Taoism

Taoism was founded by Lao-Tse, a contemporary of Confucius in China. Taoism began as a combination of psychology and philosophy which Lao-Tse hoped would help end the constant feudal warfare and other conflicts of his time. His writings, the Tao-te-Ching, describe the natuie of life, the way to peace and how a ruler should lead his life. Taoism became a religion in 440 CE when it was adopted as a state religion.

Tao, roughly translated as *path*, is a force which flows through all life and is the first cause of everything. The goal of everyone is to become one with the Tao. Tai Chi, a technique of exercise using slow deliberate movements, is used to balance the flow of energy or "chi" within the body. People should develop virtue and seek compassion, moderation and humility.[56] One should plan any action in advance and achieve it through minimal action. Yin (dark side) and Yang (light side) symbolize pairs of opposites which are seen through the universe, such as good and evil, light and dark, male and female. The impact of human civilization upsets the balance of Yin and Yang. Taoists believe that people are by nature, good, and that one should be kind to others simply because such treatment will probably be reciprocated.[57]

Buddhism

Many Buddhists believe that world peace can only be achieved if we first establish peace within our minds. Sidhartha Gautama, the founder of Buddhism, said, "Peace comes from within. Do not seek it without."[58] The idea is that anger and other negative states of mind are the cause of wars and fighting. Buddhists believe people can live in peace and harmony only if we abandon negative emotions such as anger in our minds and cultivate positive emotions such as love and compassion.

Buddhism began in India about 500 years before the birth of Christ.[59] Buddhism started its career as a protest against the formalism of Brahmanism and opposed its essential theories concerning the nature of soul and God. The religion was started by Gautama Buddha who was a contemporary of Mahavira.[60]

Gautama or sidhartha was born in the year 566 B.C. He was the son of Shudhodana, the chief of the Shakya clan of Kapilavastu.[61] He belongs to a royal Hindu family, but from his very chilhood he seemed to have no attraction for his princely life and was always found in a pensive and despondent mood. He was very much concerned about the unabated suffering of man throughout his life-time. Birth, various diseases, old age and death—all are signs of suffering and Gautama wanted to find out a paremanent cure to all these sufferings of man. Being overpressed by such concern, one night while all were engaged in rejoice connected with the birth of a son to Gautama's wife Yashodhara, he himself left the house forever and went out in search of real knowledge—Bodhi or prajna—with the help of which people will be saved. He got intuitive light or Bodhi while he was in a samadhi beneath a tree in Bodh-Gaya. Thence forward, he was begun to be called the Buddha, the enlightened one. Buddha worked day and night to instruct people regarding the path through which they could save themselves from the pangs of worldly suffering. He pointed out that birth was at the root of all suffering and therefore it was to be avoided. The real cause behind man's suffering was the result of ignorance (Ajnama). If this ignorance could be removed, man could attain a state which was called the sate of Nirvana.

This state is a state of permanent cessation of all suffering and positively a state of perfect peace and equanimity. For the attainment of this state and removal of ignorance, Buddha pointed to an eight-fold path (Astangika marga) to be followed by each and every man.

This eight-fold path was neither one of complete indulgence nor one complete asceticism. It was a middle path (Majjhima nikaya) Mitch consisted of eight disciples—Right understanding (Samyaka Karmanta), Right livedihood (Samyaka ajiva), Right effort (Samyaka Vyityarna), Right mindfulness (Samyaka Smrti) and Right concentration (Samyaka Samadhi).

Buddhism, in its original form, a practical religion of pure ethical discipline. It is a man-centered religion, totally humanistic in its outlook, approach and aim. It concerns itself with human life and puts forth ways and means so as to tide over the present problems of conditioned existence. In its essence, therefore, Buddhism gives us a way of life intended not for persons belonging to any particular caste or nationality but universally for all. It believes that every man can be a light unto himself (Atma Dipo Bhava), a saviour of himself. Man is not to seek the grace of any power superior to him. He is himself sufficient for improving his condition and that by adopting the eight-fold path.

Buddhism does not believe in any God and so does not follow any rituals. Buddha himself was begun to be treated as God and was believed to have incarnated himself on earth.

Buddhism accepted certain values of Hindu religion while it rejected certain other values. It gave no place to God and soul. Yet it gave place to *"Karma"*, *"Dharma"*, "Sansar" and "Maya", etc. According to Buddha, "Karma" links us from one life to another and not the soul. He accepts rebirth but does not accept soul. He does not believe in the authority of God but believes in "Nirvana." He rejected wnticity and divine nature of Vedas. He opposed animal sacrifice in Yajanas. He opposed caste system and the dominance of Brahmins. He thought that all human-beings are equal. None was high or low.

Buddhism is a righteous path purely dedicated to the acquisition of world peace. The fundamental principles of Buddhism is bring about peace and harmony in the world. The doctrine of emancipation as expounded in Buddhism can be categorized in terms of peace into two stages. The first stage is called relative peace and is technically known as Lokiya Shanti. This can be achieved in this complex-world by organizing one's own mental dispostion and keeping oneself fit to Buddha. The second stage is absolute peace or Parama Shanty, the achievement of this parallel and simultaneous with the attainment of Nibbaba, the ultimate goal in Buddhism.

Peace in Buddhism in its relative sense is an end by itself but a means to an end. In the absolute sense it is end by itself. The Buddhist answer to world peace is very clear but difficult to achieve, yet without having it, on amount of treaties and pacts written on paper can produce real peace in the world. The first stanza of the Dharmapana teaches that all unrest, all conflicts, and all disturbances are first born in the mind. War and conflicts are nothing but external manifestations of greed, hatred, ill will, violence, and ignorance born in the minds of men.

Buddha has preached that it is an arduous task to be born as human being and that no effort should be spared to make life happy and gay on a virtuous footing. A person deprived of the comforts of life will not have the peaceful environment which is essential for the achievement of absolute peace.

Poverty, disease, and ignorance have been referred to as three impediments to peace. In the Chakkvatti Sihanada Sutra, stealing falsehood, and violence are referred to as three offenses resulting from poverty. It is also stated that in establishing peace in a country, the virtues, temperaments, schemes, and programs of the ruler could play a part of great importance. When the ruler becomes just and righteous, his ministers, soldiers, and subjects would also follow suit and their turn ensure total peace. When the ruler becomes unjust, impatient, and unrighteous, the whole country becomes unrighteous and the extinction of peace will result.

Because there were oppressive rulers during the Buddha's time as there are today, the Buddha preached ten-fold virtues which should be adhered to by every good ruler:

- The treasury of the state should be utilized for the welfare of the masses, according to necessity and without avarice. A ruler should not distribute the state income among his chosen friends, selfishly or with prejudice.
- He should be of excellent character; he should act honesty and desist from falsehood.
- He should sacrifice his surplus wealth and excessive comforts for the sake of the state.

- He should not be prejudiced by craving, malice, fear or delusion and should act in a straight forward manner.
- He should be kind-hearted toward the subjects.
- He should lead a life of austerity.
- He should not harbor malice.
- He should not inflict pain on anyone and should never wreak vengeance.
- He should be of moderate temperament, and should bear censure and praise alike.
- He should respects public opinion.

When a ruler endowed with these ten-flod virtues administers a country, it is certain that the people will enjoy peace and harmony. We come across several regions of such in world history, of these, the great Ashoka era of India remains unsurpassed.

Another important factor for the establishment of peace is to rid the people of poverty. Buddha says it is the duty of a state to fulfil the preliminary requirements of the people food, clothing, and shelter. It is not possible for a person in hunger to observe virtuous principles. The Dharmapada gives a reference to an instance where the Buddha preached the dharma to a hunger stricken person only after providing win with a good meal to satiate his hunger.

The health of the public is another important factor in the maintenance of a society. Buddha said that health is the greatest of man. Education is yet another factor that is indispensable the peace of a country. The Buddha has said that the uneducated like an uncollected person.

The breach of peace culminated in war between two countries. In analyzing the root cause of war, it may be observed that the cause is mainly the result of the wrongful path followed in consequence of defilements such as craving, ill will and hatred. War is either the result of desire for prestige or of territorial ambition. The cause for war also may be the result of craving for conquering a country or a regional border dispute. More often than not, mighty kings, being intoxicated with their power and wealth, wage war against small kingdoms governed by puny rulers.

According to Buddhism, perpetual peace in this world could be obtained by dispelling these defilements. The major part of Buddhist Philosophy comprises discourses designed for the formation of a happy and peaceful nation. Buddhism emphasizes the following requirements to be fulfilling in order to stabilize peace in the world

- A Program should be formulated to rid society of poverty.

- Action should be taken to inaugurate schemes to produce ample supplies of foodstuffs for the people, schemes to be sponsored by both the state and the private sector.
- While advice as to the prevention of diseases should be given, steps should also be taken to convince the people that cleanliness is an integral of good living.
- Facilities should be provided which would enable everyone to get a sound education.
- People should be enlightened as to the ways of electing rulers electing capable of following the ten-fold royal precepts.
- A social reformation should be effected with a view to curbing defilements such as lust, hatred, and ignorance. All modes of propaganda should be used to achieve this end. Efforts should be made to build a society of men with very high ideals. For this purpose, school books, newspapers, and periodicals should be used.
- Necessary steps should be taken to negotiate peace talks among the countries not at war.[62]

From the very outset Buddha unambiguously proclaimed ahimsa and universal love for the other beings being the basis of living and human lifestyle. The principles of metta (friendliness), karuna (compassion), and anukampa (sympathy) state an attitude in which killing of another person, another life becomes unthinkable. Between the 7th and 5th century B.C., Jainism and Buddhism made their historical contributions. The old tribal structure was disintegrating. A number of small regional kingdoms appeared. The development of organised states and the advance of material culture in relative terms, were accompanied by the spread of ideas which were soon to become fundamental to India's thought and way of life.

These times in India were marked by continuing social change and intellectual ferment. It will be relevant for our purpose to note that "Rightmindfulness" is an important element in Buddha's teachings, and give 'bhavanas', or states of mind that is a part of the noble eight-fold path.[63] In the sphere of interpersonal relations, Buddhism inculcated a gentle and a humanitarian ethic based chiefly on duty and fellowship, as it did in the relations between human-beings and animals. The message was both for the monastic community and the people at large. Buddhism certainly had, and still has, that message travelling far beyond the monastery to the millions of ordinary people who may yet rise in the scale of being by love, compassion and non-injury and by fair dealing with "the others." Historically, it will be true to say that the practice of "metta," mindfulness of friendliness poured out by those who directly followed Buddha did have a very positive effect on the life of the people and on the then society.[64] It moulded the behaviour and attitudes of the people.

The idea of love and forbearance in one's personal relations is another emphasis of the Buddhist way condemning acts of violence on the parts of individuals. "Never in this world is hate appeased by hatred. It is only appeased by love—This is an eternal law."[65] A clear condemnation of warfare stands out in such lines as "Victory breeds hatred for the defeated lie down in sorrow; above victory or defeat, the calm man dwells in peace."[66]

There was a peace movement (not in the sense of agitation or protest processions) that helped the then society work for peace through such acts which declared men to be worthy of respect, not through birth, but through spiritual or moral merit. This movement tended obviously against the extreme manifestations of inequality in the then society. The free discussion system among the monks, among the people tended towards democracy and certainly mitigated autocracy of the rulers of those days. It created a more rational attitude towards the state.

Although Buddhism did not concentrate only on the question of war, a number of passages clearly oppose war. There is little doubt that Buddhism positively contributed to the change in the direction of mildness and non-violence that had taken place between 300 B.C. when Megasthenes (Greek) visited India and wrote his accounts of conditions in ancient India and 400 A.D. when Fa-hien (Chinese) left an account of his visit to India. Buddhism was the greatest single factor for the peace movement that affected the life of the people and the rulers, and promoted tolerance and non-violence as a part of their lifestyle.

Panchsheel, or the code based on five principles, which is well accepted in India and has influenced her present-day international relations, originates from the Buddhist concept that underlines peace,[67] ahimsa, friendship, love and compassion.

The Emperor Ashoka (268-233 B.C) of the Maurya dynasty according to his own testimony on the rock edict XIII[68] was deeply influenced by the non-violent and "the other concerned" way of life that the words and examples of Buddha inspired. Earlier, he was a ruler who did not reject war for expansion.

But he was so moved by remorse at the bloodshed and killing caused by an aggressive war which he had waged in Kalinga that he looked for a way to redeem himself from this terrible violence in which he as a king had enmeshed himself. He experienced a complete change of heart and the worth of non-violence. He adopted the Buddhist way of life the basis of which was universal love and ahimsa. He internalized the teachings of Buddha. His inscriptions on rocks, the earliest written records in India's history, testify to his dedication to peace and non-violence. Peace and non-violence as a way of life received a tremendous impetus from Ashoke. He built stupas, endowed monasteries and spread the message of peace and non-violence, throughout his empire. For the first time, the message of peace and love, the message of Buddha was carried over the whole of India by a number of messengers and teachers (also called 'missionaries' by historians of the English world). Shri Lanka accepted the message of Buddha after Mahinda spread it there. The promotion of forgiveness[69] in interpersonal relations and in relations between different people[70] moderation in everything, and peace[71] as far as possible made an impact on the way of life of his people his own life acting as a model and an example. The Buddhist way was against animal sacrifice and encouraged vegetarianism though it did not impose it. Ashoke promoted this way of life and people responded.

The social impact of all this was great. Harmony within the family, consideration for the older people and the teachers (guru), compassion for all creatures became a part of lifestyle.[72] Giving gifts, friendly ways with relatives and companions were important and considered moral.[73] Medicines were provided for human-beings and animals. The ruler felt a responsibility, moral and ethical, for his people and cared for their happiness and well-being. In numerous passages Ashoke speaks of the hard work that all this demanded of him. He gave up many of the traditional pleasures of the then kings in order to further his policy of peace and kindliness, and to inspire his people in to do so.[74] Tolerance of other ways of life, and of people of other religions was a special feature of Ashoke's understanding of non-violence. He called on the people to do likewise and himself set the example.[75] He believed progress lay in being Righteous, consciously.

At the end of the eighteenth year of his change of heart, Ashoke reviewed his work as a leader of his people and said: "In many ways the kings of olden time have worked for the welfare of the world but what I have done has been done that many may conform to Righteousness."[76] Ashoke was rewarded with the knowledge that people did accept the "good deeds" and noble thoughts he did and conveyed respectively. A change for better relations and harmony within the family and society, tolerance for others, compassion for the weak and an awareness of these thoughts and values came about.[77] "But the greatest progress... comes from exhortation in favour of non-injury to life and abstention from killing living things."[78]

Christianity

The basic Christian ideal promotes peace through goodwill and by sharing the faith with others, as well as being proactive and doing good works and forgiving those who do try to break the peace. Below are selections from two gospels:

"But I say unto you, Love your enemies, bless them that curse you, do good to them that hate you, and pray for them which despitefully use you, and persecute you; That ye may be the children of your Father which is in heaven: for he maketh his sun to rise on the evil and on the good, and sendeth rain on the just and on the unjust."[79]

"A new commandment I give unto you, That ye love one another; as I have loved you, that ye also love one another. By this shall all men know that ye are my disciples, if ye have love one to another."[80]

Due to the words of Jesus Christ in John 14:6, which says, *"I am the way, the truth, and the life. No one comes to the Father except through Me"*, many Christians are unable to accept any other way to God other than Jesus Christ. Therefore, a true act of Christian love would be to proclaim that there is but one God, and one savior. Christians are called to love their enemies, and to preach the good news of the gospel.

Although Jesus did say, "No one comes to the father except by him" and the Bible teaches that you have to confess with your mouth that "Jesus is Lord," in order to be saved, some people believe that the Bible teaches that everyone will eventually accept Jesus and be saved verses like Philippians 2:9-11 are used to support this belief "...at the name of Jesus every knee should bow, in heaven and on earth and under the earth, and every tongue confess that Jesus Christ is Lord, to the glory of God the Father." Jesus also said, "when I am lifted up from the earth (i.e. his death on the cross), I will draw all people to myself."[81] And while John 3:16 is arguably the most famous Bible verse, it is almost always quoted out of context the very next verse says, "God did not send his Son into the world to condemn the world, but to save the world through him."[82] In this verse Jesus seems to be saying that the very reason He came to world was to save it. "For the Son of Man came to seek and to save the lost."[83]

One important topic of discussion when it comes to the concept of world peace and the teaching of Christianity is Christian Universalism which is a school of Christian theology that believes in the doctrine of universal reconciliation. The Doctrine teaches that God will eventually establish world peace and redeem all people unto Himself. Some Bible verses used to support this belief are: "All the ends of the earth shall remember and turn to the LORD, and all the families of the nations shall worship before you. For kingship belongs to the LORD, and he rules over the nations,"[84] and (1 John 2:2) "And He Himself is the propitiation for our sins; and not for ours only, but also for those of the whole world." and Colossians 1:19-20 "it was the Father's good pleasure for all the fullness to dwell in Him, and through Him to reconcile all things to

Himself, having made peace through the blood of His cross; through Him, I say, whether things on earth or things in heaven."

Christianity started out as a breakaway sect of Judaism nearly 2000 years ago. Jesus, the son of the Virgin Mary and her husband Joseph, but conceived through the Holy Spirit, was bothered by some of the practices within his native Jewish faith and began preaching a different message of God and religion. During his travels he was joined by twelve disciples who followed him in his journeys and learned from him. He performed many miracles during this time and related many of his teachings in the form of parables. Among his best known sayings are to "love thy neighbor" and "turn the other cheek." At one point he revealed that he was the Son of God sent to Earth to save humanity from our sins. This he did by being crucified on the cross for his teachings. He then rose from the dead and appeared to his disciples and told them to go forth and spread his message.

Since Christianity and Judaism share the same history up to the time of Jesus Christ, they are very similar in many of their core beliefs. There are two primary differences. One is that Christians believe in original sin and that Jesus died in our place to save us from that sin. The other is that Jesus was fully human and fully God and as the Son of God is part of the Holy Trinity: God the Father, His Son, and the Holy Spirit. All Christians believe in heaven and that those who sincerely repent their sins before God will be saved and join Him in heaven. Belief in hell and satan varies among groups and individuals.

Christianity is the religion based on the life and teachings of Jesus Christ. Most followers of Christianity, called Christians, are members of one of three major groups—Roman Catholic, Protestant, one Eastern Orthodox. These groups have different beliefs about Jesus and His teachings. But all Christians consider Jesus central to their religion. Most Christians believe that God sent Jesus into the world as the Saviour. Christianity teaches that humanity can achieve salvation through Jesus.

Jesus lived in Palestine, a Middle Eastern land ruled by the Romans. Jesus Christ is worshipped among Christians as the incarnation of the heavenly Father and as the greatest Saviour of mankind. It is believed that he was born on the 25th December of a virgin Mother at Bethlehem about two thousand years ago.[85]

The Romans crucified Jesus in about A.D. 30. Jesus followers were convinced He rose from the death after three days, and they soon spread Christianity to major cities throughout the Roman Empire. Today Christians make up the largest religious group in the world. Christianity has about 1.5 billion followers—about a fourth of the world's population. Christianity is the major religion in the Europe, the Western Hemisphere, and Australia. Many Christians also live in Africa and Asia.[86]

The peace in Christianity is to be understood in the light of at least three historical factors.

First, the ethical teaching of Jesus of nszareth grew out of the Jewish heritage in to which he was born and in which he was raised. His concern for peace includes, therefore the ancient Hebrew prophetic emphasis of human dignity and social Justice.

Second, Christian moral theology through the ages had offered not a single but a variety of interpretations concerning how the peace ethic of Jesus should be applied to the problems of war. Although the interpretations seek to be faithful to Christ's gospel of peace contrasts between them have often resulted in the tragedy of Christians being pitted against Christians in a particular war.

Finally, Christians and sometimes their churches over the years have all too often failed to practice what their moral theology professes. Unholy wars have often been called holy. Even the name or Christ's cross has been used for unchristian conquest as in the crusades.

Whatever could be the historical factors, there is a strong imperative for peace or to be more precise for the making of peace at the heart of the Christian faith. This, Jesus Christ made abundantly clear. "Blessed are the peacemaker" in the opening lines of his most celebrated sermon. Blessedness not simply for the peace lover, or those with peace in their hearts, but blessed are those who in this strife-torn world make the peace settle the strife achieve the reconciliation. "Be ye doers of the word and not hearers only." Jesus showed no bitterness even towards those who put him there and said: "Father, forgive them for they know not what they do."

There were other ethical imperatives which Jesus embraced with a fervor equal to that of peace. Social justice is one. He made it clear that peace is no substitute for seeing to it that the hungry are fed, the flaked are clothed and shelter is given to the homeless. Freedom for human dignity is another imperative elevated to Pre-eminence.

The peace which Jesus preached was not simply an inner peace, or a form of retreat from intense identification with the conflicts of the world. It was a peace based on justice. Moreover, his ethics for both peace and justice had universal dimension they are for everyone. Therefore, Jesus final demand to his disciples was not "go into Palestine or the suberbs of Jerusalem." It was "go into all the world and preach the gospel"—the gospel of peace.

This preaching, Jesus made clear, is costly. One must sacrifice for peace. Jesus said: "If anyone would be my disciple let him take up his cross and follow me... He who would save his life for my sake must lose it... Behold send you as sheep into the midst of wovels, be ye therefore wise as serpent and harmless as doves."

Most of us are familiar with the Old Testament word for "peace." It is *shalom*. For Hebrew speakers, *shalom* has a much richer and fuller significance than the English word "peace." Whereas we sometimes limit the idea of peace to the absence of conflict, *shalom* includes far more. It comprises the notions of wholeness, completeness, soundness, and prosperity. The Psalmist sings, "Those who are gentle and lowly will possess the land; they will live in *abundant peace*."[87] God's promise of blessing to Israel through Isaiah uses similar language: "I will make your towers of sparkling rubies and your gates and walls of shining gems. I will teach all your citizens, and their *peace* will be great."[88]

In the Old Testament, peace is also inseparable from righteousness and justice. These latter concepts are embodied in one Hebrew word that connotes right-relationship between two or more parties. This word is usually translated as "righteousness," referring not only to doing morally correct deeds, but also to living rightly in relationship with others. Righteousness is also closely connected to justice, because the righteous person acts with justice in the civil or judicial sphere. The necessary link between righteousness and peace can be seen, for example, in Isaiah's vision of a future day when a righteous king will reign over Israel and God's Spirit will be poured out upon the people:

"Then the wilderness will become a fertile field, and the fertile field will become a lush and fertile forest. Justice will rule in the wilderness and righteousness in the fertile field. And this righteousness will bring peace. Quietness and confidence will fill the land forever."[89] With a similar picture in mind, the Psalmist looks forward to a time with God's salvation pervades the nation. It that day one will proclaim, "Unfailing love and truth have met together. Righteousness and peace have kissed![90]

In biblical perspective, therefore, the absence of conflict is only the bare beginning of peace. True peace includes personal wholeness, corporate righteousness, political justice, and prosperity for all creation. That's exactly the way God intended things to be when he created his garden, his paradise. (Our word "paradise" comes from a Greek word that described the elegant parks of ancient Persian kings.) Perhaps no term better describes God's perfect paradise than "peaceful," a world full of wholeness, righteousness, justice, and prosperity.

Hinduism

Traditionally Hinduism has adopted a saying called *Vasuda eva kutumbakam*,[91] which translates to "The world is one family." The essence of this saying is the observation that only base minds see dichotomies and divisions. The more we seek wisdom, the more we become inclusive and free our internal spirit from worldly illusions or *Maya*. World peace is hence thought by Hindus to be achieved only through internal means—by liberating oneself from artificial boundaries that separate us but it is good in acquiring peace.

The origins of Hinduism can be traced to the Indus Valley civilization sometime between 4000 and 2500 BCE. 'Hindu' is the Persian word for 'Indian' Hinduism is the most ancient. It was not founded by any individual prophet and is not composed of the teachings of any particular group of them.[92] Sir Charles Eliot remarks, "Hinduism has not been made, but has grown. It is jungle, not a building." Similarly, K.M. Sen makes the following observations in his book Hinduism, "Hinduism is more like a tree that has grown gradually than like building that has been erected by some architect at some definite point in time. It contains within itself the influences of many cultures and the body Hindu thought thus offers it much variety as the Indian nation itself."[93]

Though believed by many to be a polytheistic religion, the basis of Hinduism is the belief in the unity of everything. This totality is called Brahman. The purpose of life is to realize that we are part of God and by doing so we can leave this plane of existence and rejoin with God. This enlightenment can only be achieved by going through cycles of birth, life and death known as samsara. One's progress towards enlightenment is measured by his karma. This is the accumulation of all one's good and bad deeds and this determines the person's next reincarnation. Selfless acts and thoughts as well as devotion to God help one to be reborn at a higher level. Bad acts and thoughts will cause one to be born at a lower level, as a person or even an animal.

In the words of Dr. S. Radhakrishnan, "the Hindu view is not motivated by any considerations of political expediency. It is bound up with its religion and not its policy. The Hindu attitude is based on the definite philosophy. Toleration is the homage which the finite mind plays to the inexhaustibility of lit infinite."

The concept of man upheld in Hinduism is the most vital source of its sanctions for peace. The discovery, by the sages of the Upanishads, of the true nature of man as the Atman, the immortal divine self, and its unity with Brahman, the infinite self of all beings, constitutes the greatest single source of the universality and humanism of Hinduism and its perennial sanction for peace. The object of human life is the steady realization, through life's effort and struggles, of this ever present truth, that many are the paths that lead to such realization, and that fellowship and harmony should be the watch word among the people wending their way to the same goal through different path, this struggle insights, tested verified by sages, saints, and statesman in the past, and by Shri Ramakrishna, Swami Vivekananda and Mahatma Gandhi in the present, capable of taking modern man on the creative path of fellowship and peace leading to the total life fulfilment.

Hindu scriptures have taught the Hindu to view man in himself and in others, in the light of what is unalienable about him, namely, his innate divine nature, the Atman, and achieving peace within, project that peace outside in forms of charity, tolerance, and fellow feeling. Peacelessness and tension are the characteristics of man as the ego, man at the sensate level. Hinduism in fact, every world religion seeks to take man above this level and lead him to the experience of the peace of God. Shantoyam atma means "this Atman is peace."

The peace that Hinduism has helped man to meditate outside is the projection of what it has helped him to generate within himself by the intellectual, moral, and spiritual disciplines that it prescribes for one all. No spiritual study or understanding is commenced without a peace invocation, the Shanti patha. The well-Known shanti patha of the katha katha and some other Upanishads breathe this spirit of peace and love in abundance: "OM: may Brahmin (God) protect us both (students and teacher); may Brahman nourish us both; may we both acquire energy (by this study); May we both become bright and illumined by the study. May we not hate other Om! Peace, Peace, Peace.

Hinduism prescribes a minimum moral and spiritual discipline for all people in what Patanjali describes as the mahavratas (great disciplines): Non-killing, truthfulness, non-stealing, continence, and non-receiving (of gifts) are called yama (self-control). These without considerations of caste (or nationality), place, time and purpose, are great disciplines of universal importance.

The preamble of UNESCO which proclaims that, since wars begin in the minds of men, it is in the minds of men that the defenses of peace should be built, is fundamentally religious proposition. If there is not peace within, there cannot be peace without. What Dr. Josiah Oldfeild said in a speech in London on the eve of the Second World War that more wars were caused by bad tempered people seeking to discuss peace propositions than by good—tempered people seeking to discuss war measures—is in tune with the essential Hindu attitudę. Disciplined in the tenets of Hinduism and its two sisters religions, namely, Buddhism and Jainism, the Indian people have been uniformly a non-aggressive people and have not engaged, even when politically and militarily organized into powerful empires, in any war of aggression outside the confines of India—but her inner weakness often tempted foreign aggressors to invade the land and despoil of its riches. This ingrained love of peace and non-aggressiveness, confronted by the challenge of repeated foreign invasions, is making for the evolution in modern Hinduism of a clearer and more cogent philosophy of peace in which non-aggressiveness is integrated with all round strength, gentleness becomes coupled with fearlessness. In fact, this is the characteristic of the true devotee of God as described by Shri Krishna in the Gita:

> "He by whom the world is not agitated and who (also) is not agitated by the world, who is liberated from excessive elation, intolerance, fear, and anxiety, such a one is dear to Me."[94]

In India's peace history, the upsurge and spread of devotional movements during the medieval period is a watershed. It is known as Bhakti Movement, a movement in which the masses played a pivotal role and the vernacular languages of the regions became the vehicles of this Bhakti movement stressing love (prem) peace, harmony and an intimate personal awakening. Poetry, satire, wit through songs and poems aroused the people. In each region of the country leaders called "teachers" (guru) appeared making the whole country resound with their songs of love for a personal deity, love for fellow human-beings all being members one of another, all god's creatures. There seemed to be a symphony of this movement covering many regions, many languages and many people of India. Although the leaders came from different parts of the country and subscribed to different schools of philosophy (for example, Sankhya or Shankara School), there was a common approach and method in their work among the people. All of them were followers of the path of bhakti (devotion) arising out of love (prem) and dedication to Ishta-Devata (personal god) and a concern for their fellow human-beings.[95]

The leaders, "teachers" (Guru), some called them Saints, did not come from the high-born, the elite, or the best educated classes of society but from every stratum of society down to the lowliest. A tremendous emphasis was laid on moral character, sincerity and bhakti (devotion).

This movement both popular and non-violent began in the Tamil-speaking area of South India from the 7th century A.D. spreading to Kannada-speaking areas, to Maharashtra. Then the Hindi-speaking area took it up, and North India was aflame with this movement for love and ahimsa and devotion evincing a fervent spirit. This spiritual aspect of the bhakti movement, the emphasis on an understanding of god as personal, transcendent as well as immanent who takes manifold forms, for the benefit of humanity lent a very delicate and sensitive touch to this movement for serving the world (Lok Sangraha) with compassion and grace rather than with faith in one's own capacity, communing with fellow creatures, venerating all humanity because "god is immanent in all beings."

The Bhakti movement humanized the society attaching high values to love for fellow creatures, concern for others and a conscious abstention from violence. It was bhakti or devotion that added stature to a human being in society, not birth. The followers of Bhakti movement did not have any caste or any distinction of high and low. Love became the keyword.

One important result of this movement has been the growth and development of vernacular languages of the Southern and Northern India as various songs on devotion, divine love between the worshipped and the worshipper, on brotherhood of man, on non-violence, and on compassion were composed. The epics of India, The Ramayana and The Mahabharata were the literary sources of this movement which enshrined in the hearts of the people the consciousness of a personality, instead of a god, adored and loved as the fountain of all excellences. Now, The Ramayana came to be retold in local languages.

Musical version of the whole texts from the epics and compositions of bhaktas (devotees) and teachers (Guru) like Vagisha (7th century A.D.), Sundar Murti (9th century A.D.); Nammalvar, Basarraja (12th century A.D.), Purnadasa (16th century A.D.), Surdas (16th century A.D.), Tulsidas (17th century A.D.), Ram Prasad (18th century A.D.), Shree Chaitanya (18th century A.D.)—all contributed to producing several stirring songs, poems and literature written in vernacular languages some of which had great impact on Mahatma Gandhi and Tagore of our time and day. Bhakti movement as can be seen, was a continuous movement of peace and love and devotion covering a vast span of years (9th century A.D. to 18th century A.D.), continuing on a smaller scale in some places even today, and spreading to a very wide area within the country from the North to the South. In point of fact, this movement brought about a literary renaissance both in the Southern and Northern India as far as the respective vernacular languages are concerned.[96]

Some of the songs and music became the forerunners of a musical renaissance in India. These songs are being sung even today in temple worship, private gatherings and meetings. They were sung at Gandhi's meetings and he had quite a few favourite songs among them, "Vaishnavo Jano" in Gujarati being one of them. Bhajans, Kirtans, Namgans emanated from this renaissance glorifying love, peace within and without, brother-hood of man and the power of the spirit. They continue to be sung in India today because of their basic unity and spiritual heritage. The impact of Bhakti movement even today is visible in the lifestyle of people in many parts of Tamil Nadu, Kannada, in the South and in Bengal in the North.

Islam

According to *Islam*, faith in only *one God* and having common parents *Adam and Eve* is the greatest reason for humans to live together with peace and brotherhood. *Islamic view of global peace* is mentioned in the *Quran* where the whole of humanity is recognized as one family. All the people are children of Adam and Eve. The purpose of the Islamic faith is to make people recognize their own natural inclination towards their fraternity. According to *Islamic eschatology* the whole world will be united under the leadership of prophet *Jesus* in his *second coming*.[97] At that time love, justice and peace will be so abundant that the world will be in likeness of *paradise*.

Added October 5, 2009 by IECRC—Islamic Educational & Cultural Research Center's research on religious involvement in world peace and the concept of the World Peace Order is expanded in great detail in its latest publication *'World Peace Order—Towards an International State.'*'[98]

Islam was founded in 622 CE by Muhammad the Prophet, in Makkah (also spelled Mecca). The word Islam is derived from the Arabic root "SIM" which means among other things, peace, purity submission and obedience. In the religious sense the word Islam means submission to the will of God and obedience to His low. Only through submission to the will of God and by obedience to His law can one achieve enjoy peace and enjoy lasting purity.

Though it is the youngest of the world's great religions, Muslims do not view it as a new religion. They belief that it is the same faith taught by the prophets, Abraham, David, Moses and Jesus. The role of Muhammad as the last prophet was to formalize and clarify the faith and purify it by removing ideas which were added in error. He was only a mortal being commissioned by God to teach the word of God and lead an exemplary life. Muslims do not worship Mohammad as god. He is the best model for man in piety and perfection. He is leaving a proof of what man can be and what he can accomplish in the realm of excellence and virtue. The Muslims worship God alone. The original founder of Islam is no other than God Himself.

The two sacred texts of Islam are the Qur'an, which are the words of Allah 'the One True God' as given to Muhammad, and the Hadith, which is a collection of Muhammad's sayings. The duties of all Muslims are known as the Five Pillars of Islam and are:

- Recite the shahadah at least once.
- Perform the salat (prayer) 5 times a day while facing the Kaaba in Makkah.
- Donate regularly to charity via the zakat, a 2.5% charity tax, and through additional donations to the needy.

- Fast during the month of Ramadan, the month that Muhammad received the Qur'an from Allah.
- Make pilgrimage to Makkah at least once in life, if economically and physically possible.

Muslims follow a strict monotheism with one creator who is just, omnipotent and merciful. They also believe in Satan who drives people to sin, and that all unbelievers and sinners will spend eternity in Hell. Muslims who sincerely repent and submit to God will return to a state of sinlessness and go to Paradise after death. Alcohol, drugs, and gambling should be avoided and they reject racism. They respect the earlier prophets, Abraham, Moses, and Jesus, but regard the concept of the divinity of Jesus as blasphemous and do not believe that he was executed on the cross.

The concept of God in Islam describes Him as the Most Merciful and Gracious, and the Most Loving and most concerned with the will being of man, and as full of wisdom and care for His Creatures.

Submission to the will of God, together with obedience to His beneficial Law, is the best safeguard of peace and harmony. It enables man to make peace between himself and his fellow men on the one hand, and between the human community and God on the other. According to Islam, everything in the world, or every phenomenon other than man is administered by God-made Laws. This makes the entire physical world necessarily obedient to God and submission to His Laws, which in turn, means that it is in a state of Islam, or it is Muslim. The physical world has no choice of its own. It has no voluntary course to follow on its own initiative but obeys the Law of the creator, the Law of Islam or submission. Man alone is singled out as being endowed with intelligence and the power of making choices. When man chooses the course of submission to the Law of God, He will be making harmony between himself and all the other elements of Nature, which are by necessity obedient to God. If man chooses to disobedience he will deviate from the Right path and will be inconsistent. Besides, he will[99] incur the displeasure and punishment of the Law-Giver.

Peace and Islam are derived from the same root and may be considered synonymous. One of God's names is peace. The concluding words of the daily prayers of every Muslim are words of peace. The greeting of the Muslim when they return to God is peace. The adjective "Muslim" means, is a sense, peaceful. Heaven in Islam is the abode of peace.

The individual who approaches God through Islam cannot fail to be at peace with God, with himself, and with his fellow man. Taking all these values together, putting man in his proper place in the cosmos, and viewing life in the Islamic perspective, men of good faith and principles cannot fall to make our world a better world, to regain human dignity, to achieve equality, to enjoy universal brotherhood, and to build a lasting peace. A Muslim is never allowed to initiate a war; he can only fight in self-defense or to defend his freedom of belief and worship. The Quran says, "Fight those who are fighting with you (in order to derive you of your liberty of conscience) but do not commit any excesses. Allah does not love those who do so."

Even in the heat and the emotional tension of war, the Muslims are enjoined never to deny the enemy water or food or to corrupt their sources of sustenance or to commit any excesses on women and children or the wounded or non-combatant civilian population. The Quran further enjoins:

> Even when you are caught up in a defensive war, if the enemy shows slightest inclination to peace, respond to it in the fullest measure. If they play you false later, God will look after you."[100] This means that even the fear of possible treachery on the part of your opponents should not stand in the way of peace negotiations, for the risk of trust is certainly better to take than the risk of suspicion.

The best contribution that Islam can make to the world is to assist in the process of the exergence of the new man who will be able to define his priorities more intelligently and compassionately and live by these priorities, who will welcome technology but not barter his soul in the process, who will be more concerned with giving than with taking, and who will strive for peace with every resource of his being. In a message which President Johnson sent to the National Inter-Religious Conference on Peace at Washington in 1966, he said:

> "The billions we appropriate to conquer poverty will be worth little unless we vanquish the most crippling poverty-man's insufficiency of understanding, his meagrness of spirit. The dollars we spend to eradicate disease will be wasted unless we isolate and control the deadliest of microbes-man's capacity for hatred, his penchant for violence. Living in such a world has taught us that our only victories will be won, not by putting more weapons in men's hands but by putting more wisdom in their hearts."[101]

Humanity is at the crossroads. There is a choice between survival and annihilation of the life. If man has to survives, he has to realize his folly and correct his actions. The advancement of science and technology has provided comfortable life. But only the rich few could enjoy their benefit. The poor on the other hand are longing and striving to enjoy the same lifestyle. As a result, there is heavy competition between the two. As a result, there is heavy competition between the people, nations and the world at large. The world has been divided into two categories—rich and poor.

The spirit of competition made man to be greedy, selfish, riotous and destructive. The result of which are startling relaxing traditions of retrains and of established law and order. The world is rent by misunderstandings, bitterness and strife. The atmosphere is charged with suspicion, uncertainty and much fear for the future. The growing distress of our race, the depending economic misery, wars on an unprecedented scale, the divided counsels in high places and the inertia of those in power and authority, who wishes to preserve the collapsing order and save crippled civilization at any cost is causing revolutionary spirit.

The reason for all such confusion in the world is because of the pursuit of materialistic philosophies and the worship of science as the savior of all problems. But the scientific-materialistic view of human life has shown gross inadequacy and proved to be incapable of helping man discovery the joy, meaning and mission of his life. As a result, there is much unhappiness and disillusionment in the modern world.

Man has now come to a realization that only the spirit of love and brotherhood can be the saviour of making into live happily. Gandhi declared that "Peace will never come until the great powers courageously desire to diarm themselves.... I have an implicit faith – a faith that today burns brighter than ever, after half a century's experience of unbroken practice of non-violence....that mankind can only be saved through non-violence."[102]

Judaism

Judaism teaches that at some future time a *Messiah* will rise up to bring all Jews back to the *Land of Israel*, followed by everlasting global peace and prosperity.[103] This idea originates from passages in the *Tanakh* and rabbinic interpretations.

In addition to this well known idea of a Messiah, there also exists the idea of *Tikkun olam* (Repairing the World). *Tikkun olam* is accomplished through various means, such as ritualistically performing God's commandments (keeping the Sabbath, kashrut laws, etc.), charity and social justice, as well as through example persuading the rest of the world to behave morally. This would result in the beginning of the Messianic Age.

Judaism, Christianity, Islam and the Baha'i faith all originated with a divine covenant between the God of the ancient Israelites and

Abraham around 2000 BCE. The next leader of the Israelites, Moses, led his people out of captivity in Egypt and received the Law from God. Joshua later led them into the promised land where Samuel established the Israelite kingdom with Saul as its first king. King David established Jerusalem and King Solomon built the first temple there. In 70 CE the temple was destroyed and the Jews were scattered throughout the world until 1948 when the state of Israel was formed.

Jews believe in one creator who alone is to be worshipped as absolute ruler of the universe. He monitors peoples' activities and rewards good deeds and punishes evil. The Torah was revealed to Moses by God and can not be changed though God does communicate with the Jewish people through prophets. Jews believe in the inherent goodness of the world and its inhabitants as creations of God and do not require a savior to save them from original sin. They believe they are God's chosen people and that the Messiah will arrive in the future, gather them into Israel, there will be a general resurrection of the dead, and the Jerusalem Temple destroyed in 70 CE will be rebuilt.

Jainism

Compassion for all life, human and non-human, is central to *Jainism*. Human life is valued as a unique, rare opportunity to reach enlightenment; to kill any person, no matter what crime he may have committed, is considered unimaginably abhorrent. It is a religion that requires monks and laity, from all its sects and traditions, to be *vegetarian*. Some Indian regions, such as Gujarati, have been strongly influenced by Jains and often the majority of the local Hindus of every denomination have also become vegetarian.[104]

The founder of the Jain community was Vardhamana, the last Jina in a series of 24 who lived in East India. He attained enlightenment after 13 years of deprivation and committed the act of salekhana, fasting to death, in 420 BCE. Jainism has many similarities to Hinduism and Buddhism which developed in the same part of the world. They believe in karma and reincarnation as do Hindus but they believe that enlightenment and liberation from this cycle can only be achieved through asceticism. Jains follow fruititarianism. This is the practice of only eating that which will not kill the plant or animal from which it is taken. They also practice ahimsa, non-violence, because any act of violence against a living thing creates negative karma which will adversely affect one's next life.

The peace movement that is usually called Jainism originated at the same time and in the same region of India as Buddhism. Mighty were the rulers who supported it, as did the common people, the teachings and works of the leader known as Mahavira, who led a disciplined order of his followers. He lived in the 5th century B.C. (596-468 B.C) and left a tremendous impact on the people of that part of India (Bihar) which resulted in a peace movement in other regions as well. Long afterwards kings like Chandra Gupta Maurva (317-293 B.C.) not only supported the movement but ultimately became a follower of Mahavira's teachings and way of life.

Jainism enumerates five great vows: Ahimsa, Satya, Astheya, Parimitha Parigraha and Brahmacharya. Non-injury, truth, non-stealing, limited possession and chastity are only approximate translations for the terms mentioned. Jainism also prescribes the three-fold path of Right knowledge, Right faith and Right conduct. Jainism emphasises that all sins emanate from Himsa—injury by thought, word or deed to any living being. The first and foremost Dharma is Ahimsa.

Parimitha Parigraha or limited possesion is the forerunner of the concept of Trusteeship envisaged and explained by Gandhiji. Self-reverence, self-knowledge and self-control lead life to Sovereign Power. Individual effort and sublimation of self is the only effective answer to the problems of the present day world.

Ahimsa as preached and practised by Jain Thirthankars is the only answer to problems of peace, poverty and pollution confronting humanity. Gandhiji rightly stated: "Non-violence is the greatest force at the disposal of mankind. It is mightier than the mightiest weapon of destruction devised by the ingenuity of man. It is remarkable that unlike Vedic religion, Jainism stands for pure Ahimsa without any reservation." Romain Rolland was courageous to come forward with a very meaningful statement: "The Rishis, who discovered the law of non-violence in the midst of violence were greater geniuses than Newton and greater warriors than Wellington. Non-violence is the law of our species, as violence is the law of the brute."

The impact of Jain movement has not disappeared from India but has survived to the present day although it has never spread beyond the land of its origin. One of the basic ideas of the Jain movement is that since the universe is an organic whole, governed by comic order, all living beings in it are fellow members. Thus any one who grasps this truth will not injure or harm any living being ever.[105] Therefore, the supreme virtue according to the followers of Jaina thought is ahimsa: "not to cause pain or tend to cause pain or destruction to any living being by thought, speech or conduct is ahimsa."[106] Hinsa cannot be justified under any circumstances, or for any end. This "solidarity of lift" was, and is, a distinctive feature of Jaina peace movement. All life is sacred. All life as such is sacred.[107] To maintain, assist and enhance life is good. To do anything contrary is evil. Life here includes soul (Jiva) that exists in human-beings, animals, plants, vegetables, waterbodies, wind bodies and in all things derived from earth.[108] The individual is free to work out his/ her own salvation. One important feature of this non-violent movement was that those who joined it were expected to submit themselves to a rigid discipline.[109] The followers had to undergo fasting, and to join in a ceremony of pardon extending to every one including the animals—a fine ethical feature.

It may be mentioned here that there was/is a kind of ascetism in this movement. For example, the chief reason for doing good is the furtherance of one's own spiritual ends. Violence is to be chiefly avoided because it harms the individual who commits it. However, this movement did help growth of moral and spiritual discipline, encouraged honesty and kindliness in personal relations and underlined the imperative of non-violence. It brought about social change in matters of equality and in the perception of all being members of one another.

Sikhism

"All beings and creatures are His; He belongs to all"[110] Gurus furthermore preached to "Sing the Praise of the One, the Immaculate Lord; He is contained within all."[111] "The special feature of the Sikh of the Guru is that he goes beyond the framework of caste-classification and moves in humility. Then his labor becomes acceptable at the door of God."[112]

The Sikh faith was founded by Shri Guru Nanak Dev Ji in the Punjab area, now Pakistan. He began preaching the way to enlightenment and God after receiving a vision. After his death a series of nine Gurus (regarded as reincarnations of Guru Nanak) led the movement until 1708. At this time these functions passed to the Panth and the holy text. This text, the Shri Guru Granth Sahib, was compiled by the tenth Guru, Gobind Singh. It consists of hymns and writings of the first 10 Gurus, along with texts from different Muslim and Hindu saints. The holy text is considered the 11th and final Guru.

Sikhs believe in a single formless God with many names, who can be known through meditation. Sikhs pray many times each day and are prohibited from worshipping idols or icons. They believe in samsara, karma, and reincarnation as Hindus do but reject the caste system. They believe that everyone has equal status in the eyes of God. During the 18th century, there were a number of attempts to prepare an accurate portrayal of Sikh customs. Sikh scholars and theologians started in 1931 to prepare the Reht Maryada—the Sikh code of conduct and conventions. This has successfully achieved a high level of uniformity in the religious and social practices of Sikhism throughout the world. It contains 27 articles. Article 1 defines who is a Sikh:

"Any human being who faithfully believes in:

- One Immortal Being,
- Ten Gurus, from Guru Nanak Dev to Guru Gobind Singh,
- The Guru Granth Sahib,
- The utterances and teachings of the ten Gurus,
- the baptism bequeathed by the tenth Guru, and who does not owe allegiance to any other religion, is a Sikh."
- Zoroastrianism was founded by Zarathushtra (Zoroaster) in Persia which followed an aboriginal polytheistic religion at the time. He preached what may have been the first monotheism with a single supreme god, Ahura Mazda. Zoroastrians belief in the dualism of good and evil as either a cosmic one between Ahura Mazda and an evil spirit of violence and death, Angra Mainyu, or as an ethical dualism within the human consciousness. The Zoroastrian holy book is called the Avesta which includes the teachings of Zarathushtra written in a series of five hymns called the Gathas. They are abstract sacred poetry directed towards the worship of the One God, understanding of righteousness and cosmic order, promotion of social justice, and individual choice between good and evil. The rest of the Avesta was written at a later date and deals with rituals, practice of worship, and other traditions of the faith.

  Zoroastrians worship through prayers and symbolic ceremonies that are conducted before a sacred fire which symbolizes their God. They dedicate their lives to a three-fold path represented by their motto: "Good thoughts, good words, good deeds." The faith does not generally accept converts but this is disputed by some members.

Notes and References

1. http://www.cultureofpeace/the_war_in_intrinsic_to_human_nature_discourages_action_for_peace.htm
2. Pasricha, Ashu, Peace Studies: The Discipline and Dimension (Delhi: Abhijeet Publications), 2003, p. 2.
3. *Ibid.*
4. Bernstein, E., *et. al.*, Peace Resource Book (Cambridge: Ballinger Publishing Company), 1986, pp. 45-50.
5. Encyclopedia of Violence, Peace and Conflict (San Diego: Academics Press), 1992, 3 Volumes.
6. Galtung, Johan and Carl G. Jacobsen, Searching for Peace: The Road to TRANSCEND (London: Pluto Press), 2000.

7. Richmond, O.P., The Transformation of Peace (London: Palgrave Macmillan), 2005.
8. Wolfgang Dietrich, Daniela Ingruber, Josefina Echavarría, Gustavo Esteva and Norbert Koppensteiner (eds.), The Palgrave International Handbook of Peace Studies: A Cultural Perspective (London: Palgrave Macmillan), 2011.
9. Galtung, Johan, Peace by Peaceful Means (London: Sage Publications), 1996, p. 9.
10. Rearden, B.A., "Comprehensive Peace Education (New York: Teachers College Press), 1988, p. 16.
11. *The Encyclopedia of Social Sciences*, Vol. 13 (New York: Macmillan Free Press), p. 487.
12. Pasricha, Ashu, Peace Studies: The Discipline and Dimension, *op. cit.*, pp. 4-5
13. Galtung Johan, Peace by Peaceful Means, *op. cit.*, p. 36.
14. Bergstrom, Lass, "What is a Conflict of Interests", in *Journal of Peace Research*, 1970, pp. 197-217.
15. Boulding, K.E., Conflict and Defence: A General Theory (New York: Harper and Row Publishers) 1963, p. 51.
16. *Ibid.*, p. 4.
17. Galtung, Johan, Peace by Peaceful Means, *op. cit.*, p. 72.
18. Pasricha, Ashu, Peace Studies: The Discipline and Dimension, *op. cit.*
19. Clausewitz, Carl Von, On War (Princeton: Princeton University Press), 1968.
20. Webster Dictionary (Scotland: Geddes and Grosset), 1999.
21. English Dictionary (London: Oxford Press), 1702
22. Spinoza, Benedict, D., Tractatus Theologico: Politics A Spinoza reader: The Ethics and Other Words (Princeton: Princeton University Press), 1994, p. 670.
23. Quincy Wright, "Changes in the Conception of War", *American Journal of International Law*, Vol. XVIII, (Oct.) 1926, p. 762.
24. *Ibid.*
25. Galtung, Johan, Violence, Peace and Peace Research, *op. cit.*, pp. 16-19.
26. Aron, Raymond, Peace and War (New York: Double Day), 1966, pp. 44-47.
27. Galtung, Johan, "On the Meaning of Non-Violence", *Journal of Peace Research*, 1965, No. 2, pp. 228-30.
28. Galtung, Johan, Peace Research for Peace Action (New Delhi: Sat Sahitya Kendra Press), 1974, p. 52.
29. Galtung, Johan, Peace by Peaceful Means, *op. cit.*, pp. 3-5.
30. The South Commission Report (Geneva: South Centre), 1990.
31. Shy, O., Industrial Organization: Theory and Applications (Cambridge, Mass.: The MIT Press), 1996.
32. *Ibid.*
33. Rummel, Rudolph, Joseph, Peace Endangered: Reality of Détente (London: Sage Publications), 1976
34. Galtung, J., Peace By Peaceful Means: Peace and Conflict, Development And Civilization (London: Sage Publications), 1996, p. 32.
35. Wilmerding, John, *The Theory of Active Peace* (London: Sage Publications), 2006
36. Wolfgang Dietrich/Wolfgang Sützl: A Call for Many Peaces; in: Dietrich, Wolfgang, Josefina Echavarría Alvarez, Norbert Koppensteiner (eds.), Key Texts of Peace Studies (Vienna: LIT Münster), 2006.
37. Wolfgang Dietrich: *Variationen über die vielen Frieden*; Vol. 1: Deutungen; VS Verlag Wiesbaden, 2008.
38. Wolfgang Dietrich, Josefina Echavarría Alvarez, Gustavo Esteva, Daniela Ingruber, Norbert Koppensteiner eds.: The Palgrave International Handbook of Peace Studies: A Cultural Approach, *op. cit.*
39. John Paul Lederach: Preparing for Peace (Syracuse: Syracuse University Press), 1996.
40. President meets with Bulgarian President Georgi Purvanov.

41. Trotsky, Leon, War and International (The Trotsky Internet Archive), 1914.
42. Rand, Ayn, Capitalism: The Unknown Ideal (United States: New American Library), 1996, pp. 35-43.
43. *Ibid.*
44. Col. Alan J. Parrington, USAF, "Mutually Assured Destruction Revisited, Strategic Doctrine in Question", *Airpower Journal*, Winter 1997.
45. Michael, Mousseau, "The Social Market Roots of Democratic Peace", *International Security*, Vol. 33, No. 4, Spring 2009, pp. 53-67.
46. Michael, Mousseau, "Market Civilization and Its Clash with Terror", *International Security*, Vol. 27, No. 3, Winter 2003-04, pp. 5-29.
47. Mousseau, Michael, 2003, "The Nexus of Market Society, Liberal Preferences, and Democratic Peace: Interdisciplinary Theory and Evidence", *International Studies Quarterly*, 47(4): 483-510.
48. *Ibid.*
49. Mousseau, Michael, 2009, "The Social Market Roots of Democratic Peace", *International Security*, *op. cit.*
50. Friedman, Milton, Capitalism and Freedom (Chicago: University of Chicago), 1970.
51. Smith, P., A Concise Encyclopedia of the Bahá'is Faith (Oxford, UK: Oneworld Publications), 1999. pp. 363-64.
52. Hatcher, W.S., Martin, J.D., The Bahá'ís Faith: The Emerging Global Religion (California: Harper and Row), 1984.
53. Shoghi Effeendi, The Advent of Divine Justice (Illinois: Bahá'í Publishing Trust), 1969.
54. De, W.T., The Liberal Tradition In China (New York: Columbia University Press), 1983.
55. Fang, T. H., Chinese Philosophy: Its Spirit And Its Development (Taipei: Linking), 1981.
56. Saso, M., The Teachings of Taoist Master Chuang (New Haven: Yale University Press), 1978.
57. Welch, H., Taoism: The Parting of the Way (Boston: Beacon Press), 1966.
58. Quoted in Siddhartha Gautama.
59. McDowell, Josh and Stewart, Don, Concise Guide to Today's Religions (England: Scripture Press), 1990, p. 288.
60. Kumar, Rajendra, World Famous Religions: Doctrines and Sects (Delhi: Pustak Mahal), 1993, p. 59.
61. Alfred Alfanso, Glimpses of World Religion (Madras: Jaico Publishing House), 1995, pp. 1-9.
62. Tiwari, K.N., Comparative Religion (New Delhi: Motilal Banarsidas), 1993, pp. 43-44.
63. Majjhima Nikaya 1, 420.
64. Sirlta Nipata, p. 143.
65. Dhanunapada 3-5, p. 201.
66. *Ibid.*
67. Jawaharlal Nehru formulated the Panchsheel code of conduct in 1954:
 (i) Mutual respect for one another's territorial integrity and sovereignty,
 (ii) Non-aggression, (iii) non-interference in one another's internal affairs, (iv) equality and mutual benefits, (v) peaceful coexistence as basis for India's relations to other nations.
68. The Edicts of Ashoke, The Adyar Library, Madras, 1950,
69. The Edicts of Ashoke, p. 43.
70. *Ibid.*, p. 63.
71. The Edicts of Ashoke, p. 49.

72. Minor Rock Edict.
73. Ninth Rock Edict.
74. Eighth Rock Edict
75. Twelfth Rock Edict.
76. Seventh Pillar Edict.
77. *Ibid.*
78. *Ibid.*
79. Mathew 5:44-45.
80. John 13:34-35.
81. *Ibid.*, 12:32.
82. *Ibid.*, 3:17.
83. Luke 19:10.
84. Psalm 22:27-30.
85. The World Book Encyclopaedia, Vol. 3, 1992, p. 483.
86. Malhotra, A.R., Philosophy of Religion—An Analysis to World Religions (Jalandhar: Sterling Publishers Pvt. Ltd.), 1985, p. 169.
87. Ps 37:11
88. Isa 54:12-13.
89. *Ibid.*, 32:15-17, NLT.
90. Psa 85:10.
91. Dharmic Wisdom Quotes, Page 3, Hindu Dharma Forums
92. Bhagavatgita, II, 20.
93. *Ibid.*, II, 23-24.
94. Jack, H. A. (ed.), World Religion and World Peace (Boston: Beacon Press), 1968, pp. 40-48.
95. Buddhist literature survive in Chinese or Tibetan translations. Complete Canon of Buddhist (Theravada) has been fully preserved in Sri Lanka. It is written in Pali language.
96. India's Constitution recognizes 15 languages. The Academy of Literature recognizes 22 languages.
97. Bukhari, Kitab Ahadith al-Ambiya; Bab: Nuzul 'Isa Ibn Maryam; Muslim, Bab: Bayan Nuzul 'Isa; Tirmidhi, Abwab-al-Fitan; Bab Fi Nuzul 'Isa; Musnad Ahmad, Marwiyat Abu Huraira. http://www.witness-pioneer.org/vil/Books/M_fop/fop11.htm
98. World Peace Order Towards an International State. http://www.iecrcna.org/publications/books/World_Peace_Order.
99. Adalati, Hammudah, Islam in Focus (Delhi: Crescent Publishing Co.), 1988, pp. 7-8.
100. *Ibid.*, p. 36.
101. Jack, H.A., World Religions and World Peace, *op. cit.*, pp. 55-57.
102. *Harijan*, Vol. 6, p. 295.
103. Rambam, Mishneh Torah, Hilkhot Melachim, Chs. 11-12.
104. Titze, Kurt, Jainism: A Pictorial Guide to the Religion of Non-Violence (Delhi: Mohtilal Banarsidass), 1998.
105. Acharanga Sutra.
106. Acharanga Sutra II, 5.
107. *Ibid.*, 1,1.
108. Sutrakartanga 1,1-9.
109. Acharanga Sutra. 1, 41.
110. Guru Granth Sahib, 425.
111. *Ibid.*, 706.
112. Bhai Gurdas Ji, 1.

United Nations and Major Peace Initiatives

All over the world, October 24, is known as United Nations' Day, but at the lofty streamlined headquarters in New York there are no celebrate birthday celebrations, for the Organizations is growing up the hard way, surrounded by countless difficulties and dangers and always short of money. The original charter was drawn up with the advice and consent of fifty-one nations. It was designed to promote but, above all, to keep the world at peace.

The United Nations is not the first attempt in history to outlaw war by international agreement. In the grim aftermath of farmer battles victorious rulers have tried to lay the foundations of permanent peace. After the 1st World War, in 1919 the leaders of the great powers gathered in the famous Hall of Mirrors at the Palace of Versailles to draw up Peace Treaties. During the Conference, President Wilson of the United States produced his draft for a League of Nations to till the urgent need of peace. He proposed that all the victorious nations should unite against aggression, and that disputes should be settled by peaceful means, by discussion instead of by violence or force. A council of nations, it was decided, would sit in Geneva and dispense universal justice and every one would disarm since there would be no need of guns.

The League of Nations never fulfilled its early promise and its influence declined steadily. In 1931, the Japanese siezed the Chinese province of Manchuria, 1935 the Italians added Ethiopia to their North African empire and in 1936 the German dictator, Adolf Hitler, defied the ruling of the Treaty of Versailles and marched and led the army into the Rhineland, on the French border. Mussolini, the Fascist dictator of Italy, joined forces with Hitler, and at the other side of the world the Japanese fought for the mastery of the Far East. The conflict spread o every continent, and people of many nations were dragged unwillingly into war. Everywhere, all over the world, people were praying for peace and security.

While the heavy responsibilities of war still rested on their shoulders, the two great leaders, Winston Churchill and Franklin Roosevelt, had turned their minds to the problems of peace.

Thus the United Nations Organization was born in the tragedy of the Second World War. While the framers of the charter were meeting in San Francisco, Allied forces were fighting beyond the German frontier and the assault on Japan could begin. The charter begins by stating that the people of the world are combining their efforts to accomplish certain objective. Understandably, the 1st objective was, "to save succeeding generations from the scourge of war, which twice in our life time has brought untold sorrow to mankind......."

The main purpose, then, of the United Nations, is the maintenance of peace. The overall method by which it is to be accomplished is the development of a dynamic international society in which nations are held together by many visible and intangible bonds of civilized adjustments and developments. The Charter suggests that the nations first of all attempt to settle disputes directly. It suggests a variety of means for dealing with them. Article 33 of the Charter states: "The parties to any dispute, the continuance of which likely to endanger the maintenance of international peace and security, shall, first of all, seek a solution by negotiation, judicial settlement, resort to regional agencies of arrangements, or other peaceful means of their own choice."

The United Nations, the world's most comprehensive and modern organization for preservation of World Peace, grew from a wartime alliance. The basic motivation for establishing the UNO while its predecessor, the League of Nations, was languishing at Geneva, was to try once again to avoid the catastrophe of war. Among the Allied Powers, the US under President Franklin D. Roosevelt was strongly in favour of a global peace-keeping agency. He was one who coined the name United Nations. Even when the World War-II was raging, the need for such an organization was proclaimed in the famous Atlantic Charter signed by President Roosevelt and Prime Minister Churchill as early as 1941. The Anglo-American initiative gained further momentum at the Moscow (October 1943) and Yalta Conference (February 1945) where consent of Soviet Union and the Republic of China was obtained.

The Moscow Communiqué released in November 1943 envisaged

"a general international organization based on the principle of sovereign equality of all peace loving states....... large and small, for the maintenance of international peace and security." At Yalta Conference of February 1945, the decision-making procedure for the UN was agreed upon, whence arose the Veto power of the big five. Also introduced was the notion of the trusteeship system.

The next major initiative was taken at the Dumbarton Oaks Conference of foreign officials (August–October 1944), where the first blueprint of UN emerged. At Dumbarton Oaks the question was raised whether economic and social matters should come within the scope of the proposed organization. The Soviet position had been that it should be devoted exclusively to security matters. However, the Anglo-American viewpoint in favor of entrusting the organization with security as well as non-security tasks ultimately prevailed.

The next and the largest Conference for framing the Charter of the new organization was held at San Francisco from April 25 to June 26, 1945. Attended by about 280 delegates from 50 invitee nations, the Conference looked like a World Constitutional Convention. At San Francisco the medium and small powers took considerable initiative to scrutinize the Dumbarton Oaks proposals and suggest important changes. The San Francisco Conference ended with the signing of the Charter on June 26, 1945. It took another four months to get the Charter ratified so that the UN of today was officially launched on October 24, 1945.

The UN was conceived as a general international organization, not only world-wide in membership but comprehensive in its tasks as well. Hence, the purposes of the organization stated in Article 1 of the Charter, refer to a great variety of political, social, economic, cultural and humanitarian objectives. The foremost objective is "to maintain international peace and security and to that end, to take effective collective measures for the prevention and removal of threats of peace...... and to bring about by peaceful means...... adjustments or settlement of international disputes or situations which might lead to a breach of the peace."

The second purpose was to "develop friendly relations among nations based on respect for the principle of equal rights and self-determination of peoples" and to take "other appropriate measures to strengthen universal peace." A third purpose was "to achieve international cooperation in solving international problems of an economic, social, cultural or humanitarian character and in promoting respect for human rights" without any invidious distinction. Finally, the UN was intended to be "a centre for harmonizing the actions of nations in the attainment of these common ends."

UN PEACE KEEPING OPERATIONS

As mentioned above the primary purpose of the UN is to maintain international peace and security, as such it is required "to take effective collective measures for the prevention and removal of threats, to the peace and for suppression of acts of aggression." The measures to be taken have been set out in Chapters VI and VII of the UN Charter, with the Security Council taking the primary responsibility. While under Chapter VI, the Security Council calls on the parties to settle their disputes either voluntarily or agreeing to the Council's directives, Chapter VII addresses more serious breaches of peace and requires the Council to take all sorts of peace enforcement measures including armed action. Remarkably, the UN so far has not engaged in a full scale collective security action, although the Korean Operation (1950s) and the Gulf expedition (1991-92) came closer to the idea. By and large, conflicts and breaches of peace have been contained and controlled by an alternative method called Peace Keeping Operation.

Peace Keeping Operations (PKO) are never partly military. They have been commonly employed to supervise and maintain ceasefire; to provide a buffer between opposing forces; to assist withdrawal of contending forces and, sometimes to help national reconciliation in civil war situations. Evidently, the PKOs are flexible instruments of policy and can be undertaken either at the initiative of the Security Council or of the General Assembly. In most cases PKO has avoided the crippling effects of the veto system. In short, the PKO stands between text-book enforcement measures and mild diplomatic means for settlement of conflicts. Aptly did Dag Hanunarskjold put it, PKO might be put in a new "Chapter VI and a half.

The PKOs are mostly initiated following agreements between the UN and the countries affected. They are intended to be provisional and involve temporary measures. Their task is essentially to stop or contain hostilities and thus create conditions in which peace-making can start. The Secretary General has all along taken the lead in organizing the PKO. United Nations peace-keeping operations can be divided into two broad categories. Observer mission which consists largely of officers who are almost invariably unarmed; and peace-keeping forces which consist of lightly armed infantry units with the necessary logistic support elements. These categories are not, however, watertight. Observer missions are some times reinforced by infantry and/or logistic units, usually for a specific purpose and a brief period of time. Peace-keeping forces are often assisted in their work by unarmed military observers.

The first use of military personnel by the United Nations was in 1947 through two United Nations bodies; the Consular Commission in Indonesia and the Special Committee on the Balkans.

The first peace-keeping operation established by the United Nations was an observer mission, the United Nations Truce Supervision Organization (UNTSO), which was set-up in Palestine in June 1948. Later *observer missions* were: the United Nations Military Observer Group in India and Pakistan (UNMOGIP) in 1949, the United Nations Observation Group in Lebanon (UNOGIL) in 1958, the United Nations Yemen Observation Mission (UNYOM) in 1963, the United Nations India-Pakistan Observation Mission (UNIPOM) in 1965, the Mission of the Representative of the Secretary-General in the Dominican Republic (DOMREP) in the sun year, the United Nations Good Offices Mission in Afghanistan and Pakistan (UNGOMAP) in 1988, the United Nations Iran-Iraq Military Observer Group (UNIMOG) also in 1988, the United Nations Angola Verification Mission (UNAVEM) in 1989 and the United Nations Observer Group in Central America (ONUCA) in 1990. Of these, UNTSO, UNMOGIP, UNIIMOG, UNAVEM and ONUCA are still in operation besides UNIMIR (1993) and UNTSO (1948).

There have been, in all, eight peace-keeping forces. The first was the United Nations Emergency Force (UNEF-I) which was in operation in the Egypt-Israel sector from November 1956 until May 1967. The United Nations Operation in the Congo (ONUC) was deployed in the 'Republic of the Congo' (now Zaire) from July 1960 until June 1964. The United Nations Security Force in West Israel (UNSF) was in operation from its establishment in September 1962 until April 1963. The second United Nations Emergency Force (UNEF-II) functioned between Egypt and Israel from October 1973 until July 1979. The United Nations Transition Assistance Group (UNTAG) was deployed in Namibia from March 1989 until March 1990. The other forces, which are still in operation, are the United Nations Peace-keeping Force in Cyprus (UNF1CYP), established in March 1964; the United Nations Disengagement Observer Force (UNDOF) established in Syrian Golan Heights in May 1974; the United Nations Interim Force in Lebanon (UNIFTL), established in March 1978. United Nations Protection Force (UNPROFOR) in Bosnia; and United Nations Operations in Somalia (UNOSOM) the last two continuing since 1992.

A United Nations peace-keeping operation is considered a subsidiary organ of the UN, established by a resolution of the Security Council, or occasionally of the General Assembly. Its military component consists of a Force Commander (sometimes called Chief of Staff) and a number of contingents provided by selected member-states of the UN who have been so requested by the Secretary General. Since 1973 selection of the contingents is being made in consultation with the Security Council and, of course, in consultation with the parties concerned. During the period of their assignment to UNPKF, the military personnel, while remaining in their national service, are treated as international personnel. As such they are to be totally under the UN authority and have to regulate their conduct with only the best interests of the UN in view.

It may be mentioned here that the UNPKF has also a civilian component. A civilian administrative staff is formed by the Secretary General from among existing staff of the UN Secretariat. In addition, some local hands may be recruited temporarily to facilitate logistics and communications. Where the UNPKF is required to perform tasks of a non-military nature, the civilian contingents constitutes the bulk of the personnel (e.g. policemen, election monitors). Overall command in such cases rests with the Special Representative of the Secretary General.

Some of the major initiatives taken by United Nations for maintaining and establishing peace in the different parts of the world.

The Korean Experience (1950-53)

To learn about the Korean war from a historical perspective, one can start early in this century with the victory of the Japanese over Russia in the Russo-Japanese war that ended in 1905 and their domination of Manchuria and Port Arthur followed by the Japan's annexation of the Korean peninsula in 1910. The Japanese occupation of Korea lasted for 35 years until Japan's defeat and surrender on 25 August 1945.[1]

In 1947, the UN declared that elections should be held throughout the entire country to choose one government to unify the country. The south rejected the proposal and held its own election and established an independent Republic of Korea in August 1947 with Syngman Rhee as its leader.

Then on 9 September 1947, the Russians proposed a mutual withdrawal of USSR and US troops from the peninsula. While making such a peaceful gesture, flows of USSR military equipment began to enter the north bolstered by 25,000 vet Chinese troops from the Manchurian campaign to replace the withdrawal of USSR troops.

For American leaders who were tired of their troops in Asia, and did not want another conflict of the mainland, this offer of withdrawal came as an opportunity to extract themselves from a potentially costly and strategically unimportant situation which they considered Korea to be. Withdrawal could go ahead. This American policy toward Korea, following World War II and the occupation of Japan by the US are linked.[2] The adding of troops, equipment and money to Korea with the occupation of Japan and the rebuilding of its economy was financially too much for Washington to handle. Therefore, it was rationalized that Korea was outside of the US line of defense in Asia. In September 1948, with the support of the USSR, Kim II Sung was elected prime minister of the new People's Republic of North Korea and the withdrawal of Russian troops began.

Such a policy made the 'Korea problem' convenient to hand over to the newly formed UN in May 1948. The UN goal was to unify the country, and if that failed, support for an independent government in the south was to proceed and the US could withdraw its 30,000 troops while providing limited economic aid to the newly formed Republic of Korea government. As US forces withdrew, however, a US military advisory group of 500 officers and men remained to train and equip the small ROK army. It was called the Korean Military Assistance Group, or KMAG, a well-trained and equipped ROK army of 100,000 troops was KMAG's goal. Once trained, 4 RCK divisions were stationed along the 38th parallel to defend against a North Korean People's Army—the NKPA intrusion.[3]

The reaction to the Communist attack called for immediate US action through the newly-established UN. Cognizant of the charge that he was 'soft on Communism,' President Truman had to act decisively and strongly. However, he acted cautiously and in proportion to NKPA aggression because of the possible involvement of the USSR, chief supplier and supporter to the North Koreans, that could lead to an expanded war, even a possible World War II. He set limited objectives for US intervention, that is, to drive the NKPA back beyond the 38th parallel. Carefully, he even down-played the gravity of America and UN Involvement by agreeing to the term 'police action' rather than war.

As a first test of the Cold War, the Communist invasion of the South had been turned around. Exacting revenge on the North by an invasion and takeover of their country remained unanswered. Underlying all planning was the question of the Chinese and their participation and what the USSR intended to do in the changing balance of military power. Would they possibly assist the NKPA and, if so, at what point?

Within America, those opposed to further involvement were branded as being 'soft oil Communism' and failure to check such aggression would encourage similar acts in other Asian countries. With consideration of the difficulties of winter warfare in the north on the minds of allied military planners, the question of continuing north became more complex. Syngman Rhee had his own reason for complete defeat of the north which was the possibility that the whole country would become his to lead.[4]

UN forces continued to drive north toward the Yalu which was reached in late October. The successes of Inchon, the recapture of Seoul and winning of Pyongyang gave military planners like MacArthur a sense of overconfidence and arrogance. As oil previous occasions, MacArthur's estimations of NKPA strength were much lower than reality. Based on such information, he assured the president that the Chinese would not enter the war, that NKPA resistance would end by thanksgiving and that his troops would be home by Christinas, a promise he would live to regret. While making, such promises to Truman at a meeting held on Midway Island and assuring him that 'victory was won in Korea,' 300,000 Chinese Communist forces—CCF, were pouring over the Yalu river into North Korea without the knowledge of the Allies.[5]

Phase three thus began, with UN forces unprepared to face the onslaught and bloodshed that was about to overwhelm them. With the entry of the Chinese, the political equation and military scope of the war changed and expanded greatly. US policy-makers at the highest levels were forced to re-think America's role and the domestic and international repercussions of the developments. The support of the Chinese by the USSR added a far deeper dimension to the role of the UN.[6]

MacArthur was shocked and astounded by Truman's order and reacted by saying that 'thousands of America lives' would be lost with the bridges left intact. One of his famous statements was uttered: 'in war, there is no substitute for victory. We cannot fight with one hand tied behind our back.' So great was his insult that he threatened to resign but his feelings of self-importance and vanity and the belief that the Army couldn't do without him overcame such thinking. Challenging the authority of the JCS and taking his case directly to the American people, MacArthur believed that UN forces were in 'grave danger' without the bombing. His strategy was successful and Truman had to yield under political pressure and authorized the bombing of the Yalu bridges.

However, to avoid a complete withdrawal from Korea, MacArthur recommended strategies designed to expand the scope of the war with provocative actions against Red China. Perhaps it was his way to retaliate against the Chinese or distract their attention away from Korea. The recommendations were for a naval blockade of the China coast; releasing the forces of Chaing Kai-shek on Taiwan to attack the Chinese in Korea and assisting anti-Communist guerillas on the Chinese mainland to fight the Communists. Such recommendations caused a greater loss of MacArthur's credibility among the JCS and the president and created more doubts about his ability to command and his mental state.

Phase four of the war began in January 1951, when the CCF re-occupied Seoul and drove the Allies south along with millions of half-frozen refugees who crossed the ice-covered Han River with the troops. Phase 4 turned out to be the longest phase of the war, lasting 18 months. Their retreat, however, ended about 25 miles south of the city due to UN superiority in tanks and heavy artillery. And, starting in late February, the Allies began to turn the tide in their favour.[7]

As Allied forces were fighting their way back to the 38th parallel, the debate about how far they should go and if the NKPA and CCF should be destroyed took place. MacArthur, on the other hand, continued to insist on inflicting heavy losses on the Chinese with massive infusions of men and equipment until (here was an all-out) victory over the enemy at no-matter what the cost. He felt humiliated by what his soldiers had endured ever since the CCF forces crossed the border and aggressively pushed south. No doubt, his ability as a leader could have been called into question with such attitudes.

MacArthur's supporters blamed Truman for the frustrating status of the war while forgiving the general for defying the Constitution, which he clearly did. Ultimately, in the next Presidential election, Truman's was bypassed as the nominee for the Democrats in favor of Adlai Stevenson who lost to Dwight Eisenhower, the hero of World War II. In a campaign promise, the former general said that he would go to Korea and bring the war to a conclusion.

From late June 1951, a UN strategy of a 'limited offensive' was to be followed, that is, defense lines were to be held without the taking of a additional enemy-held territory. Despite it, Americans advanced to an area called the Iron Triangle, located just north of the 38th parallel. There they engaged in savage fighting in which 60 Marines were killed in one week alone. Unlike previous battles, very little news coverage was given this event and subsequent fights, indicating the indifference which most Americans had toward the war.

However, later the same month, Jacob Malik, USSR Ambassador to the UN, called for a cease-fire and peace negotiations on the Korean War. Such news was welcomed by Americans and provided hope that the US could leave Korea under honorable circumstances. By July, US casualties had mounted to 69,000 troops.[8]

The back and forth course of the war had shown very little positive results because the stalemate in which both sides were at approx the same point where they started. Without reports of newsworthy fighting for the newspapers in America, Korea began to drop-off the pages and historians in later years began to call it 'the forgotten war' and the term is still used today.

Soon after Malik's proposal, peace talks began on 10 July 1951, in Kaesong and lasted until July 1953. The warring armies continued to fight while peace talks were in progress. The violence, however, did not lessen as the casualty count continued to build and, at the war's end, was greater during the two years of the talks than during the one year before they began.

As the negotiations began, no agreement was reached on an immediate cease-fire despite the static battle lines. The fighting continued as it would for almost two years. The Ist Communist demand was the insistence that the UN pull back to the 38th parallel from their positions north of it. Had the UN done so, there would have been absolutely no net gain. In reality, all sides—the Russians, Chinese and Americans wanted to end the conflict but the hostility was too great to reach an agreement.[9]

After nearly two months of negotiations and bickering over petty issues, the talks were suspended for two months. Talks resumed after the two-month delay. A new site, Panmurnjorri was chosen because Kaesong was no longer acceptable to General Ridgway, the head of the UN delegation. The Communists seemed to offer an end to the fighting at the existing battle line and not at the 38th parallel. Ridgway was a hard liner who personally distrusted the enemy and insisted on the existing battle line. Even though the talks resumed, the fighting continued, much of it instigated by the Chinese in a failed effort to influence America voters with a military victory and thereby turn more public opinion against the war. Their efforts, however, turned into failure at the battle of White Horse Hill when more than 10,000 Chinese soldiers were killed.

The US was charged with engaging in bacterial warfare by dropping disease carrying insects over North Korean cities resulting in thousands of deaths. Though denounced by the US as propaganda, 39 America POWs who were pilots or flight crews 'confessed' to the charges after being tortured and brainwashed. The charge was never proven by an independent organization such as the Red Cross.

Finally, in the spring of 1953, after the death of Joseph Stalin, there were signs of hope as the Communists became more flexible. Whether Stalin's death and the influence of the USSR was directly related to the change in attitude is not fully known. However, in April, both sides agreed to Operation Little Switch which was the exchange of wounded and sick POWs on both sides, 6,670 Communists and 684 UN prisoners including 149 Americans.

Despite the opposition of Syngrnan Rhee who resisted peace of any kind with the Communists and tried to undermine the process, Operation Little Switch went ahead, followed by Operation Big Switch, the major exchange of all POWs on both sides.[10]

After months of negotiation, it was agreed that repatriated prisoners held by the UN were free to choose to return to Communism or be turned over to a commission composed of neutral nations. After further questioning by Communist officers to try to persuade them to remain, they were free to go to a non-Communist country.

In the Big Switch exchange, which proceeded after the signing of the cease-fire, 12,773 UN POWs including 3,597 Americans and 7,862 ROK, 945 British, 229 Turks and 140 others were returned. For the

Communists, 75,823 POWs were returned, including 70,183 NKPA and only 5,640 Chinese. Even up to the last days of the war with the final agreement near, a major Communist offensive against ROK positions was undertaken, only to be driven back by a massive artillery response. Although 27 July 53 was agreed upon for the signing of the cease fire, fighting continued during the final hours before 10:00 am, the hour of signing.

There is much that can be said about the war. The casualty figures are enormous and very tragic: at least 2 million Korean civilians and 2.4 military casualties on both sides, which shows that 4.2 million men, women and children were killed or wounded with lives and families destroyed. The country, north and south was almost completely devastated.

Differing political systems, which the fighting was all about, remain essentially the same on the Korean peninsula which remains divided in two almost along the same line as it was before the war, a 151 mile long Demilitarized Line. Only a small gain of about 1,500 square miles above the 38th parallel is now in the south's hands that wasn't theirs before the war. The added territory is hardly worth what it cost.[11]

Direct enforcement action with organized combat units against an alleged aggressor has been few and far between in the history of the UN so far. The first and perhaps the only instance when it took classic proportions was during the Korean crisis. Four distinct phases can be identified in the UN collective security action in Korea.

(a) Fixation of responsibility for breach of the peace—The Security Council, taking advantage of the absence of the Soviet delegate on 25 and 27 June 1950, held North Korea responsible for an armed intrusion into the territory of South Korea. It determined that this was a breach of the peace and decided to take enforcement action against North Korea if it did not withdraw its troops to the norm of the 38th parallel. Non-compliance by North Korea was taken as the basis for a punitive action which the US and its western allies were only too eager to carry through. Considering the fact that North Korea enjoyed Soviet support, the Security Council had to choose between passive acquiescence and endorsing US action that was likely to produce a major confrontation with the Soviet Union. There being no option for a negotiation with North Korea, a firm action seemed to be unavoidable, particularly to avoid the stigma of being ineffective like the League of Nations.

(b) Dispatch of UN forces under US command—Following the 27th June resolution a combined armed force drawn from UK, US, Australia, South Korea and New Zealand was placed under the unified command of the American General Mac Arthur with Headquarters at Tokyo. A few other pro-western, members agreed to make only some token contribution while many Afro-Asian members maintained a position of detachment. The actual authorization to use UN force however came by way of a maneuver called Uniting for Peace Resolution in the General Assembly (November 3, 1950).

(c) Chinese intervention—while the UN military action dragged on in the face of fierce North Korean resistance, entry of China into the fray was precipitated by Mac Arthur's decision to enlarge the theatre of war. A security council attempt to condemn China was vetoed by the Soviet Union. Many at this stage had the apprehension that instead of managing the original, limited crisis the UN was getting embroiled in a major war. Moreover, the military reverses suffered by the UN forces in the bands of the North Koreans and the Chinese undermined the prospect of an early settlement.

(d) Move towards armistic—With the ground realities showing some stability, the General Assembly adopted a resolution in February 1951 to explore the possibilities of a peaceful settlement, followed by a contrary resolution in May imposing embargo on shipment of war materials likely to reach the North Koreans and stepping up UN combat operations, soon, an exasperated UN decided to negotiate an armistic, primarily with a view to arranging repatriation of thousands of western soldiers held captive in the Chinese and the North Korean camps. Certain neutral nations were assigned the role of running an armistic supervision commission with India at its head. Finally, in July 1953 the armistic was signed with armed forces of the two Koreas receding to their pre-war positions and prisoners of war released in several batches.

Thus, the first test case of collective Security seemed to end in too much ado about too little achieved. The territorial integrity of South Korea was preserved no doubt but the characterization of an alleged aggression from the North remained ambiguous. Neither was the ability of the UN to take a concerted and effective action clearly established.

Going far beyond his mandate, the American General turned a police action into a military expedition. There was indeed little justification to provoke a Chinese retaliation. A virtually one-nation enterprise, the UN operation did not reveal "independent statesmanship in making the most critical policy decision."[12] It had all the smell of a cold war fought in disguise of collective security. National interests got mixed up with community concerns. Above all, the whole enterprise was undertaken without developing a proper military-diplomatic apparatus to give it a sense of direction. In any case, the preponderance of forces was definitely not on the side of the UNO.[13] Finally, the only abiding legacy of the Korean operation was the Uniting for Peace Resolution which redefined the institutional balance between the Security Council and the General Assembly.

Indonesia

After the liberation of Indonesia from Japanese troops, the Indonesian nationalists set-up a republic and declared independence. So the Dutch government launched military attack on Indonesia. The matter was brought before the Security Council by the Indian representative and a ceasefire was arranged. Both the Dutch government and Indonesia accepted goods offices of the committee of Australia and Belgium. Australia on behalf of Indonesia and Belgium on behalf of the Dutch carried on negotiations for peace. In January 1948 an eighteen point settlement programme was accepted but this agreement was violated by the parties and there was further clash. The Security Council called for cease-fire and established UN committee to settle the issue. The Dutch government was asked by the Security Council to recognise the Independence of Indonesia which she did on 27th December 1949.[14]

Greece

British troops were in Greece at the end of the Second World War and were supporting the conservative provisional government. The Soviet Union challenged the presence of British forces and contended that Britain was interfering in the internal affairs of Greece and the military presence of Britain was threat to peace. The matter was referred to the Security Council, which simply took notice of the views expressed. The Greek question became serious when the neighbouring countries helped the guerillas against the Greek government. The Security Council appointed a commission of investigation. On the Greek question the UK and the United States were on one side whereas the Soviet Union was on the other side. It was observed that the Security Council could be paralyzed in the exercise of security functions by the veto. However, the Greek case could not be regarded as a triumph for the UNO but it set a precedent for increased reliance on the General Assembly in future disputes in case Security Council is paralysed by exercise of veto power.[15]

Issue of Merger of Trieste

According to the Italian peace treaty after the end of the Second World War, Trieste was internationalised and the Security Council accepted responsibility for its government. In the meanwhile Trieste was occupied by joint Anglo-American and French troops in Zone A where as the forces of Yugoslavia had occupied the Zone B of Trieste. In 1948, the USA and the UK expressed their desire to revise the treaty and handover the territory to Italy. In 1953, an Anglo-American plan to handover Zone A to Italy, was announced. Marshall Tito, the head of Yugoslavia government threatened to march into Trieste. In the meanwhile Italy and Yugoslavia reached an amicable solution by which Italy, occupied Zone 'A' and Yugoslavia occupied Zone 'B' of the disputed territory.[16]

Cuban Missile Crisis

The Cuban missile crisis and its aftermath was the most serious U.S.-Soviet confrontation of the Cold War although the crisis itself was short, it was so intense that it absorbed the entire attention of President Kennedy and his closest advisers. The Cuban missile crisis, the "sixteen days in October," ending with the Kennedy-Khrushchev "agreement" of October 28, 1962, has been studied extensively by scholars and has been described in a variety of published works.

According to Nikita Khrushchev's memoirs, in May 1962 conceived the idea of placing intermediate-range nuclear missiles in Cuba as a means of countering all emerging lead of the United States in developing and deploying strategic missiles. He also presented the scheme as a means of protecting Cuba from another United States-sponsored invasion, such as the failed attempt at the Bay of Pigs in 1961.[17]

After obtaining Fidel Castro's approval, the Soviet Union worked quickly and secretly to build missile installations in Cuba. On October 16, President John F. Kennedy was shown reconnaissance photographs of Soviet missile installations under construction in Cuba. After seven days of guarded and intense debate in the United States administration, during which Soviet diplomats denied that installations for offensive missiles were being built in Cuba, President Kennedy, in a televised address on October 22, announced the discovery of the installations and proclaimed that any nuclear missile attack from Cuba would be regarded as an attack by the Soviet Union and would be responded to accordingly. He also imposed a naval quarantine on Cuba to prevent further Soviet shipments of offensive military weapons from arriving there. In response to the threat the US military began a rapid mobilization for possible use against Cuba. The Ist Armored Division was ordered to Fort Stewart. In the short span of two weeks the population of the post rose from 3,500 personnel to over 30,000.

During the crisis, the two sides exchanged many letters and other communications, both formal and "back channel." Khrushchev sent letters to Kennedy on October 23 and 24 indicating the deterrent nature of the missiles in Cuba and the peaceful intentions of the Soviet Union. On October 26, Khrushchev sent Kennedy a long rambling letter seemingly proposing that the missile installations would be dismantled and personnel removed in exchange for United States assurances that it or its proxies would not invade Cuba. On October 27, another letter to Kennedy arrived from Khrushchev, suggesting that missile installations in Cuba would be dismantled if the United States dismantled its missile installations in Turkey. The American administration decided to ignore this second letter and to accept the offer outlined in the letter of October 26. Khrushchev then announced on October 28 that the would dismantle the installations and return them to the Soviet Union, expressing his trust that the United States would not invade Cuba.

Further negotiations were held to implement the October 28 agreement, including a United States demand that Soviet light bombers also be removed from Cuba, and to specify the exact form and conditions of United States assurances not to invade Cuba. A second dangerous crisis emerged over the removal of Soviet IL-28 bombers from Cuba, which the United States insisted were "offensive weapons" and thus subject to the October 28 agreement. By January 1963 it was clear that no formal agreement would result.[18]

Suez Crisis and the UNEF (1956)

With Korean experience still fresh in memory, the UN was soon confronted with unprecedented crisis. On October 29, 1956 two permanent members of the Security Council, (Britain and France) and Israel combined to forcefully oust Egypt from the Suez canal area over which the latter had asserted its sovereignty but the aggressors wanted to get back control over the canal. In response to Egypt's petition, the General Assembly in its emergency special session of November 1956 sent out an appeal for ceasefire and created the UN Emergency Force (UNEF) to resolve the crisis in the Middle East. It was a unique peace effort in which the Secretary General played the central role. The force was not intended so much for combat operation as for truce supervision and to prevent the redemption of hostilities. This was particularly necessary in view of the fragile character of the Arab-Israeli truce since the 1948 flare up in the middle-East. To ensure that the Force was unquestionably impartial, its contingents were to be drawn from states other than the permanent members of the Security Council.[19] It was made accountable direct to the Secretary General and its terms of reference were fixed by the General Assembly. The force was essentially meant for emergency operation and had nothing to do with the military balance in the conflict. Moreover, all operations of the force including its stationing and duration of stay, were subject to the consent of the host country, i.e. Egypt. Finally, the force was to be financed by the nations who contributed troops and logistics. However, the cost of their transportation, maintenance and administration were to be met out of a special fund to which all member-states must make contributions in proportion to their share of the regular UN budget. At no point of time the UNEF included more than 6000 men.

Once in the field the UNEF formed a buffer zone between the Anglo-French-Israeli forces and the Egyptian army. Following withdrawal of the invading forces UNEF restored the lost patch of territory to Egypt. In the Sinai Peninsula, it took prolonged diplomatic pressures to make Israel evacuate. The 273 kilometer long border between Israel and Egypt had to be patrolled by UNEF till May 1967—a period marked by occasional breach of truce, UNEF was withdrawn at a time when Egypt no longer wanted it in view of the offensive it was planning against Israel.

In May and June 1967 the ONEF withdrew, leaving the Truce Supervision group to witness the 1967 flare up. Later, the October 1973 war between Israel and Egypt aided by other Arab nations led to the formation of UNEF-II to serve more or less the same purpose as its predecessor. It was kept alive for about six years and was not extended after 1979.

West New Guinea (West Irian)

The territory of West New Guinea (West Irian) had been in the possession of the Netherlands since 1828. When the Netherlands formally recognized the sovereign independence of Indonesia in 1949, the status of West Irian remained unresolved. It was agreed in the Charter of Transfer of Sovereignty C concluded between the Netherlands and Indonesia at The Hague, Netherlands, in November 1949 C that the issue would be postponed for a year, and that "the status quo of the presidency of New Guinea" would be "maintained under the Government of the Netherlands" in the mean time. The ambiguity of the language, however, led the Netherlands to consider itself the sovereign Power in West New Guinea, since this would be a continuation of the "status quo." Indonesia, on the other hand, interpreted the Dutch role there to be strictly administrative, with the implication that West Irian would be incorporated into Indonesia after a year.

The status of the territory was still being disputed when Indonesia brought the matter before the United Nations in 1954. Indonesia claimed that the territory rightfully belonged to it and should be freed from Dutch colonial rule. The Netherlands maintained that the Papuans of West New Guinea were not Indonesians and therefore should be allowed to decide their own future when they were ready to do so. The future of the territory was discussed at the General Assembly's regular sessions from 1954 to 1957 and at the 1961 session, but no resolutions on it were adopted.

In December 1961, when increasing rancour between the Indonesian and Dutch Governments made the prospect of a negotiated settlement even more elusive, Secretary-General U Thant, who had been appointed Acting Secretary-General following the death of Secretary-General Dag Hammarskjöld, undertook to resolve the dispute through his good offices. Consulting with the Indonesian and Dutch Permanent Representatives to the United Nations, he suggested that informal talks take place between the parties in the presence of former United States Ambassador Ellsworth Bunker, who would act as the Secretary-General's representative. The parties agreed, and talks were begun in early 1962.

A sharpening of tension between the two Governments occurred shortly thereafter, however, when Indonesia landed paratroops in West New Guinea. The Netherlands charged that the landings constituted an act of aggression, but Indonesia refuted this on the grounds that "Indonesians who have entered and who in future will continue to enter West Irian are Indonesian nationals who move into Indonesia's own territory now dominated by the Dutch by force." Secretary-General U Thant urged restraint by both parties but declined a Dutch request to send United Nations observers to the scene, noting that such action could only be considered if both Governments made the request. Further incidents were reported by the Netherlands during the first months of 1962, and there were intermittent lulls in the progress of Ambassador Bunker's talks.

The Acting Secretary-General was at last able to announce, on 31 July 1962, that a preliminary agreement had been reached, and that official negotiations were to take place under his auspices. The final negotiations were held at United Nations Headquarters under the chairmanship of the Secretary-General, with Ambassador Bunker continuing to act as mediator. An agreement was signed at New York by Indonesia and the Netherlands on 15 August 1962. Ratification instruments were exchanged between the two countries on 20 September 1962 and, the next day, the General Assembly took note of the agreement in resolution 1752 (XVII) of the same date, authorizing the Secretary-General to carry out the tasks entrusted to him therein.

The agreement provided for the administration of West New Guinea (West Irian) to be transferred by the Netherlands to a United Nations Temporary Executive Authority (UNTEA), to be headed by a United Nations Administrator who would be acceptable to both parties and who would be appointed by the Secretary-General. Under the Secretary-General's jurisdiction, UNTEA would have full authority after 1 October 1962 to administer the territory, to maintain law and order, to protect the rights of the inhabitants and to ensure uninterrupted, normal services until 1 May 1963, when the administration of the territory was to be transferred to Indonesia.

The agreement also stipulated that the Secretary-General would provide a United Nations Security Force (UNSF) to assist UNTEA with as many troops as the United Nations Administrator deemed necessary. In "related understandings" to the main agreement, it was established that United Nations personnel would observe the implementation of the ceasefire that was to become effective before UNTEA assumed authority. The United Nations was therefore entrusted with a dual peace-keeping role in addition to its administrative responsibilities as the executive authority.

Establishment of UNSF

With the cessation of hostilities, the next step was to ensure the maintenance of law and order in the territory. In addition to supervising the observer team, General Rikhye had been charged with making preliminary arrangements for the arrival of UNSF.

Article VIII of the Indonesian-Netherlands agreement stipulated the role and purpose of such a force:

The Secretary-General would provide the UNTEA with such security forces as the United Nations Administrator deems necessary; such forces would primarily supplement existing Papuan (West Irianese) police in the task of maintaining law and order. The Papuan Volunteer Corps, which on the arrival of the United Nations Administrator would cease being part of the Netherlands armed forces, and the Indonesian armed forces in the territory, would be under the authority of, and at the disposal of, the Secretary-General for the same purpose. The United Nations Administrator would, to the extent feasible, use the Papuan (West Irianese) police as a United Nations security force to maintain law and order and, at his discretion, use Indonesian armed forces. The Netherlands armed forces would be repatriated as rapidly as possible and while still in the territory will be under the authority of the UNTEA.

UNSF was thus essentially an internal law and security force C the "police arm" of UNTEA C whose responsibilities would range from ensuring the smooth implementation of UNTEA's administrative mandate to supervising the buildup of a viable, local police force.

In the memorandum of understanding on the cessation of hostilities, it was provided that UNSF would commence its duties as soon as possible after the General Assembly adopted an enabling resolution, but no later than 1 October 1962. In fact, the UNSF Commander arrived in West Irian weeks before the Assembly resolution was passed.

Major-General Said Uddin Khan (Pakistan), appointed by the Secretary-General as Commander of UNSF, arrived in Hollandia on 4 September for preliminary discussions with Netherlands authorities and for a survey of future requirements. Similar efforts had already been exerted to some extent by General Rikhye, who had been charged earlier with making preliminary arrangements for the arrival of UNSF. The two men cooperated closely before and after the establishment of UNSF in West Irian.

UNSF comprised 1,500 Pakistan troops, made available at the request of the Secretary-General, as were the support units of Canadian and United States aircraft and crews.

By 3 October, an advance party of 340 men of UNSF had arrived in the territory. On 5 October, the balance of the Pakistan contingent took up its positions. Also included in UNSF were some 16 officers and men of the Royal Canadian Air Force, with two aircrafts, and a detachment of approximately 60 United States Air Force personnel with an average of three aircrafts. These provided troop transport and communications. The Administrator also had under his authority the Papuan Volunteer Corps, the civil police, the Netherlands forces until their repatriation, and Indonesian troops, totalling approximately 1,500.

Establishment of UNTEA

UNSF was created to uphold the authority of UNTEA. Whereas groundwork for the arrival of UNSF troops had been laid in West Irian prior to the General Assembly's recognition of the agreement, it was not until Assembly resolution 1752 (XVII) was adopted that personnel associated with UNTEA were dispatched. This resolution, which would make the United Nations directly responsible for the administration of the western half of New Guinea, was approved by a vote of 89 to none, with 14 abstentions.

In the resolution, the Assembly took note of the agreement between Indonesia and the Netherlands concerning West New Guinea (West Irian), acknowledged the role conferred by it upon the Secretary-General, and authorized him to carry out the tasks entrusted to him in the agreement.

Upon adoption of the resolution, the Secretary-General noted that for the first time in its history the United Nations would have temporary executive authority established by and under the jurisdiction of the Secretary-General over a vast territory. He dispatched his Deputy Chef de Cabinet, Mr. José Rolz-Bennett, as his Representative in West New Guinea (West Irian), where he would make preliminary arrangements for the transfer of administration to UNTEA. Mr. Rolz-Bennett arrived in the territory on 21 September 1962, the date the enabling resolution was passed.

Under the agreement, neither Dutch nor Indonesian officials were to hold any of the top administrative positions during the seven-month transition period. In addition, three quarters of the Dutch civil servants of lesser rank had decided to leave the territory before 1 October, thereby creating a vacuum that would have to be filled to prevent a disruption of essential functions and services. In some instances, this was accomplished by promoting Papuan offrcials to the vacant posts. There was, however, a great shortage of adequately trained Papuans.

Mr. Rolz-Bennett immediately set about assembling an emergency task force to be deployed in key areas of the administration, recruiting international as well as Dutch and Indonesian personnel. The Netherlands Governor of the territory and his senior officials assisted in this effort; measures were also taken by the Netherlands Government to encourage Dutch officials to remain and serve the Temporary Executive Authority. In addition, the Indonesian Government was requested to provide urgently a group of civil servants to fill certain high-priority posts. This request was made with a view to the gradual phasing in of Indonesian officials, whose presence thus facilitated the subsequent transfer of administrative responsibilities to Indonesia. In all, 32 nationalities were represented in UNTEA, among them both Dutch and Indonesian personnel.

The transfer of the administration from the Netherlands to UNTEA took place on 1 October 1962 and, in conformity with Article VI of the agreement and its related aide-mémoire, the United Nations flag was raised and flown side by side with the Netherlands flag.

Before his departure from the territory on 28 September, the Netherlands Governor, Mr. Peter Johannis Plateel, appealed to the population to give its support to the United Nations administration. In messages from the Secretary-General and from Mr. Rolz-Bennett (who was designated as Temporary Administrator for approximately six weeks), the population was informed that UNTEA would endeavour to ensure the welfare of the inhabitants. The Temporary Administrator signed an order effective 15 October granting amnesty to all political prisoners sentenced prior to 1 October 1962.

On 1 October, Indonesia and the Netherlands established liaison missions to UNTEA in Hollandia/Kotabaru. An Australian liaison mission replaced one which had formerly served in Hollandia/Kotabaru as an administrative liaison between the authorities of the territory of Papua/New Guinea and West New Guinea, and now provided effective liaison with UNTEA on matters of mutual interest.

The United Nations Administrator, Mr. Djalal Abdoh (Iran), was appointed by the Secretary-General on 22 October 1962, under Article IV of the agreement. On 15 November, he arrived in the territory to take up his assignment and Mr. Rolz-Bennett returned to Headquarters the following day.

UN in Kashmir: The UNCIP (1948), the UNIPOM (1965)

Regular raids by Pakistan-sponsored marauders into the princely state of Kashmir which had acceded to join the Indian Union led to an Indian complaint in the Security Council in January 1948. Without specifically branding Pakistan an aggressor, the Council sent a UN Commission for India and Pakistan (UNCIP) to investigate and report on the situation as well as assist mediation efforts. By mutual consent, a ceasefire was effected to assist truce supervision. A group of military observers became operational. They were known as UNMOGIP. Since Indo-Pak relations frequently led to crises and hostilities with Kashmir remaining the bone of contention, the presence of the UN troops has at least marginally assisted in keeping the conflict localized and practically freezing the line of actual control (LAQ).

Again when war broke out between Pakistan and India in 1965 the Security Council was apprised of the matter. It imposed a ceasefire and ordered immediate withdrawal of forces by both sides. The UNMOGIP was upgraded to UN India-Pak Observation Mission to patrol the borders.

UN in Lebanon: UNOGIL (1958)

In May 1958, armed rebellion broke out in Lebanon when President Camille Chamoun (a Maronite Christian) made known his intention to seek an amendment to the Constitution which would enable him to be re-elected for a second term. The disturbances, which started in the predominantly Moslem city of Tripoli, soon spread to Beirut and the northern and north-eastern areas near the Syrian border, and assumed the proportions of a civil war.

On 22 May, the Lebanese Government requested a meeting of the Security Council to consider its complaint "in respect of a situation arising from the intervention of the United Arab Republic in the internal affairs of Lebanon, the continuance of which is likely to endanger the maintenance of international peace and security." It charged that the United Arab Republic was encouraging and supporting the rebellion by the supply of large quantities of arms to subversive elements in Lebanon, by the infiltration of armed personnel from Syria into Lebanon, and by conducting a violent press and radio campaign against the Lebanese Government.

On 27 May, the Security Council decided to include the Lebanese complaint on its agenda but, at the request of Iraq, agreed to postpone the debate to permit the League of Arab States to try to find a settlement of the dispute. After the League had met for six days without reaching agreement, the Council took up the case and, on 11 June, adopted resolution 128 (1958), by which it decided to dispatch urgently to Lebanon an observation group "so as to ensure that there is no illegal infiltration of personnel or supply of arms or other matériel across the Lebanese borders." The Secretary-General was authorized to take the necessary steps to dispatch the observation group, which was asked to keep the Council informed through him.

Resolution 128 (1958), supported by both Lebanon and the United Arab Republic, formed the basis for the establishment of the United Nations Observation Group in Lebanon (UNOGIL).

Creation of UNOGIL

Following adoption of the Security Council's resolution 128 (1958), Secretary-General Dag Hammarskjöld told the Council that the necessary preparatory steps had already been taken. The Observation Group proper would be made up of highly qualified and experienced men from various regions of the world. They would be assisted by military observers, some of whom would be drawn from the United Nations Truce Supervision Organization (UNTSO) and could be in Beirut on the very next day. The Secretary-General stressed that the Group would not be a police force like the United Nations Emergency Force (UNEF) deployed in Sinai and the Gaza Strip.

Following the adoption of the resolution, the Secretary-General appointed Mr. Galo Plaza Lasso of Ecuador, Mr. Rajeshwar Dayal of India and Major-General Odd Bull of Norway as members of UNOGIL. Mr. Plaza acted as Chairman.

In order to start the operation without delay, 10 observers were immediately detached from UNTSO for assignment with UNOGIL. Five of them arrived in Beirut on 12 June and began active reconnaissance the following morning. The plan was to cover as many areas as possible and to probe further each day in the direction of the Syrian border so as to observe any illegal infiltration of personnel and supply of arms across the border. The number of observers were rapidly increased with new arrivals and reached 100 by 16 June. Two helicopters were placed at the disposal of the Group on 23 June, and they were supplemented shortly thereafter by four light observation aircrafts.

Method of Operation

The three members of UNOGIL assembled in Beirut on 19 June under the personal chairmanship of Dag Hammarskjöld, who had arrived in the area the day before. As outlined by the Secretary-General, the role of UNOGIL was strictly limited to observation, to ascertain whether illegal infiltration of personnel or supply of arms or other matériel across the Lebanese borders was occurring. It was not UNOGIL's task to mediate, arbitrate or forcefully to prohibit illegal infiltration, although it was hoped that its very presence on the borders would deter any such traffic. The borders meant those between Lebanon and Syria, since the Armistice Demarcation Line between Israel and Lebanon was covered by UNTSO and not involved in the present case.

It was decided that the Group should discharge its duties by the following methods:

(a) The UNOGIL military observers would conduct regular and frequent patrols of all accessible roads from dawn to dusk, primarily in border districts and the areas adjacent to the zones held by the opposition forces.

(b) A system of permanent observation posts was to be established and manned by military observers. There were initially 10 such stations. The observers at these stations attempted to check all reported infiltration in their areas and to observe any suspicious development.

(c) An emergency reserve of military observers was to be stationed at headquarters and main observation posts for the purpose of making inquiries at short notice or investigating alleged instances of smuggling.

(d) An evaluation team was to be set-up at headquarters to analyse, evaluate and coordinate all information received from observers and other sources.

(e) Aerial reconnaissance was to be conducted by light aeroplanes and helicopters, the former being equipped for aerial photography.

(f) The Lebanese Government would provide the Observation Group with all available information about suspected infiltration. The Group would also request the military observers to make specific inquiries into alleged activities as occasion required.

In a letter dated 1 October, the United Kingdom informed the Secretary-General that it had agreed with the Jordanian Government that the withdrawal of British troops should begin on 20 October. On 8 October, the United States announced that, by agreement with the Lebanese Government, it had been decided to complete the withdrawal of United States forces by the end of October. The withdrawal of United States troops was completed by 25 October, and of the British troops by 2 November.

Operations in the Congo: ONUC (1960-64)

Although post-Westphalian enforcement is often regarded as a phenomenon that started in the 1990s UN peace-keepers used significant amounts of force in the Congo in the early 1960s. The crisis in the Congo demonstrates how a combination of hasty (Belgian) decolonization, state fragility, weakness of central government authority, and ethnic and regional fragmentation drew the UN into using force against a secessionist movement and foreign mercenaries, and covertly supporting the overthrow of the elected Prime Minister, Patrice Lumumba.[20]

On 30 June 1960 the Congo gained its independence from Belgium. Only five days later, however, the Congolese army mutinied, causing extensive civil unrest, which included a number of attacks against Belgian citizens. In response to these attacks, on 11 July Belgium deployed paratroopers without the consent of the Congolese government. To make matters more complicated, on the very same day, local politician Moïse Tshombé declared Katanga, Congo's most mineral-rich province, to be independent, and the following month South Kasai also attempted to secede. It soon became apparent that Tshombé had considerable support from both the Belgian government and the vast industrial mining complex Union Minière du Haut-Katanga, headquartered in Brussels.[21]

In response to Belgium's intervention, both President Kasavubu and Prime Minister Lumumba called upon the UN to send military assistance, declaring that Belgium had committed an act of aggression against the Congo. Invoking Article 99 of the Charter, Secretary-General Dag Hammarskjöld called an urgent meeting of the Security Council. The Security Council agreed with the Congolese government and in Resolution 143 of 14 July 1960 called for Belgium to withdraw its troops. The Council authorized the deployment of a peace-keeping force, ONUC, which included troops from 30 states and at its peak, in July 1961, comprised 19,828 soldiers and some 2,000 civilian experts and technicians. ONUC personnel were initially intended to act as peace-keepers to oversee the withdrawal of Belgian troops and to help the Congolese government restore law and order; they were not supposed to get involved with Congolese politics in general and the Katangan secession in particular. But this is precisely what happened. Arguably, this was because ONUC's underlying goal was to restore an acceptable degree of Westphalian order by maintaining Congo's territorial integrity, peacefully if possible but by force if necessary.[22] Although Belgian troops quickly withdrew from the majority of Congolese territory, they did not withdraw from Katanga. This prompted the Security Council to call for their immediate withdrawal from the province (Resolution 146, 9 August 1960). This was duly done within six weeks.[23] ONUC was left to support the Congolese government restore law and order in the country. The problem was that the issue of Katanga's secession remained unresolved and approximately 510 Belgian officers and foreign mercenaries remained within Katanga to support Tshombé .[24]

In retrospect, it is clear that the UN actively took sides within Congolese politics in two senses. Covertly, the Secretary-General and the United States employed strategies designed to weaken Lumumba's position, especially after August 1960 when he had requested and received military assistance from the Soviet Union to suppress the regional rebellions in Katanga and South Kasai.[25]

Lumumba was subsequently abducted and later murdered by opposition politicians in January 1961. The UN also authorized ONUC to use force, ostensibly to prevent civil war in the Congo (Resolution 161, 21 February 1961). UN peace-keepers used force shortly afterwards against Tshombé's gendarmes and various mercenary and 'foreign' (mainly Belgian) elements in Katanga (although ONUC troops were also killed by rogue and undisciplined factions of the Congolese army in several incidents during 1961). The use of force to remove all mercenaries from Katanga was reiterated in November 1961 (Resolution 169). ONUC was eventually terminated in stages after February 1963 when Katanga was reintegrated into the national territory of the Congo. The last ONUC troops were withdrawn by 30 June 1964, although the country continued to receive civilian aid.

ONUC's use of force had important repercussions for UN peace-keeping more generally. As Alan James[26] has suggested, the mission was widely perceived as a tool of US foreign policy.[27] It also generated a financial crisis which has plagued UN operations ever since: ONUC's annual cost was $66 million at a time when the UN's overall budget was only $70 million and France and the Soviet Union refused to pay.[28] The operation also encouraged the UN to ensure that henceforth the role of the Secretary-General would be far more circumscribed. Finally, all subsequent UN forces were given six month long mandates in order to allow the Security Council to periodically review ongoing operations. ONUC's role in the Congo thus highlights two important points. First, given the opportunity, the UN was willing and able to engage in intra-state conflicts well before the 1990s.[29] Second, even when dealing with problems exacerbated by Westphalian systems of governance, in this case the retention of state borders imposed during colonialism, the UN refused to countenance political solutions that were not based on the territorial integrity of the state in question.

The Congo Crisis confronted the world community with all possible complexities — internal instability, intrusion of external forces, deliberate subversion, secession, tie-up of local and foreign economic interests and above all obstructive cold war politics. All these arose from the chaos that followed Congo's independence from a reluctant Belgium in July 1960. As the national any mutinied and the uranium rich Katanga province seceded due to foreign instigations, the central government requested UN intervention. Urgent action was recommended by Secretary General Dag Hammarskjold for the first time in a civil war situation which required a new form of peace-keeping. The Security Council authorized the UN Congo Operation (ONUC). A large contingent with civilian and military personnel was sent to the Congo as per host-country agreement with the immediate objective of ending Belgian intervention and restoring law and order. But the UNEF with its pure and simple posture of self-defense and non-interference could not cope with a fast deteriorating situation. Consequently the principles of non-interference had to be 'stretched, modified and at times, by passed'[30] to flush out the obstinate foreign mercenaries and to strengthen Central Government grip on the seceding Katanga Province. For about four long years, the UN went on helping the Congolese Government to maintain the country's political independence and territorial integrity as well as maintain law and order. After the assassination of the Prime Minister Patrice Limumba, the ONUC mandate had to be more assertive. The parliament was reconvened under its protection (August 1961) and regular forces were dispatched to chase away the mercenaries employed by the Tshombe Government in Katanga (December 1962). The initiative for expanded ONUC now came from Mr. U Thant who succeeded Dag after the latter died in a plane crash. In February 1963 Katanga came to be reintegrated into the Congo State. At the peak, part of its operation, ONUC forces consisted of a total strength of 20,000 personnel. Before it was finally withdrawn by June 30, 1964, a nation-wide political reconciliation had been effected.

It was stated that "when ONUC ended its mandate, the Congo was a united country in name only; One-fifth of its territory was under Leftist rebels ...what the UN intervention in the Congo accomplished was the restoration of *status quo ante.* There was a central government friendly to the western Countries."[31] No wonder, therefore, US diplomatic and financial support was readily available throughout the UN operations while the Soviets were thoroughly opposed to the expansion of UN mandate and refused to share the burden of peace-keeping expenses.

UN Peace-keeping in Cyprus: (UNFICYP 1964-87)

UN role in ethnic strife in a newly independent small state was illustrated for the first time in the Cyprus crisis. With Greek and Turkish Cypriots seriously defending their interests under the new Constitution of 1960, the island state was in acute tension. On receiving Cyprus governments' charge of Turkish intervention in its internal affairs, the Security Council recommended the sending an UN peace-keeping force in Cyprus (UNFICYP) intended to prevent recurrence of communal fighting and restore law and order The mandate was initially for six months at a time but has been continuously renewed to date. Apart from peace restoration, the UN also undertook the task of helping a settlement of the Cyprus problems, for which a UN mediator was appointed by the Secretary-General. With the communities finally persuaded to come to the negotiating table, stability gradually returned to the island. Ten years later, the General Assembly passed a resolution urging end of outside interference, safe return of all refugees and continuation of in Ere-communal dialogue assisted by UN mediator. Since a mutually acceptable solution was hard to arrive at, UNFICYP took care that the cease fire was not violated. The operation lasting for more than two decades and involving a force level of 2,328 with expenses running into a huge deficit. The multinational force also included a large contingent from a permanent Security Council member, i.e. UK.

Vietnam War

US involvement in Vietnam began during the administration of Dwight D. Eisenhower (1953-61), which sent US military to South Vietnam. Their numbers increased as the military position the Saigon government became weaker. In 1957, Communist rebels—Viet Cong—began a campaign of terrorism in South Vietnam. They were supported by the government of North Vietnam and later by North Vietnamese troops. Their goal was to overthrow the anti-communist government in the South.

John F. Kennedy (1961-63) decided to commit American support troops to South Vietnam. Four thousand troops were sent in 1962. After John Kennedy was murdered, Vice-President Lyndon Johnson served the last fourteen months of Kennedy's term. He then was elected to his own full term. It began in January 1965. Much of his time and energy would be taken up by the war in Vietnam. By early nineteen-sixty-four, America had about seventeen-thousand troops in Vietnam. The troops were there to advise and train the South Vietnamese military.

Under President Lyndon B. Johnson (1963-68), US intervention mushroomed both militarily and politically. Johnson asked for a resolution expressing U.S. determination to support freedom and protect peace in Southeast Asia. Congress responded with the Tonkin Gulf Resolution, expressing support for "all necessary measures" the President might take to repel armed attacks against US forces and prevent further aggression.[32]

Under the strategy developed by General William C. Westmoreland, Commander, U.S. Military Assistance Command, Vietnam, American divisions would seek out and destroy North Vietnamese and Viet Cong (South Vietnamese Communist) formations, while air power carried the war to the North, attacking both the will of Hanoi's leaders to continue the fight and, to an increasing extent, their ability to do so. The list of targets expanded to include transportation, oil storage, and the nation's few industries. In theory, Westmoreland's strategy of search and destroy would force the Communists to expend supplies and thus make the logistics establishment in North Vietnam all the more vulnerable to bombing.[33]

In 1966, more than 200,000 troops were committed to Vietnam. The United States escalated its participation in the war to a peak of 543,000 troops in April 1969. American forces in Southeast Asia operated under some stringent restrictions, including being forbidden to invade enemy territory in North Vietnam and, for many years, likewise being barred from ground operations against enemy sanctuaries in bordering Laos and Cambodia. The "body count" of Vietcong killed was the centerpiece of the American approach to waging the war, conducted through search and destroy operations in remote jungle regions. By 1966, it became increasingly clear that this strategy of attrition was not working and could not work because of the enemy's capacity to replace losses far higher than those the allies were able to inflict.

The political challenge of the war stemmed from the belief of the rural Vietnamese that the Government of Vietnam will not stay long when it comes into an area, that the Government was indifferent to the people's welfare, that the low-level officials were tools of the local rich; and that the Government was excessively corrupt from top to bottom. The American search and destroy military operations didn't solve these problems, and were at best irrelevant to security in rural Vietnamese villages. At worst, indiscriminate aerial attacks and artillery fire exacted a toll on village allegiance to the Saigon government.[34]

Concern that China might react as it had fifteen years earlier in Korea argued powerfully for relying on air power rather than invasion to convince Hanoi to call-off the war in the South. Having turned to air power, the Johnson administration chose to apply it in a gradually escalating fashion. President John F. Kennedy's recent success in compelling the Soviet Union to withdraw bombers and ballistic missiles from Cuba bred confidence in the gradual application of force.

The individual services, for the most part, controlled their own air arms. The Army maintained control of its large helicopter fleet as organic air assets. Marines followed their traditional organizational path of assigning an Air Wing to each Marine division. The Navy maintained complete control of its air assets and Admiral Sharp, as Commander-in-Chief of Pacific Command (CINCPAC), implemented the Route Pack system for all air operations over North Vietnam. General Clay, the Pacific Air Forces (PACAF) commander, was assigned coordinating authority for de-conflicting air operations, but he felt that the existing command arrangements (route packaging and assigning the air component only coordinating authority) did not provide a sound means to control the overall air effort.

The Route Pack system divided responsibility within North Vietnam into seven different geographic areas, with the Air Force and the Navy each receiving responsibility for portions of the route packs. Commander-in-Chief of Pacific Fleet (CINCPACFLT), the naval component of Pacific Command (PACOM), maintained control of carrier air assets. Even within the Air Force there was no single air commander. Seventh Air Force was responsible for Air Force air operations in Vietnam, while Thirteenth Air Force was responsible for Thailand, and Strategic Air Command (SAC) never relinquished command or control of its B-52 bombers.

The targeting process further complicated this patchwork of responsibility. Targets were selected in Washington by a small team on the joint staff and approved only at the presidential level. The result was a major misuse of air power. Air power application came to be simply the servicing of targets, with little regard for whether or not they were the "right" targets, and without an air campaign plan. Service parochialism dominated the air effort. Lacking a single responsible air commander, a clear set of objectives, and a common concept of operations, even the most skilled operations of the separate components tended to work at cross-purposes and give respite to the enemy.

Initially, most Americans backed Washington's Vietnam policy. A dangerous situation seemed to be developing, one which the US government referred to as the "domino theory"—if South Vietnam was allowed to fall to communism, so eventually would the rest of Southeast Asia.[35] But as the war dragged on and a military victory appeared more and more elusive, public opposition became more vocal.

President Johnson believed that the United States had to support South Vietnam. Many other Americans agreed. They believed that without American help, South Vietnam would become communist. Then, all of Southeast Asia would become Communist, too. As Johnson's term began, his military advisers told him the Communists were losing the war. They told him that North Vietnamese troops and Viet Cong forces would soon stop fighting. On February sixth, however, the Viet Cong attacked American camps at Pleiku and Qui Nhon. The Johnson administration immediately ordered air attacks against military targets in the north.

In March 1965 the first American ground troops arrived in South Vietnam. Congress supported the president's actions at that time. However, the number of Americans who opposed the war began to grow. These people said the war was a civil war. They said the United States had no right, or reason, to intervene. For six days in May, the United States halted air attacks on North Vietnam. The administration hoped this would help get the North Vietnamese government to begin negotiations. The North refused. And the United States began to build up its forces in the South. By July, one-hundred twenty-five thousand Americans were fighting in Vietnam.

In December 1965 the United States again halted air attacks against North Vietnam. Again, it invited the North Vietnamese government to negotiate an end to the fighting. And again, the North refused. Ho Chi Minh's conditions for peace were firm. He demanded an end to the bombing and a complete American withdrawal. Withdrawal would mean defeat for the South. It would mean that all of Vietnam would become Communist. President Johnson would not accept these terms. So he offered his own proposals. The most important was an immediate cease-fire. Neither side would compromise, however. And the fighting went on.

Johnson strongly defended the use of American soldiers in Vietnam. In a speech to a group of lawmakers he said: "Since world war two, this nation has met and has mastered many challenges—challenges in Greece and Turkey, in Berlin, in Korea, in Cuba. We met them because brave men were willing to risk their lives for their nation's security. And braver men have never lived than those who carry our colors in Vietnam this very hour."[36]

On 31 January 1968 combat erupted throughout the entire country in the Tet [new year] Offensive. Thirty-six of 44 provincial capitals and 64 of 242 district towns were attacked. They even struck at the American embassy in the capital, Saigon. Once the shock and confusion wore off, most attacks were crushed in a few days. During those few days, however, the fighting was some of the most violent ever seen in South Vietnam. Fifty-thousand Communist soldiers were killed during the Tet Offensive. Fourteen-thousand South Vietnamese soldiers were killed. And two-thousand American soldiers were killed. Thousands of Vietnamese civilians were killed, too.

On 31 March 1968 the President spoke to the American people on television. He told of his proposal to end American bombing of North Vietnam. He told of the appointment of a special ambassador to start peace negotiations. And he told of his decision about his own future: "I do not believe that I should devote an hour or a day of my time to any personal partisan causes or to any duties other than the awesome duties of this office—the presidency of your country. Accordingly, I shall not seek, and I will not accept, the nomination of my party for another term as your president."[37]

Hanoi had suffered a military defeat in the Tet Offensive, but had won a political and diplomatic victory by shifting American policy toward disengagement.

By 1969 the unsatisfactory results in Vietnam compelled U.S. leaders to reconsider their approach to the Cold War. Consequently, assumptions regarding Cold War adversaries were revised. In their own strategic innovation, Nixon and Kissinger transformed the nature of superpower relations, inaugurating detente with the Soviet Union and rapprochement with the People's Republic of China. Recognizing the United States altered economic and strategic position, Kissinger introduced the concept of "interdependence" to explain significant changes in American relations with the less-powerful countries of the world. Such developments led many observers to conclude that the Cold War had ended. Others believed that the change was one of form rather than substance. Some Cold War assumptions and appearances had changed, in their view, but superpower confrontation remained the basis of international affairs.

By the spring of 1972 the Vietnam War was at a low ebb. The 1968 Communist Tet Offensive had given way to a gradual winding down by mid-1969, and after the invasion of Cambodia in May 1970, there was little fighting in South Vietnam. Yet, while the United States was in the process of withdrawing it's forces from a war that was becoming increasingly unpopular with its citizens, the North Vietnamese were rebuilding their forces in preparation for another massive offensive in hopes of overrunning the southern half of the divided country. In April 1972, heavily armed North Vietnamese divisions crossed into the South at several points, including from out of Cambodia.

Beginning in late 1972, National Security Advisor Henry A. Kissinger's negotiations with North Vietnam began to move seriously towards a settlement. To build-up the military of South Vietnam,

Secretary of Defense Melvin R. Laird initiated, "Project Enhance Plus" on 20 October 1972. The Pentagon ordered rush deliveries of some $2 billion worth of military equipment including over 600 aircrafts. The program gave South Vietnam the fourth largest air force in the world, with over 2,000 aircrafts. Only the United States, the Soviet Union, and the Peoples' Republic of China maintained larger air forces. By this time South Vietnam also floated the fifth largest navy in the world (with 1,500 ships) and fielded the fourth largest army in the world (with 1.1 million troops).

Nixon resumed bombing of North Vietnam in response to the North Vietnamese 1972 Easter offensive, and mined North Vietnamese ports and bombed Hanoi and Haiphong in late 1972. Such pressure was intended, at least in part, to force North Vietnam to sign an armistice. In early 1973 the United States, North and South Vietnam, and the Viet Cong signed an armistice. American military activities in Cambodia and Laos, which had continued after the cease-fire in South Vietnam went into effect, ended in 1973 when Congress cut off funds.

South Vietnam's military defeat tended to obscure the crucial inability of this massive military enterprise to compensate for Saigon's political shortcomings. Over a span of nearly two decades, a series of regimes failed to mobilize fully and effectively their nation's political, social, and economic resources to foster a popular base of support. North Vietnamese main force units ended the war, but local insurgency among the people of the South made that outcome possible and perhaps inevitable.[38]

The setback suffered by the United States in the Vietnam War was rooted in a failure of strategy. Indeed, perhaps no war in American history shows more clearly both the difficulties of making sound strategic judgments and the dire consequences of a lack of clear strategic vision.

The Vietnam War thus provides a cautionary tale for American political and military decision-makers about the crucial importance of thinking clearly about strategy. By incorrectly relating military strategy to national policy and by improperly understanding the nature of the conflict, the United States exhausted itself against a secondary enemy in South Vietnam. The American failure in Vietnam also stemmed from trying to fight a traditional conventional war when the conflict's nature demanded a counterinsurgency effort. Top military commanders, unable to fathom the problem, refused to implement such a strategy despite evidence of its effectiveness.

Problem of Racial Discrimination in South Africa

In the first session of the General Assembly India complained that the government of the Union of South Africa had enacted certain discriminatory laws to the disadvantage of the people of Indian origin there. For example, Asiatic Land Tenure and Representation Act of 1946 placed the people of Indian origin in a disadvantageous position. India requested the General Assembly to recommend that the government of South Africa should abandon the policy of apartheid and enact legislation in conformity with the principles of UN Charter. South Africa contended that the matter lay within her domestic jurisdiction. This view was rejected by the Assembly which called upon the parties to settle the matter peacefully. But the disputants failed to reach an agreement. On May 14, 1949 the General Assembly asked India, Pakistan and the Union of South Africa to hold a round table conference and explore the ways and means to settle the issue. But the differences continued to persist. The parliament of South Africa passed yet another stringent measure known as Group Areas Act. The sixth session of the General Assembly provided for the establishment of commission to help the disputants in solving the long standing controversy. The Assembly also called on the South African government to suspend the implementation of the Group Areas Act since it was based on the doctrine of racial discrimination. The seventh session of the UN General Assembly commenced in 1952 and it set-up UN Good Offices Commission to arrange negotiations between India, Pakistan and the Union of South Africa but the commission did not succeed in its mission because the South African government insisted that the commission had no jurisdiction in the matter. In June 1955 the UN Secretary General designated ambassador Louis de Faro of Brazil to assist the parties. India and Pakistan agreed to co-operate but the South African Government declined to collaborate. In December 1955 and again in November 1956 the General Assembly appealed to the parties to negotiate but the Union of South Africa refused to respond to the appeal. The Assembly recommended later the economic and trade boycott of South Africa. Unfortunately Britain and the United States had adopted partisan approach to question of imposition of comprehensive mandatory sanctions on the racist white regime of South Africa which had audacity to flout the world public opinion. However, the UNO had also failed to force South Africa to dismantle the edifice of apartheid because of continued support of the Western Powers to the White regime there.[39]

Civil War in Cyprus

Cyprus is an Island republic in eastern Mediterranean with a population of about 6 lakhs including 77% Greeks and 18% Turks. The trouble started in Cyprus with the demand raised by Greek Cypriots for union with Greece. The Arab nationals were opposed to this plan and so both the communities clashed in 1965. The UN General Assembly adopted a resolution calling upon all the states to refrain from interference in the internal affairs of Cyprus. The situation in Cyprus deteriorated again in November 1967. Ultimately three peace makers representing the USA, the UNO and NATO brought about an agreement in Cyprus. This agreement provided for withdrawal of Greek and Turkish expeditionary force from Cyprus, UN guarantee of territorial integrity and sovereignty of Cyprus and disarmament of all armed forces in Cyprus except for a 5000 strong police force. On July 16, 1974 President Makarios of Cyprus fled when a coup was staged against him. Turkey now intervened in favour of the Turkish Cypriots and landed her troops in Cyprus. The UN General Assembly adopted resolution asking for the withdrawal of all foreign troops. UN emergency force was stationed in Cyprus and Indian military officers participated in peace-keeping operations there. President Makarios was able to regain his authority and refugees returned to their homes. In 1977 the Greeks and Turkish Cypriots had agreed to set-up a federation in Cyprus.[40]

Arab-Israel Wars

During the First Arab-Israeli War (1948-49), an Egyptian invasion force of 7,000 men crossed the Palestinian border at Rafah on the Mediterranean coast and at Al Awja (Nizzana) farther inland. They soon reached Ashdod, less than thirty-five kilometers from Tel Aviv. But by the time the first truce ended in mid-July, the Israelis had reinforced their positions, beating-off Egyptian attacks and recovering territory to protect Jewish settlements in the Negev. By the fall of 1948, the Israelis put Egypt's 18,000 troops deployed in Palestine oil the defensive and penetrated the Sinai Peninsula. Egypt and Israel concluded an armistice under United Nations (UN) auspices at the end of 1948 and later agreed on a cease-fire line that generally followed the pre-war boundary between Palestine and Sinai.[41]

After President Gamal Abdul Nasser's seizure of the Suez Canal in July 1956, the British, French, and Israelis began coordinating an invasion which triggered the Second Arab-Israel War. On October 29, 1956, the Israelis struck across Sinai toward the canal and southward toward Sharm ash Shaykh to relieve the Egyptian blockade of the Gulf of Aqaba. At the crossroads of Abu Uwayqilah, thirty kilometers from the Israeli border, and at the Mitla Pass, Egyptian troops resisted fiercely, repelling several attacks by larger Israeli forces. British and French forces bombed Egyptian air bases, causing Nasser to withdraw Egyptian troops from Sinai to protect the canal. At the heavily fortified complex of Rafah in the north-western corner of Sinai and at other points, the Egyptians carried out effective delaying actions before retreating. Egypt vigorously defended Sharm-al-Shaykh in the extreme south until two advancing Israeli columns took control of the area. At Port Said (Bur Said), at the north end of the canal, Egyptian soldiers battled the initial British and French airborne assault, but resistance quickly collapsed when allied forces landed oil the beach with support from heavy naval gunfire.[42]

In the eleven years leading up to the Third Arab-Israel War in June 1967 (also seen as the Six-Day War), the military had been intensively trained for combat and outfitted with new Soviet weapons and equipment. Despite these preparations, the war proved to be a debacle for Egypt.

On February 4, 1971, Sadat announced a new peace initiative that contained a significant concession: he was willing to accept an interim agreement with Israel in return for a partial Israeli withdrawal from Sinai. A timetable would then be set for Israel's withdrawal from the rest of the occupied territories in accordance with UN Resolution 242. Egypt would reopen the canal, restore diplomatic relations with the United States, which had been broken after the June 1967 War, and sign a peace agreement with Israel through Jarring. Sadat's initiative fell on deaf ears in Tel Aviv and in Washington, which was not disposed to assisting the Soviet Union's major client in the region. Disillusioned by Israel's failure to respond to his initiative, Sadat rejected the Rogers Plan and the cease-fire.

In May 1972, President Nixon met Soviet President Leonid Brezhnev, and Sadat was convinced that the two superpowers would try to prevent a new war in the Middle-East and that a position of stalemate—no peace, no war--had been reached. For Sadat this position was intolerable. The June 1967 War had been a humiliating defeat for the Arabs. Without a military victory, any Arab leader who agreed to negotiate directly with Israel would do so from a position of extreme weakness. At the same time, the United States and the Soviet Union were urging restraint and caution. However, the United States refused to put pressure on Israel to make concessions, and the Soviet Union, which had broken-off diplomatic relations with Israel as a result of the June 1967 War, had no influence over Israel.[43]

On October 17th Arab oil producers announced a program of reprisals against the Western backers of Israel: a 5 percent cutback in output, followed by further such reductions every month until Israel had withdrawn from all the occupied territories and the rights of the Palestinians had been restored. The next day, President Nixon formally asked Congress for US $ 2.2 billion in emergency funds to finance the massive airlift of arms to Israel that was already under way. The following day, King Faisal of Saudi Arabia decreed an immediate 10 percent cutback in Saudi oil and, five days after that, the complete suspension of oil shipments to the United States.

Israel was shocked and unprepared for the war. After the initial confusion and near panic in Israel followed by the infusion of United States weaponry, Israel was able to counterattack and Succeeded in crossing to the west bank of the canal and Surrounding the Egyptian Third Army. With the Third Army Surrounded, Sadat appealed to the Soviet Union for help. Soviet Prime Minister Alexei Kosygin believed he had obtained the American acceptance of a cease-fire through Henry Kissinger, (United States secretary of state). On October 22, the UN Security Council passed Resolution 338, calling for a cease-fire by all parties within twelve hours in the positions they occupied. Egypt accepted the cease-fire, but Israel, alleging Egyptian violations of cease-fire, completed the encirclement of the Third Army to the east of the canal. By nightfall on October 23, the road to Suez, the Third Army's only supply line, was in Israeli hands, cutting-off two divisions and 45,000 men.[44]

The Soviet Union was furious, believing it had been double crossed by the United States. On October 24, the Soviet ambassador handed Kissinger a note from Brezhnev threatening that if the United States was not prepared to join in sending forces to impose the cease-fire, the Soviet Union would act alone. The United States took the threat very seriously and responded by ordering a grade-three nuclear alert; the first of is kind since President John F. Kennedy's order during the Cuban missile crisis of 1962. The threat came to naught, however, because a UN emergency force arrived in the battle zone to police the ceasefire.

Meanwhile, Syria felt betrayed by Egypt because Sadat did not inform his ally of his decision to accept the cease-fire. Two days after Sadat had accepted the cease-fire, President Hafiz al Assad of Syria also accepted the cease-fire.

Neither side had, won a clear-cut victory, but for the Egyptians, it was a victory non-etheless. The Arabs had taken the initiative in attacking the Israelis and had shown that Israel was not, invincible. The stinging defeats, of 1948, 1956, and 1967 seemed to be avenged.

In Egypt the casualties included about 8,000 killed. The effect of the war on the morale of the Egyptian population, however, was immense. Sadat's prestige grew tremendously. The war, along with the political moves Sadat had made previously, meant that he was totally in control and able to implement the programs he wanted. He was the hero of the day.

Negotiations toward a permanent cease-fire began in December 1973. In January 1974, Kissinger began his shuttle diplomacy between

Egypt and Israel. On January 18, the first disengagement agreement was signed separately by Sadat and Golda Meir. A second disengagement agreement was signed on September 1, 1975. The agreement provided for a partial Israeli withdrawal in Sinai and limited the number of troops and kinds of weapons Egypt could have on the eastern side of the canal. Israel agreed to withdraw from the Abu Rudays oil fields in Western Sinai, which produced small but important revenue for Egypt. Egypt also agreed not to use force to achieve its aims, a concession that in effect made Egypt a non-belligerent in the Arab-Israeli conflict. As the price for its agreement, Israel extracted important concessions from the United States. Kissinger's secret promises to Israel included meeting Israel's military needs in any emergency, preserving Israel's arms superiority by providing the most advanced and sophisticated weaponry, and pledging not to recognize or to negotiate with the PLO.[45]

On June 5, 1975, the Suez Canal was reopened. This was a great moment for Sadat, not only politically but economically, because the canal provided Egypt with considerable revenues.

The stark defeat of the Arab states in the 1967 war gave new popularity to Palestinian resistance groups organised among the Palestinian refugee community. These groups took control of the Palestine Liberation Organization, formed in 1964 by the Arab states. Yasser Arafat, head of the Fateh group, became the Chairman of the PLO. The PLO became the institutional vehicle for attracting and directing the national aspirations of the Palestinians, and quickly established itself as the central force in the Palestinian Diaspora. The Summit of Arab Heads of State in Rabat in October 1974 recognised the PLO as the sole legitimate representative of the Palestinian people. This United Nations General Assembly bolstered this status by inviting Arafat to give a speech before it on 13 November 1974; the same General Assembly session admitted the PLO as an observer at the UN and its specialised agencies.

Until the outbreak of the Gulf crisis in 1990, Arab, European and American leaders introduced various initiatives for a comprehensive settlement to the Arab-Israeli conflict. Although none of these achieved a breakthrough, many of their suggestions served as the basis for the Middle-East Peace Conference that convened on 30 October 1991 in Madrid.

At the end of the Madrid Peace Conference the delegations from Israel, Egypt, Syria, Lebanon, and the joint Palestinian Jordanian delegation agreed to hold rounds of bilateral and multilateral. negotiations, which began in late November and December 1991. Secret Palestinian-Israeli talks also commenced on 20 January 1993 in Norway. On 9-10 September, Chairman Arafat and Israeli Prime Minister Yitzhak

Rabin exchanged letters of mutual recognition, and on 13 September, the two leaders signed the Israeli-Palestinian Declaration of Principles of Interim Self-Government Arrangements in Washington, D.C. The Declaration of Principles introduced significant changes in the governance of the occupied West Bank and Gaza Strip. Under that agreement, the parties agreed to Israeli military withdrawal from portions of Palestine, where control was to be assumed by the Palestinian Authority (an entity distinct from the PLO). These arrangements were to endure for a five-year interim period, during which the parties were to negotiate and implement a permanent status agreement. Issues deferred to the permanent status negotiations are borders, security arrangements, water, Jerusalem, refugees, relations and cooperation with neighbors and settlements.[46]

Israel's first military withdrawal, beginning in April 1994, ceded control over the West Bank town of Jericho and approximately two-thirds of the Gaza Strip to the Palestinian Authority. Under the Palestinian-Israeli Interim Agreement of 28 September 1995 the Israeli army re-deployed from all the large Palestinian towns in the West Bank (except Hebron) as well as from other smaller towns and villages. The Interim Agreement created three categories of areas in the West Bank: Area A, where the Palestinian Authority had authority for public order and internal security; Area B, where the Palestinian Authority assumed responsibility for public order for Palestinians while Israel ensured internal security; and Area C, where Israel maintained exclusive control. Israel also maintained exclusive control over borders, external security, Jerusalem and settlements.

Under the Interim Agreement, Israeli military forces were to carry out three further redeployments from all areas of the West Bank other than specified military locations, Jerusalem and witlements. These were to be completed by July 1997, although by January 2000 Israel had not completed its second redeployment.

On January 20, 1996, Palestinians of the West Bank (including Jerusalem) and the Gaza Strip elected an 88-mernber Palestinian Legislative Council as well as the President of its Executive Authority. Following Israel's opening of a tunnel under the Haram al Sharif, the holiest Islamic site in Palestine, demonstrations and armed clashes broke out over a four-day period leaving 62 Palestinians and 14 Israelis dead and 1,600 Palestinians and 50 Israelis wounded. Despite the tense relations that prevailed during the government of Birlyarnin Netanyahu, the two sides initialed the Hebron Protocol of January 15, 1997 which provided for Israeli redeployment from 80% of Hebron, while Israel maintained control over the portions of the city in which Jewish settlers lived.

Palestinian-Israeli relations were also negatively affected by Israel's rapid expansion of illegal Israeli settlements in Palestinian occupied territories, which occurred in the face of Palestinian and international condemnation. In February 1997, the government of Israeli Prime Minister Binyamin Netanyahu announced its intention to construct a Jewish settlement on Jabal Abu Ghneim, south of Jerusalem. This settlement, which reinforced the ring of Jewish settlements around East Jerusalem, prompted fierce confrontations between protesters and Israeli troops in the West Bank and the Gaza Strip, an angry reaction from the Palestinian Authority and a several months-long breakdown in peace negotiations. This hiatus ended with the signing of the Wye River Memorandum on 23 Oct. 1998, which provided for the implementation of the second phase of further redeployment from the West Bank and for heightened security-related obligations on the part of the Palestinian Authority.[47]

The Netanyahu government, which signed the Wye River Memorandum with great reluctance, quickly bowed to internal political pressures and declared Israel's refusal to implement the Wye River Memorandurn, plunging Palestinian-Israeli relations into a new state of crisis. Netanyahu's defeat by Ehud Barak in Israel's May 1999 elections led to improve relations with the Palestine Liberation Organization. The Palestine Liberation Organization and Israel signed the Sharm El-Sheik Memorandurn of September 4, 1999 which established a timeline for the implementation of outstanding commitments of existing Palestinian-Israeli agreements, including further redeployments, prisoner releases, the construction of the Gaza Sea Port and the opening of West Bank-Gaza Strip safe passage corridors. Israel conducted two phases of further redeployments from 7% and 3% of the West Bank in September 1999 and January 2000, respectively, in accordance with the obligations of the Sharm, El-Sheik Memorandum. At the end of the latter redeployment, 11.3% of the total area of the West Bank was comprised of Area A and 25.6% of the West Bank comprised Area B, while the rest (63.1%) remained under exclusive Israeli control.

The permanent status negotiations formally started in May 1996, although serious discussions only commenced in earnest in November 1999. As of January 2003, no concrete progress had been made in the negotiations. Meanwhile, several issues still plague relations between Palestine and Israel, including continued Israeli settlement activity, the presence of hundreds of Palestinians in Israeli jails and Israel's Judaization policy in Jerusalem.

Afghanistan War

More than two decades after its commencement and over a

decade after its cessation, the Soviet-Afghan War remains an enigma in the West. Earlier successful Soviet military interventions in the Ukraine (1945-51), East Germany (1953), Hungary (1956), and Czechoslovakia (1968) and intermittent Soviet military pressure on Poland demonstrated that the stark military power of the Soviet state was an irresistible tool of Soviet political power. The West was thankful that nuclear deterrence maintained the Cold War balance and reluctantly accepted Soviet intervention within its socialist commonwealth and in the Soviet border regions as one cost of that balance.[48]

The Soviet invasion of Afghanistan was a repeat of their invasion of Czechoslovakia. For months after the invasion, hardly a political or military expert in the world doubted that Afghanistan was now forever incorporated as a part of the Soviet Empire and that nothing short of a large-scale global war could alter the *status quo.*

And global war was most unlikely as both super powers intended to avoid it. Some Westerners recalled the British experiences in Afghanistan and waited for a Soviet "Vietnam" to emerge, but most Westerners believed that the Soviets would ultimately prevail. Some even projected their European fears to southern Asia and envisioned a bold Soviet strategic thrust from southern Afghanistan to the shores of the Persian Gulf, to challenge Western strategic interests and disrupt Western access to critical Middle Eastern oil.

The initial active resistance by the Afghan military was confined to a short battle against the Soviet Spetsnaz unit storming the Presidential Palace. However, the stunned citizens of this geographically isolated land immediately rose to defend their land. In defiance of the wisdom of conventional warfare, the citizens armed themselves, gathered into loose formations and began to attack and sabotage the superior occupying force's personnel, installations, depots and transport with any available weapons (to include flintlock muskets).

Open resistance flared so quickly that only two months after the invasion, (on the night of 23 February 1980) almost the entire population of Kabul climbed on their rooftops and chanted with one voice "God is Great." This open defiance of the Russian generals who could physically destroy their city was matched throughout the countryside. The Afghan warrior society sent thousands of warriors against their northern invader.

Communist power was established in Afghanistan on 27 April 1978 through a bloody military coup. President Nur M. Taraki, the new president, announced sweeping programs of land distribution, emancipation of women and the destruction of the old Afghanistan social structure. The new government enjoyed little popular support. The wobbly new government was immediately challenged by Armed resistance fighters. The Army of the Democratic Republic of Afghanistan began to disintegrate as bloody purges swept the officer ranks. In March 1979, the city of Herat rose in open revolt. Most of the Afghan 17th Infantry Division mutinied and joined the rebellion. Forces loyal to Taraki advanced and occupied the city while the Afghan Air Force bombed the city and the 17th Division. Over 5,000 people died in the fighting, including some 100 Soviet citizens. This event may have lead the Soviet General Staff to start intervention planning. Soldiers, units and entire brigades deserted to the resistance and by the end of 1979, the Afghan Army had fallen from about 90,000 to about 40,000. Over half the officer corps were purged, executed or had deserted. In September 1979, Taraki's Prime Minister, Hafizullah Amin, seized power and executed Taraki. Amin's rule was no better and the Soviet Union watched this new communist state spin out of control and out of Moscow's orbit. The Soviet Politburo moved to stabilize the situation.

The Soviet Union had significant experience with stability operations to maintain its socialist empire. Their experiences in subjugating the Hungarian revolution of 1956 (where they suffered 669 killed, 51 missing and 1540 wounded) led to improved methods and techniques. In the 1968 invasion of Czechoslovakia, the Soviet Army lost a total of 96 killed. The elements of their invasion plan included the establishment of an in-country Soviet military and KGB element to assist the invasion force and the production of a cover or deception operation to divert attention away from the future invasion. A General Staff group would tour the country in advance of the invasion, under some pretense, in order to assess and fine-tune invasion plans.[49]

When the invasion began, the in-country Soviet military and KGB element would disarm or disable the national military forces. Airborne add Spetsnaz forces would spearhead the invasion and seize major airfields, transportation choke points the capital city, key government buildings, and Communications facilities. They would seize or execute the key government leaders. Soviet ground forces would cross into the country, seize the major cities and road networks, suppress any local military resistance, and occupy the key population centers. A new government would then be installed, supported by the armed might of the Soviet Armed Forces.

This invasion plan was also used in Afghanistan. Soviet military and KGB advisers permeated the structure of the Afghanistan Armed Forces. In April 1979, General of the Army Aleksly A. Yepishev, the head of the Main Political Directorate, led a delegation of several generals in a visit to Afghanistan to assess the situation. General Yepishev made a similar visit to Czechoslovakia prior to the 1968 invasion. In August 1979, General of the Army Ivan G. Pavlovski, CINC

Soviet Ground Forces, led a group of some 60 officers on a several weeks long reconnaissance tour of Afghanistan. General Pavlovski commanded the invasion force in Czechoslovakia in 1968.

The invasion of Afghanistan was launched on Christmas eve, not a major Muslim holiday, but a time when the Western governments were not prepared to react. Soviet advisers disabled equipment, blocked arms rooms and prevented a coordinated Afghan military response. Soviet airborne and Spetsnaz forces seized the Salang tunnel, key airfields, and key government and communications sites in Kabul. Soviet Spetsnaz soldiers killed President Amin. The Soviet ground invasion force crossed into the country, fought with a few pockets of Afghan military resistance and occupied the main cities while the Soviet government installed their Afghan puppet regime.

The Soviets expected the resistance to end here, but it had only begun. The ability to rationalize an intolerable situation that pervades the West did not hold in the mountains of Afghanistan. The Afghans' values, faith and love of freedom enabled them to hold out against a superpower, even though they suffered tremendous casualties in doing so.

The Afghan war was fought under four General Secretaries Brezhnev, Chernenko, Andropov and Gorbachev. Many senior Soviet military officers want to blame the Afghanistan debacle solely on the Soviet political leadership, yet, there were high ranking military accomplices who carried out Politburo directives without protest. And, although many in the West view Gorbachev as a liberal democrat and point out that he ordered the Soviet withdrawal from Afghanistan, the bloodiest years of fighting in Afghanistan (1985-86) were under his leadership.

Ideologically, the Soviet leadership was unable to come to grips with war in Afghanistan. Marxist-Leninist dogma did not allow for a "war of national liberation" where people would fight against a Marxist regime. So, initially the press carried pictures of happy Soviet soldiers building orphanages—and did not mention that they were also engaged in combat and filling those very orphanages. By the end of 1983, the Soviet press had only reported six dead and wounded soldiers, although by that time, the 40th Army had suffered 6,262 dead and 9,880 combat wounded. Soviet solutions for Afghanistan were postponed, as one general secretary after another weakened and died and the military waited for a healthy general secretary who could make a decision. It was only during the last three years of the war, under Gorbachev's glassnost policy, that the press began to report more accurately on the Afghanistan war.

The Afghanistan War forced the 40th Army to change tactics, equipment, training and force structure. However, despite these changes, the Soviet Army never had enough forces in Afghanistan to win. Initially, the Soviets had underestimated the strength of their enemy. Logistically, they were hard-pressed to maintain a larger force and, even if they could have tripled the size of their force, they probably would still have been unable to win. Often, they could not assemble an entire regiment for combat and had to cobble together forces from various units to create a make-shift regiment. Base-camp, airfield, city and lines of communication (LOC) security tied-up most of the motorized rifle forces, but still, the mujahideen constantly interdicted the road and pipelines supplying the Soviet and Afghan forces. The Soviets were never able to completely control their LOCs, although their forces were performing an important international mission. Consequently, they were never able to consistently transport sufficient supplies into the country to support a larger force.[50]

Gulf Adventure (1990-91)

The occasion for UN action in the Persian Gulf region arose by early 90s, following a sudden Iraqi occupation of Kuwait, which met with practically no local resistance and led to temporary annexation of the oil-rich kingdom by Baghdad. As usual, such a shocking turn of events stirred world conscience and the UN as the conscience-keeper was immediately activated. The Security Council in a 14 to 1 vote (Yemen against) branded Iraq an aggressor (resolution 660 of August 1990) and imposed all out economic sanctions (Res 661 of 6 August) against it.

Initial reaction of President Saddam Hussain was one of intransigence as he laboured under a misguided impression regarding possible US moves. These were revealed one after another in subsequent sessions of the Security Council. To implement UN measures of sanction, exclusive authority was given to "member-states cooperating with the government of Kuwait", in other words US and other western powers who had already got their forces deployed in adjacent areas, earlier in the context of tensions arising from Iran-Iraq and Arab-Israeli confrontations (Res. 665 of 25 August).

The decision finally to use force against a recalcitrant Iraq came with the adoption of Resolution 678 (29 November) authorising the use of "all necessary means" to uphold and implement Security Council resolution 660 and all subsequent relevant resolutions." This time as many as 12 members supported the US drafted resolution. Soviet Union included, with China abstaining and only Cuba and Yemen opposing it. This meant two things viz. (a) the UN enforcement action was to be applied through a chosen group of states with special interests in the gulf region, and (b) there would be no restraints on the kind of measures these states would themselves like to decide upon.

Action followed with amazing speed. About a dozen resolutions were carried in record time by a highly energized Security Council, between 29th November 1990 and 15th January 1991. A massive multinational 'armada' was dispatched by air and sea to roll back the invading Iraqi troops. The mode of operation was also unprecedented. UN combat forces were placed under the command and control of US General Schwarzkopf and Mr. Colin Powell. Armed with teary; artillery and latest missiles and anti-missile devices they not only pushed the Iraqi forces back but entered deep into the sovereign territory of Iraq with round the clock air attacks against Iraqi military installation. No serious attempt was made to take a second chance at peaceful resolution for which signals did come from President Hussain when he was met by the French President and an ex-British Prime Minister and later also by President Gorbachev. Neither was any mid-operation review allowed regarding the admissibility of the punitive actions taken in the name of the UN but actually conducted in accordance with the war plans of the Pentagon codenamed operation "Desert Storm". There was no questioning if the UN mandate was being exceeded, which indeed it was. After all, the proclaimed US objectives were to shatter Iraq's defense capability, eliminate Saddam from the seat of power and cripple Iraqi economy by choking the commercial outlet of its oil resources. Added to this was the unrelated dimension of Kurd revolt for which again, a strictly monitored "no fly zone" was imposed inside Iraqi territory. Patently, the US has been using the UN mandate to fulfil its own game-plan of power politics in the region where its primary interest has always been to control the vital supply line of oil.

So far as international intervention at the behest of the US is concerned, the UN was virtually 'hijacked'. Although the Security Council legitimized the actions and was still not ready to relent so far as economic sanctions against Iraq were concerned, it was definitely against the true spirit of the UN to make a rather vindictive use of the enforcement measures. It is one thing to punish and undo aggression but it is altogether different to engage in unrestrained violence totally out of proportion with the original offence. Once Iraq agreed to honor all UN resolutions, it was unduly harsh to prolong the economic sanctions. The use of deadly weapons not only caused untold damages but severely affected the ecological conditions around the Gulf.

The Gulf operations, the latest in UN collective Security activities, have thus unleashed certain forces and given rise to certain tendencies that may not augur well for the world organization. They amounted to recognition of US hegemony and paved the way for what subsequently came to be called a uni-polar world. To use the UN in the partisan interest of a big power and its allies without due regard to the limits and legitimacy of the actions taken by them is clearly doing a disservice to its ideals. It would have been defensible if the actions did not go beyond liberation of Kuwait imposition of financial and other penalties on Iraq to compensate for its illegal occupation of Kuwait and general restoration of the regional order.

UNIKOM: UN-Iraq-Kuwait Observation Mission 1991 (Continuing)

Iraqi invasion and occupation of Kuwait on 2nd August 1990 attracted immediate UN attention. The Security Council condemned the invasion and demanded unconditional withdrawal. This was followed by imposition of economic sanctions against Iraq with a deadline of 15th January, 1991 within which Iraq must comply with all the resolutions of the Security Council. Otherwise member-states cooperating with the government of Kuwait were authorized to use "all necessary means" to uphold the Council's resolution and restore international peace and security in the area.

As the deadline passed, armed forces of several states led by USA began air attacks against Iraq and a severe ground offensive. Hostilities were suspended on 27th February, 1991 as Iraqi forces had by then, been rolled back. On 3rd April, 1991, the Security Council, while still maintaining economic sanctions against Iraq, adopted resolution 687 (1991) which set detailed conditions for a cease-fire and established a machinery for securing implementation of those conditions. Following Iraq's acceptance of the provisions of the resolution, the ceasefire came formally into force.

By the same resolution (687/91) the Council established a demilitarized zone along Iraq-Kuwaiti boundary. A UN Observer Unit (UNIKOM) was posted to monitor the situation on the basis of the plan submitted by the Secretary General and approved by the Security Council (Res. 689/91).

The mandate of the mission was:

(1) to monitor the 40 km. Khawr-Abd Alien Waterway dividing Iraq and Kuwait, and
(2) to deter violations of the boundary by constant surveillance of the 200 km DMZ, running 10 km, inside Iraqi territory.

By 6th May, 1991, the mission was fully deployed and is still continuing from its HO at Umm Qasr. Initially to provide essential security UNIKOM included five infantry companies. The military observers initially remained unarmed. They would simply engage in ground and air patrol and maintain liaison with the parties-They are to verify that no military personnel and equipments move through the Zone and no fortification or bases are maintained there. UNIKOM is also providing technical support to (i) the Iraq-Kuwait Boundary Demarcation Commission, (ii) transfer of property from Iraq to Kuwait, and (iii) relocation of Iraqi citizens on the Kuwaiti side of the border.

Following some reported intrusions in 1993, the UNIKOM was reinforced. An infantry strength of 3 battalion was sanctioned and they were to use force in self-defense (S.C. Res. 806 of 5th Feb., 1993), two fixed wing aircrafts and some helicopters are at the disposal of the UNIKOM. Participating countries include among others, India, China, Bangladesh, Pakistan, Indonesia, and Malaysia.

The annual cost of the UNIKOM is approximately $ 70 million. Two-thirds of the amount is being paid by Kuwait Government. The remainder comes from assessed contributions of UN members.

Peace-keeping in Bosnia-Harzegovina (March 1992 Continuing)

Reports of serious fighting after Croatia and Slovania declared themselves independent from Yugoslavia while Serbs living in Croatia opposed this move. Efforts of the European Community to stock the hostilities proved unsuccessful. UN got involved in September 1991 when the Security Council unanimously adopted its resolution 713/91 calling all States to implement a "general and complete embargo on all deliveries of weapons and military equipments to Yugoslavia."

Cyrus Vance, then US Security of Stale, was appointed by Secretary General Perez de Cuellar as his personal envoy. Lord Carrington, then chairman of the European Community Conferences on Yugoslavia also offered his good offices. The initial purpose was to discuss the feasibility of deploying a UN Peace-keeping Operation. Despite an agreement reached by the Yugoslav parties at a meeting in Geneva, the temporary truce was broken soon after.

On 27th November Security Council resolution 721(91) endorsed the deployment of a UN PKO in Yugoslavia. With a small group of military officers, civilian police and UN Secretariat staff moved to Yugoslavia for maintaining ceasefire. Following a second agreement at Saraxevo between Die UN Special envoy and the warning factions the new Secretary-General B.B. Ghali sent a group of 50 military liaison officers to promote the conditions of ceasefire. On 25th February, 1992, the Security Council by resolution 743/(92) approved the setting up of the UNPROFOR initially for one year and on 7th April authorized full deployment of force (resolution 749/92).

The operational mandate of UNPROFOR extends to 5 Republics of former Yugoslavia—Croatia, Bosnia, Macedonia, Montenegro and Serbia. In Croatia die task was to secure withdrawal of fighters from all

Croatia and demilitarization of UN protected areas. By later resolutions of the Security Council, UNPROFOR was also authorized to undertake monitoring functions in the 'pink zones', and control entry of civilians into UN protected areas and perform immigration and custom functions. On January 25, 1993 a semblance of peace was restored as the Croatian Government and Serb local authorities informed the UNPROFOR that they would withdraw forces.

Then came the turn of Herzegovina and Bosnia. About 100 observers were redeployed therefrom Croatia. But by May 1992 the situation went almost beyond control as Bosnian, Serbs and Muslims intensified their conflict threatening even the lives of the UNPROPOR personnel.

A series of appeals from the Security Council to all countries for a ceasefire proved ineffective. On 30th May, 1992, acting under Chapter VII, the Security Council imposed wide-ranging sanctions on Yugoslavian federal authorities (then located in Serbia and Montenegro) in its resolution 757(92). It demanded cooperation for unimpeded delivery of all humanitarian supplies to Sarajevo and other destinations in Bosnia and Herzegovina. UNPROFOR also tried to stop fighting around the airport of Sarajevo. Necessary military personnel were also sent by UN to supervise the withdrawal of anti-aircraft weapons. By early July, UNPROFOR was partly able to achieve its objectives around Sarajevo. Hence by resolution 776(92) the Council called on states to take "necessary measures" to facilitate delivery of humanitarian assistance, UNPROFOR mandate was, accordingly, expanded to support efforts of the UNHCR to ensure relief supplies and protect convoys of civilian detainees. A no-fly zone was declared in October 1992 to ban all military flights in the airspace of Bosnia and for strict monitoring of all other flights. Next month, by resolution 787, The Council demanded that all forms of interference from outside Bosnia and Herzegovina must stop immediately—evidently in view of the adverse reaction of some Muslim states outside the region. To achieve this Secretary General wanted a larger mandate for UNPROFOR to include the right not only to search but to turn back all provocative military elements as well as confiscate all contraband goods. He wanted some 10,000 additional troops to carry on operations at 123 crossing points on the borders of Bosnia-Herzegovina.

However, the operation to protect humanitarian convoys throughout the territory had been persistently thwarted by obstruction, mines, artillery fire, and total non-cooperation of the Serbs. Violations of no-fly zone were also frequent, although no combat air-mission was detected by NATO AWAC-s until March 1993. Air support coming from NATO members from April 1993 onward with France, UK, USA, Turkey and Netherlands providing aircrafts for the operation somewhat stemmed the deteriorating situation. Simultaneously, Srebrenica, and the area around was declared a 'safe zone' wherefrom the Serb forces had to withdraw their paramilitary forces. Systematic searches were carried on to collect and seize unauthorized weapons and ammunitions.

In his 20th September, 1993 report, the Secretary General admitted that the task was becoming extremely difficult and short of a political solution, the UN mandate was not possible to implement. Air strikes around Sarajevo were also deemed necessary. NATO did the job with amazing enthusiasm. Russia, however, registered its objections to the veiled ultimatum of NATO against Serbs. Ultimately the threat of bombing had some effect. By February 1994, informal consultations resumed, largely due to Russian initiative and the warring sides, particularly the Serbs, agreed to observe cease-fire and comply with the UN directive to withdraw their troops from Bosnia.

Commenting on the overall experience of the UNPROFOR Stanley Meisler, a leading American journalist wrote:

"The UN mission to Bosnia was hapless and star-crossed but not wholly a failure. In 1994, 2,740,000 Bosnians received relief aid. Many lives were saved, and the war did not spread. As the fiftieth anniversary of the UN approached, however, aggression remained unpunished, and peace elusive. The mission and the war had also frayed relations between NATO and the UN, the United States and Europe, the Clinton administration and UN bureaucrats. The gravest error made by Boutros-Ghali was to accept the veto on bombing. That made it difficult for the UN to rationalize its two roles as peace-keeper and peace enforcer.... Yet given the nervousness of troop suppliers, France and Britain and the refusal of the United States to commit soldiers on the grounds, the UN accomplished as mush as it could of a confused and limited mandate.[51]

UN in Somalian Civil Strife (UNOSOM, 1992)

The power struggle following the ouster of President Siad Barre in January 1991 led to severe clan clashes in different parts of Somalia, Mogadishu, the capital witnessed intense fighting between one faction supporting the interim President Ali Mahdi Mohamed and the other supporting General Mohamed Farah Aidid. Infiltration of numerous bandit groups aggravated the situation. The hostilities resulted in widespread casualties, destruction, homelessness, malnutrition and pestilence—killing about 300 thousand people upto 1994.

As political chaos mounted, the UN continued its humanitarian assistance and was later fully engaged in finding out a peaceful solution of the civil strife. The then Secretary-General Javier Perez de Cuillar sent visiting team under a senior UN official, Mr. James O.C.-Jonah in January 1992. Then on the advice of the next Secretary General Boutros-Boutros Ghali the Security Council by resolution 733 of January 23, 1992 urged all parties to the conflict to cease hostilities and imposed a general and complete embargo on all deliveries of weapons and military equipments to Somalia. To assist the process of political settlement, the Secretary General convened a meeting of the representatives of LAS, OAU, OIC as well as the contesting factions. The talks succeeded in gelling the factions accept a cease-fire agreement (3rd March, 1992). It also instituted UN convoys of humanitarian assistance and approved deployment of a few military observers on both sides of Mogadishu, The Security Council also authorized the dispatch of a technical team for monitoring cease-fire (resolution 746 of 1992) and set-up a UN operation in Somalia (resolution 751 of 1992) to run emergency humanitarian assistance. About 500 security personnel were drawn from ten third world countries and placed under Pakistani Brigadier General Imuaz Shaheen. But the UN troops could not tackle the widespread lawlessness and looting of supplies by armed gangs. The UN convoys themselves now required protection. For safe deliveries of relief airlift was also necessary. Hence, an enhanced UNOSOM with some 4219 personnel was authorized and a 100-day action programme for accelerated humanitarian assistance was launched to prevent famine, death and deprivation. About $ 82 million was requested for implementation of the programme. But the urgent need of the hour was to stop the unabated violence against international relief effort. Hence, on 3rd December 1992, the Security Council adopted, unanimously, resolution No. 794 authorizing the use of "all necessary means to establish as soon as possible a secure environment." A 3500-su-ong Task Force was engaged and it successfully secured major population centers. At the same time a national reconciliation meeting was held at Addis Ababa in January and March 1993. Simultaneously, in view of mounting attacks on UN personnel and reported casualties, UNOSOM was endorsed with enforcement powers to monitor cessation of hostilities, prevent resumption of violence, disarm the factions and transfer the weapons to a newly constituted national army (Security Council resolution 814 of 1993). End to the hostilities was in sight by middle of the year allowing a two-year transition period to set-up a viable structure of civilian administration. In the meantime an operation carried by US Rangers on 3 October 1993 in South Mogadishu tried to capture the key areas held by General Aidid for his alleged complicity in the June attack on UN personnel. During the course of the operation two US helicopters were shot down by Somalia militiamen and about 18 US soldier had died in the cross-fire. This led to the retaliatory attack by US Quick Reaction Force by air, navy and artillery. Finally, the forces were withdrawn in March 1994 but Mogadishu remained tense and many African states were unhappy over the bitter end of the conflict.

UN in Cambodian Turmoil (UNTAC)

Cambodia which has gone through bouts of civil war and prolonged instability received UN attention only towards the final phase of its crisis. Ouster of the charismatic left-oriented Prince Norodom Sihanouk in 1970 by a US-backed military coup led by Loh Not whose dictatorship was replaced by a more ruthless government of the Khmer Rouge, a pro-Chinese guerilla band led by Pol Pot in 1975. Deep scaled public discontent against the terrorist regime occasioned intervention of Vietnamese forces with full Soviet backing, leading to the installation of a moderate communist government headed by Heng Samrin in January 1979. But the die-hard Khmer Rouge elements did not allow peace and stability to return to the country until the legendary prince in self-exile in Beijing agreed to lead a national coalition government which was facilitated by an international initiative under the UN auspices. The Paris Agreement of October 1991 laid the ground work for restoration of peace.

On 28th February, 1992, the Security Council authorised by a unanimous resolution for the establishment of a UN Transitional Authority in Cambodia (UNTAC) and adoption of necessary measures by the Secretary General for rapid deployment of the forces. A tentative plan for a 15-month long action involving an estimated cost of $2 billion was also approved so that conditions could be created for holding a nationwide election in which parties to the civil war were free to participate once they abjured violence and made complete demobilization as well as surrender of arms.

Evidently it was politically a rather delicate task to try to restore public confidence after about two decades of sporadic warfare and widespread destruction. However, UNTAC with more than 22,000 personnel having expertise in human rights, civil and military administration as well as constitutional matters successfully completed its mission under the competent command of the UN Special Representative from Japan. Free and fair elections took place under UNTAC auspices in Spring 1993, law and order was restored, refugees were rehabilitated and displaced persons repatriated. Of course, the UNTAC failed to achieve complete demobilization due to non-cooperation of the Khmer Rouge on the pretext that all Vietnamese forces had not left Cambodia. Actually the UN needed more lime to reach out to the key areas of the Cambodian administration. Nevertheless it successfully repatriated about 3.6 lakh refugees and held a free and fair election in May 1993, although the Khmer Rounge boycotted the election. After the election, the Constituent Assembly proclaimed Sihanouk as Head of the State, with Prince Norodom Ranaridh of FUNCINPEC and Hun Sen of CPP as Co-Chairmen of the

Council of Ministers. The Constituent Assembly was also helped by UN experts in drafting the Constitution, especially its human rights provisions. Thus, the travails of a small Asian Country were mitigated, thanks to a rather extraordinary intervention by the UN.

The UN Role in Darfur

As a response to the escalating crisis in Darfur, the Security Council, on 30th July 2004, assigned additional tasks to UNAMIS by its resolution 1556 (2004).

Darfur had long experienced localized violence exacerbated by ethnic, economic and political tensions and competition over scarce resources. Beginning in February 2003, attacks on government targets by the Sudan Liberation Movement/Army (SLM/A) and the Justice and Equality Movement (JEM), and the Government's decision to respond by deploying its national armed forces and mobilizing local militia, took the violence to unprecedented levels. Indiscriminate air bombardment carried out by Sudan's armed forces, accompanied by attacks by the Janjaweed and other militias, left villages across the region razed to the ground. Often during these attacks civilians were murdered, women and girls raped, children abducted and food and water sources destroyed. The cycle of terror inside Darfur also threatened regional peace and security.

At the same time, the United Nations and a collection of non-governmental organizations launched a massive humanitarian operation in Darfur, constantly expanding activities to respond to the needs of an increasing number of people displaced by violence.

In its resolution 1556 of 30 July 2004, the UN Security Council, among other things, reiterated its grave concern at the ongoing humanitarian crisis and widespread human rights violations, including continued attacks on civilians. In addition to requesting a monthly report on the Government's implementation of commitments *vis-a-vis* the Janjaweed militias and their leaders, the Council also requested the Secretary-General to incorporate into the mission contingency planning for the Darfur region, including by assisting the African Union with planning and assessments for its mission in Darfur and by preparing to support the implementation of a future agreement in Darfur in close cooperation with the African Union. Accordingly, the mission initiated such contingency planning.

Comprehensive Peace Agreement

On 9th January 2005, in an event that marked a turning point in the history of the Sudan, the Government of the Sudan, represented by Vice-President Ali Osman Taha, and the Sudan People's Liberation Movement/Army (SPLM/A), represented by Chairman John Garang, signed in Nairobi, Kenya, the Comprehensive Peace Agreement (CPA).

The CPA included agreements on outstanding issues remaining after the Machakos Protocol and had provisions on security arrangements, power-sharing in the capital of Khartoum, some autonomy for the south, and more equitable distribution of economic resources, including oil.

Though, the United Nation's initiatives in direction of World Peace has not achieved its goal, but this does not mean that UN is a total failure in this direction. Right from its inception, UN did a commendable job in various conflicts such as Korean crisis, Congo and Lebanon crisis, etc. As per its commitment towards the World Peace, UN has established and running peace-keeping operations around the world. The United Nations is carring or carried out more than 60 peace-keeping operations around the world till date.

If we took the positive meaning of peace which include social and economic justice, basic human needs such as food, shelter, health and education, United Nations is doing a good job in this direction. The UN charter states that one of the organization's central purpose is to achieve international cooperation in solving international problems of an economic, social, cultural, or humanitarian character. Through a series of high profile international conferences over the last few decades, the UN has shown the spotlight on emerging issues of global concern and helped to propel action to address them globally and nationally. New understandings on the range of issues addressed by global conference ultimately found expression in the Millennium Development Goals (MDGs), adopted unanimously at the 2000 UN Millennium Assembly. And the 2002 World Summit on Sustainable development in Johannesburg, South Africa, brought renewed political attention to sustainable development challenges, including the adoption or reaffirmation by government of a broad range of targets related to water, energy, health, agriculture and biological diversity. The UN is currently finding a growing role for itself in encouraging governments to implement the policy reforms needed to achieve these goals and targets and in tracking their progress along the way.

The UN system has also proved adoptable in the face of new challenges. For instance, as the seriousness of problems such as rapid population growth and environmental degradation become apparent, new institutions like the UN fund for population and the UN Environment Programme were organized. Today the UN is being called on to play a growing role in combating the spread of terrorism and weapons of mass destruction.

In sum, it is hard to accept the idea that the conventional power political model merely represents the past, the remnants of which linger in the present, whereas the alternative approaches represent the future. We cannot foresee how much of these new perspectives will materialize, although it would be foolish to deny that some of them are already making an impact on the operation of the international system; it is possible that this impact may greatly increase, although, as has been argued, scarcely leading to an international government. Consequently only a vague and impressionistic prediction is possible about the shape of things to come at the end of the century: it seems likely that the international system will remain pluralistic and untidy, with states continuing to play a leading though probably increasingly more circumscribed role.

Notes and References

1. Sondhi, Sunil, International relations: A Framework for Analysis (New Delhi: Sanjay Prakashan), 2004, pp. 64-65.
2. Russett, Bruce and Haivey Stars, World Politics: The Menu for Choice (Bombay: Vakils, Feffer and Simon Ltd.), 1986, p. 296.
3. Frankel, Joseph, International Relations in a Changing World (Delhi: Oxford University Press), 1990, p. 55.
4. *Ibid.*, p. 122.
5. *Ibid.*, p. 150.
6. Deustch Merton, The Analysis of International Relations (Englewood Cliff, NJ.: Prentice Hall), 1998, p. 138.
7. *Ibid.*, p. 240.
8. Frankel, Joseph, International Relations in a Changing World, *op. cit.*, pp. 43-44.
9. *Ibid.*, p. 55.
10. *Ibid.*, p. 122.
11. *Ibid.*, p. 209.
12. Jacow, P. E. Atherton, L., The Dynamics of International Organization (Illinois: Dorsey), 1965, p. 100.
13. Goodrich, Leland, M., "Korea: Collective Measures against Aggression." International Conciliation No. 495, October 1953, p. 146.
14. Keshwani, Khemchand B., International Relations in Modern World (1900-1995) (New Delhi: Himalaya Publishing House), 1996, p. 627.
15. Chabra, H.K., Relations of Nations (Delhi: Surjeet Publications), 1980, p. 280.
16. Keshwani, Khemchand B., International Relations in Modern World (1900-1995), *op. cit.*, p. 365.
17. Deustch Merton, The Analysis of International Relations, *op. cit.*, p. 154.
18. Alison, Geaham, Essence of Decision: Explaining the Cuban Missile Crisis (Boston: Little Brown), 1970, pp. 192-94.
19. The ten contributory states were: Brazil, Canada, Colombia, Denmark, Finland, India, Indonesia, Norway, Sweden and Yugoslavia
20. Gibbs, D., 'The United Nations, International Peace-keeping and the Question of 'Impartiality': Revisiting the Congo Operation of 1960', *Journal of Modern African Studies*, 2000, 38(3): 359-82.
21. UN, The Blue Helmets: A Review of United Nations Peace-keeping (New York: UN Department of Public Information), 1990, p. 239.
22. James, A., Peace-keeping in International Politics (Basingstoke: Macmillan with the IISS), 1990, p. 296.

23. Howard, M., 'The Historical Development of the UN's Role in International Security' in A. Roberts and B. Kingsbury (eds.), *United Nations, Divided World* (Oxford: Oxford University Press), 2000, pp. 63-80.
24. UN, The Blue Helmets: A Review of United Nations Peace-keeping, *op. cit.*, p. 242.
25. Abi-Saab, G., The United Nations Operation in the Congo: 1960-64 (Oxford: Oxford University Press), 1978, p. 67.
26. James, A., Peace-keeping in International Politic, *op. cit.*, p. 299.
27. Gibbs, D., 'The United Nations, International Peace-keeping and the Question of 'Impartiality': Revisiting the Congo Operation of 1960', *op. cit.*, pp. 380-82.
28. Nicholas, H.G., The United Nations as a Political Institution (Oxford: Oxford University Press), 1974, p. 65.
29. Morphet, S., 'UN Peace-keeping and Election-Monitoring' in A. Roberts and B. Kingsbury (eds.), *United Nations, Divided World* (Oxford: Oxford University Press), 2000, pp. 183-239.
30. Saksena, K.P., The United Nations and Collective Security: A Historical Analysis (Delhi: D.K. Publishing), 1974.
31. Bilgrani, S.J.R., International Organization (New Delhi: Vikas Publishing), 1977, p. 160.
32. Frankel, Joseph, International Relations in Changing World Allison, *op. cit.*, p. 41.
33. Russett, Bruce and Haivey Stars, World Politics: The Menu for Choice, *op. cit.*, p. 135.
34. Vasquez, John, A., Classics of International Relations, *op. cit.*, p. 320.
35. *Ibid.*, pp. 54-55.
36. Sondhi, Sunil, International Relations: A Framework for Analysis, *op. cit.*, pp. 93-95.
37. *Ibid.*
38. Vasquez, John, A., Classics of International Relations, *op. cit.*, pp. 59-67.
39. Deustch Merton, The Analysis of International Relations, *op. cit.*, p. 78.
40. Keshwani, Khemchand B., International Relations in Modern World (1900-95), *op. cit.*, p. 55.
41. Lakhanpal, P.L., Documents and Notes on the Arab-Israeli Question (New Delhi: International Book Publication), 1968, pp. 232-33.
42. *Ibid.*
43. Frankel, Joseph, International Relations in a Changing World, *op. cit.*, pp. 76-77.
44. Sondhi, Sunil, International Relations: A Framework for Analysis, *op. cit.*, p. 102.
45. Frankel, Joseph, International Relations in a Changing World, *op. cit.*, pp. 76-79.
46. Russett, Bruce and Haivey Stars, World Politics: The Menu for Choice, *op. cit.*, p. 171.
47. Sondhi, Sunil, International Relations: A Framework for Analysis, *op. cit.*, p. 110.
48. Deustch Merton, The Analysis of International Relations, *op. cit.*, pp. 184-85.
49. *Ibid.*
50. Sondhi, Sunil, International Relations: A Framework for Analysis, *op. cit.*, p. 124.
51. Meisler Stanley, UN: The First Fifty Years (New York: Atlantic Monthly Press), 1995, p. 329.

3

Gandhi's Approach to World Peace

History has proved that Mohandas Karamchand Gandhi and the World Peace are inseparable. Gandhi first employed his idea of peaceful civil disobedience in the Indian community's struggle for civil rights in South Africa. Assuming leadership of the Indian National Movement, Gandhi led a national campaign for the alleviation of poverty, for the liberation of women, for brotherhood amongst differing religious and ethinicities, for the end of untouchability and caste discrimination, and for the economic self-sufficiency of the nation, but above all for Swaraj, the independence of India from foreign domination. It was during his peaceful agitation for the cause of the people, Gandhi was addressed by the people fondly as Bapu (Father of the Nation) and Mahatma (Great Soul).

Non-violence and Truth were his time tested weapons throughout his life and he had applied them meticulously even in the extreme situations. He lived on a simple vegetarian diet and kept rigorous fasts for long periods, for both self-purification and protest in support of his justified demands. By means of a hunger strike, Gandhi had helped bringing about India's Independence from British rule, inspiring colonial people to work for their own independence and ultimately dismantle the British Empire. Gandhi's principle of Satyagraha (truth force) has inspired generation of democratic and antiracists activists including Martin Luther King (Junior) and Nelson Mandela.

G. Ramachandran, a close associate and interpreter of Gandhi, once said about Gandhi's non-violence: "In Gandhi's mind, truth incarnates as love, and love translates itself into action and incarnates as non-violence. It was strong as steel, heritable but unbreakable." As could be seen, Gandhi's thoughts and actions were indivisible and as he himself said in his autobiography, "What I want to achieve—what I have been striving and pinning to achieve these thirty years—is self-realization, to see God face to face."

Admitting that what he was trying to propagate was not anything new and that truth and non-violence were as old as the hills, he averred: "My non-violence does not admit of running away from danger and leaving dear ones unprotected. Between violence and cowardly fight, I can only prefer violence to cowardice. I can no more preach non-violence to a coward than I can attempt a blind man to enjoy healthy scenes. Non-violence is the summit of bravery. And in my own experience, I have had no difficulty in demonstrating to men trained in the school of violence and superiority of non-violence. As a coward, which I was for years, I harbored violence. I began to prize non-violence only when I began to shed cowardice." Many may not admit openly that the real problem is this, our lack of courage to face challenges which would definitely demand facing difficulties of that sort. We become votaries of violence, for it is easy there for every one to hide his or her real self while non-violence requires infinite courage, suffering for which many may not be ready.

Gandhi's approach to life itself needs to be understood if one wants to realize how he perceived human problems and solutions. He began to realize as he perceived human problems and solutions. He began with the assertion that 'God is Truth', but after several years he changed it to 'Truth is God', signifying the importance he attached to man's relation to infinite. Gandhi asserted that humanity has to progress towards non-violence if it has to survive and he was convinced that humanity is gradually moving towards non-violence.

Gandhi through his numerous campaigns in South Africa and India (21 years in South Africa and 33 years in India) demonstrated that Satya, Ahimsa and Satyagraha could become the base of a new concerted effort on the part of humanity to discover its roots and more steadfastly to an era of amity and goodwill which will promise continuation of life in harmony with nature. He said, "We have to make truth and non-violence not matters for more individual practice but for practice by groups and communities and nations. Ahimsa is the attribute of the soul, and therefore, to be practiced by everybody in all the affairs of life. It cannot be practiced in all departments, it has no practical values. The one refrain of most of his arguments has always been that society is largely regulated by expressions of non-violence in its mutual dealings and that non-violence is not merely personal virtue, it is social virtue to be cultivated like other virtues.

He pointed out, "If one does not practice non-violence in one's personal relations with others and hopes to use it in large affairs, one is vastly mistaken. Also, one cannot be non-violent in one's own circle and violent outside it. Or else one is not truly non-violent in one's circle. Often the non-violence is only in appearance." Gandhi believed that "the world of tomorrow will be, must be a society based on non-violence." He reminded his countrymen and others that non-violence cannot be preached, it has to be practiced.

Admitting that what he was trying to propagate was not anything new and that truth and non-violence were as old as the hills, he said, "My non-violence does not admit of running away from danger and leaving dear one unprotected. Between non-violence and cowardly flight, I can only prefer violence to cowardice. I can no more preach non-violence to a coward than I can tempt a blind man to enjoy healthy scenes.

However, humanity's urge for peace is innate and insatiable. Today, as never before, the urgency of securing it on a lasting basis is at once desperate and attainable. Gandhi's thought and action flowed from this deep-rooted conviction. "Not to believe in the possibility of permanent peace," he held, was to "disbelieve in the Godliness of human nature. Methods hereto adopted—have failed because rock bottom sincerity on the part of those who have striven has been lacking. Not that they have realized this lack.

In unconditional acceptance of non-violence and its methods Gandhi saw the possibility of raising foundation pure and strong for an enduring peace in the world—through the concept of non-violence. The philosophy of non-violence was rooted in and permeated by truth. The difference between nations arose over the perception of their interests. The moral force of Satyagraha would oblige a nation to ascertain its true interests and in a spirit of cooperation rather than selfishness or malice. Once this is done, interstate relations could come to be founded upon mutuality and accommodation rather than competition, aggrandizement and domination. The choice of Satyagraha would transform the very character of the state and thus of interstate relations and the consequent state of the world. It is hoped that Non-violence and Satyagraha together can usher in a lasting peace.

Gandhi fervently hoped for a world federation of free and "independent state." His concept of World Government transcended the traditional thinking, the pattern of conventional international organisations could not satisfy the conditions for bringing genuine peace. He held that peace could not be established through mere conferences. He was not optimistic about the League of Nations and the U.N. Since they lacked the spirit of non-violence and failed to serve as vehicles of peace in the absence of a force to enforce their decisions.

Gandhi believed that the doctrine of non-violence held good in the matter of relationship between states and states also. This conviction impelled him to unequivocally recommend total disarmament. He was optimistic enough to advocate unilateral disarmament. "If even one great nation were unconditionally to perform the supreme act of renunciation many of us unconditionally to perform the supreme act of renunciation, many of us would see in our life-time visible peace established on earth. His call for unilateral disarmament betrayed his idealism, while the realist Gandhi appreciated that with the establishment of a democratic world federation disarmament would be practicable in all countries.

Gandhi believed that disarmament was possible only through "the matchless weapon of non-violence," and it was his hope that "India will ... prove herself worthy of being the first nation in the world to give lead to other nations for the delivery of earth from the burden of war. He wanted the great powers lead the rest by disarming themselves: they should give up ambitions and exploitation and revise their mode of life. Thus, according to Gandhi disarmament cannot crystallise, unless the nations of the world cease to exploit one another. Exploitation must go ... that is the essential pre-condition for the establishment of a world free from blood-spilling and destruction.

Accordingly, he advocated Satyagraha as the sure and potent weapon of combating Inter-state aggression. Satyagraha is universally acceptable. Non-violence, according to him, excludes war and ushers in peace. Gandhi's ideas about peace suggest that the solution he offered for effecting world peace transcended the frontiers of international diplomacy. The chief limitation of international diplomacy is that it is based up on recognition of the power-system. The Gandhian way claims to stand for non-violent and non-exploitative Social order which alone can ensure just and enduring peace. It may be argued that the Gandhian declarations on peace bristle with some practical difficulties. But Gandhi would ask that—if an individual could practice non-violence why whole nations could not do so. He believed that one must make a beginning and the rest would follow. The Gandhian concept of world peace should be viewed within the general framework of his philosophy of ahimsa. A proper appreciation of his doctrine of ahimsa would facilitate comprehension of the logical application of that doctrine.

Sceptics consider Gandhian plea for disarmament Utopian. In fact, it is not so. Its success depends on the nature of human-beings. Gandhi has great faith in the godliness of human nature. Human nature is essentially peace loving. Even when man fights violently, he does so out of a desire to live in peace. The way of world peace lies in cultivating the spirit of non-violence and peace in the hearts of men. As the individuals are built, so the nations are also built. And as the nations are built, so the world is built. Gandhi says: "there is not one law for the atom and another for the universe."

The life-style of Mahatma Gandhi is quite enough to prove that he was able to reduce himself virtually to "the level of the poorest of the poor." As for an ordinary human being, it would be too much to expect what would have been possible for a great man like Gandhi. We must however have to learn a lesson from Gandhi's style of living, for as an effective means to achieve Socialism. There is no alternative to simple living and noble thinking and this is more so for a developing country like ours.

It goes without saying that a world of peace and prosperity can never be achieved by the use of force. It was Mahatma Gandhi who invented a new weapon that alone could save mankind from a war of total annihilation. Gandhi and the atom bomb were intact "the two originalities of our time and one would defeat the other before it ended."

Jayaprakash Narayan has very aptly said about Mahatma Gandhi that "He was specifically a prophet of the atomic age in which the engines of violence which man has invented for the first time in history threaten to destroy the whole of mankind. Gandhiji not only preached non-violence as a Philosophy and an ideal but practiced it on a very colossal scale and did it if not with complete success, with very great success. As long as there is violence which threatens the very future of the human race, the relevance of Gandhiji would continue. Gandhiji will remain relevant till the changes of total annihilation of the human race are removed."

Peace is a relationship between people and people. Peace begins with a harmony between individuals. Gandhi lived and worked for the establishment of such relationship among individuals and groups. His is a unique contribution to peace in the modern context. Gandhi's style of life and the techniques he propounded deserved to be studied and applied so that the world may be a safe place to live.

Gautama Buddha preached the message of Ahimsa and Compassion—Asoka one of the greatest emperors had followed the Buddha's teachings in giving up wars and to tread the path of peace though only after being vexed with the carnage which the Kalinga was brought about. Jesus Christ whom the Christians worship as the Saviour and Lord is described as the prince of peace. He had lived and preached the message of love, forgiveness and peace. In contemporary times Gandhi has relentlessly voiced the efficacy of non-violence as against violence.

H.G. Wells in one of his last writings had predicted that man is unfit to live in this world as he knows what is good but does not know how to do good. Man wants peace but does not know how to achieve it. Hence, he being incapable of doing what he knows to be the right would destroy himself. The future would show whether H.G. Wells is right or wrong. However, a survey of the contemporary world is ominous. Since man has perfected the weapons of war and nations have manufactured and stored them in enough numbers to such an extent that an outbreak of war would not only destroy the living and the products of civilization, but also would make the surface and atmosphere of the earth uninhabitable for hundreds of years if not for ever. Leaders of nations and man in general are aware of this fact and they dread another war. War is an international nightmare. Man would like to avoid or escape wars if possible.

It is known that Gandhi is opposed to violence and wars. Gandhi has been an advocate of non-violence and peace. Though non-violence is "as old as the hills", Gandhi's exposition, clarification and forceful advocacy of non-violence is unique. The Gandhian way of peace springs from the basic concept of non-violence.

Though for many war is said to be a way of ending wars. As a matter of fact the Second World War was fought by the allies with a view to end all wars. Gandhi is of the firm opinion that war can never end wars. Violence breeds only violence but can never end violence. War is destructive whereas peace is constructive. They are two opposite processes. Further, violence, being destructive, is a negative process, whereas peace, being constructive is a positive process. Peace is a positive force of cementing people. War which is a destroying and divisive force can never contribute to the establishment of peace. Hence, the search for peace should be in the way of non-violence alone. What Napolean had said to the emperor of Austria in a personal appeal after a fierce battle is worthy of note:

> "Thousands of Frenchmen and Austrians have been killed. The prospect of continuance of such horrors distresses me so greatly that I make a personal appeal to you. Amid grief and surrounded by 15,000 corpses, I implore your Majesty, I feel bound to give you an urgent warning. Let us give our generation peace and tranquility. If the men of later days are such fools as to come to blows, they will learn wisdom after a few years of fighting and will then live at peace with one another."

Napolean had sent this appeal for peace at the height of his glory and success. He saw the futility of war to end hostilities and appealed for peace. Napolean subscribed to the Gandhian view when he said, "There are only two powers in the world, those powers are the spirit and the sword. In the long-run the sword will always be conquered by the Spirit."

Gandhi writes, "There will be international league only when all the nations big or small, composing it are fully independent." An International league based on non-violence leads to the establishment of world peace. Such a league implies and it is possible only when it consists of independent nations.

As long as any nation is not independent, there would not be world peace. It is necessary that all nations should be independent to be equal partners in the League of Nations in order to have peace.

Gandhi in adopting non-violent means to get Swaraj for India aimed at achieving international peace by doing so. Gandhi said, I suggest to the friends of peace for the world, that the Congress in 1920 took a tremendous step towards peace when it declared that it would attain her own, namely Swaraj, by non-violent and truthful means. And I am positive that if we unflinchingly adhere to these means in the prosecution of our goal, we shall have made the largest contribution to the world peace."

According to Gandhi, there are certain conditions which are conducive for international peace. They are:

(i) All nations should be independent;
(ii) The equality of all nations should be recognized; and
(iii) Disarmament should be accepted by the nations both in principle and their practice.

Wars are the result of lust for power. In some way or other some nations want to establish supremacy over at least some of the other nations. They derive to create and perpetuate inequalities so as to maintain their superiority. Self-aggrandizement gives rise to inequality and inequality in return affords scope for self-aggrandizement. It is a vicious circle which can be broken only by an international law by which all nations are treated as equal. The spirit of self-aggrandizement is killed to some extent, though it requires to be more nullified by education, by the proclamation of equality of all nations by an international law. Such a law in the course of time would become a convention and *de-facto* accomplishment. Equality of nations would go a long way to establish peace in this world.

However, his philosophy of peace is to be sharply distinguished from the conservative plea for "Peace at any cost" which is in essence a plea for the maintenance of *status quo*. Peace as Gandhi advocated is integrally related to justice. As he wrote: "Peace must be just." Peace is not mere cessation of hostilities. Gandhi did not share the diplomatic view of peace. Peace for him connoted a positive state of affairs, the pre-condition being freedom from exploitation. What he advocated was non-violence and just peace which alone in his opinion, could ensure lasting peace. Accordingly his ideas about peace suggest that the solution he offered for effecting world peace transcended the frontiers of international diplomacy. The chief limitation of international diplomacy is that it is based upon recognition of the power-system.

Further, the Gandhian way claims to stand for non-violent and non-exploitative social order which alone can ensure just and enduring peace. Non-violence, according to Gandhi, excludes war and ushers in peace.

As a result, Gandhi's concept of peace on earth and goodwill among mankind leads to the development of Sarvodaya Social order which is India's distinctive contribution to the world of thought. The application of moral truth to the facts of social life is the essence of Gandhian and Valluvar's way of life. Their dynamic Philosophy can make possible the advent of a radically transformed society. They serve as a system of norms and moral values that can guide our conduct and action in society and state. The truth or a few will count, the untruth of millions will vanish even like a chaff befole a whiff of wind. The message of Gandhi and Tiruvalluvar will remain permanent in the hearts of one and all. Tiruvalluvar really transcends Jesus who only wants to forgive them. In advising to forget the trespasses Valluvar is only in the positive degree, Mahatma Gandhi and Tiruvalluvar have become the symbols of peace, truth, non-violence and dharma. If an individual can practice non-violence, why not whole groups of individuals and whole nations? Gandhi believed that one must make a beginning and the rest would follow. Gandhian concept of world peace should be viewed as an integral part of his philosophy of life and one should try to appreciate his attitude within the general framework of his philosophy of ahimsa.

TRUE INTERNATIONALISM

Nations, according to Gandhi, must learn to live for each other, and they are quite capable of doing so—even the defeated Germans: "all that is needed is a transmutation of their marvellous energy for the promotion of the progress of the world. as a whole, rather than its application for their own against that of the whole world."[1] He asserted that the great powers assembled at San Francisco for the founding of the United Nations ought to work for "parity among all nations—the strongest and the weakest—the strong should be the servants of the weak not their masters or exploiters."[2] Brotherhood of all peoples in the world, which is the ultimate goal of humanity or at any rate should be, could only be based on the plinth of their national freedoms, according to Gandhi: "Hinduism insists on the brotherhood not only of all mankind but of all that lives. . . . The moment we have restored real living equality between man and man, we shall be able to establish equality between man and the whole creation. When that day comes we shall have peace on earth. . . ."[3]

Evidently, then, Gandhi had no doubt whatsoever that nationalism, instead of being narrow or exclusive, is a vital prerequisite for internationalism. The passion with which he made India's independence the linchpin of world peace exemplifies this belief. According to Gandhi, one could not be an internationalist without being a nationalist. Internationalism would come only if nationalism became a reality, that is, only when peoples of different countries and cultures were organized in such a way that they were capable of acting as one being.

Nationalism was not bad in itself, of course. It was the selfishness, the spirit of exploitation that inhered in those with power that, in Gandhi's view, impelled them to fight others and grow bigger at the latter's expense and ruin. He was emphatic that India's nationalism had broken new ground insofar as it was "seeking full self-expression for the benefit and service of humanity at large. I cannot possibly go wrong so long as I do not harm other nations in the act of serving my country."[4]

Even in the mid-1920s, Gandhi wanted "to think in terms of the whole world," for his patriotism include [d] the good of mankind in general."[5] He proclaimed, "My nationalism is intense internationalism." That is how, in his logic, hatred need not be an attribute of nationalism. Those who believed it were to be pitied, for they were laboring under the grossest of delusions:

> So long as they retain that attitude the progress of this country [India], the progress of the world is retarded. . . .

The world is weary of it. We see the fatigue overcoming the Western nations. We see that this song of hate has not benefited humanity. Let it be the privilege of India to turn a new leaf and set a lesson to the world.

Gandhi's views of nationalism are expressed thus:

> Internationalism pre-supposes nationalism—not the narrow, selfish, greedy spirit that often passes under the name of nationalism that, whilst it insists upon its own freedom and growth, will disdain to attain them at the expense of other nations.[6]

Apparently, in Gandhi's version of nationalism, there is a strong undercurrent of cooperation born of and necessitated by the understanding of one people by the others in a spirit of humility and sympathy rather than arrogance. He wants insolence and ignorance to be banished forever in the concerns and calculations of nations when it came to interacting with one another. Gandhi's nationalism was as broad as the universe. It includes in its sweep even the lower animals . . . all the nations of the earth. He said: "If I possibly could convince the whole of India of the truth of the message, then India would be something to the whole world for which the world is longing. My nationalism includes the well-being of the whole world. I do not want my India to rise on the ashes of other nations. I do not want India to exploit a single human being. I want India to become strong in order that she can infect the other nations also with her strength. Not so with other nations of the world, not so with a single nation in Europe today."[7]

Gandhi was certain that internationalism did not mean the loss of national identity: "we do not want to follow the frog-in-the-well policy, nor, in seeming to be international, lose our roots. We cannot be international, if we lose our individuality, i.e. nationality." Nations must promote nationalism, of course, but such promotion should always be in the spirit of universal brotherhood and should always "depend on the rule [that the] stronger should help the poor."[8]

Such a spirit, Gandhi had no doubt, could really and quite easily be developed by means of positive nationalism: unless people could serve their family and their village, they could not serve the world. Nationalism had no malice, no ill-will or contempt—it had only goodwill and peace in it. Unless one learned to love one's neighbors, one could not possibly cultivate the spirit of love for the rest of the world.

Gandhi described himself as a cosmopolitan. He could not possibly be anything else, if he wanted his credo and gospel to have universal relevance. And his mission was to unite the world by "grouping unities": Unless I group unities I shall never be able to unite the whole world. Tolstoy once said that if we would but get-off the backs of our neighbours the world would be quite all right without any further help from us. And if we can only serve our immediate neighbour by ceasing to prey upon them, the circle of unities thus grouped in the right fashion will ever grow in circumference till at last it is co-terminus with that of the whole world. More than that it is not given to any man to try or achieve.[9]

It is not surprising, therefore, to find Gandhi expressing his revulsion against the idea of "Asia for Asians" as an anti-European combine. Brimming with the vision of world unity, he could not bear the thought of being a "frog in the well." Takaoka, a member of the Japanese Parliament, sought a message from Gandhi at Sevagram for his party, which was just founded with the motto "Asia for Asians." Gandhi's response was blunt and firm: I do not subscribe to the doctrine Asia for the Asiatics, if it is meant as an anti-European combination. How can we have Asia for the Asiatics unless we are content to let Asia remain a frog in the well? But Asia cannot afford to remain a frog in the well. I have a message for the whole world, if it will only live up to it. There is the imprint of Buddhistic influence on the whole of Asia, which includes India, China, Japan, Burma, Ceylon and the Malaya States. I said to the Burmese and the Ceylonese that they were Buddhist in name; India was Buddhist in reality. I would say the same thing to China and Japan. But for Asia to be not for Asia but for the whole world, it has to learn the message of Buddha and deliver it to the world. Today, it is being denied everywhere.[10]

In Gandhi's view "for a non-violent person the whole world is one family." If Gandhi had his way, the post-war policy of the free National Government of India would be to promote commonwealth of all world states including, if possible belligerent states also, so as to reduce to the minimum the possibility of an armed conflict between different states.[11]

The League of Nations, he thought accordingly, could not further the ideal of one world, for it was not universal. A truly international League could exist only when all its members, big or small, were independent, with the nature of that independence corresponding to the extent of non-violence assimilated by the nations concerned. Gandhi is absolutely clear about one thing: "In a society based on non-violence the smallest nation will feel as tall as the tallest. The idea of superiority and inferiority will be wholly obliterated."[12]

THE IMPERATIVE OF SWADESHI

In a literal sense swadeshi means "home manufacture." But the main thrust of Gandhi's advocacy and insistence of swadeshi was on the need for self-reliance, which in turn contributed to world peace. Seething poverty in India naturally moved Gandhi to conclude that independence did not mean mere political emancipation from foreign rule. He believed that in order to be meaningful independence must have a substantive economic content and criterion. Indeed, fiscal autonomy and health were very vital for the life of a nation. And that, he was confident, could be attained through swadeshi, particularly in the case of India.

The history of nations, Gandhi said, bore testimony to the fact that nations unable to preserve their economic independence for want of a policy of swadeshi had fallen, whereas those that could had always enjoyed swaraj. Citing the example of the smaller European states of his time, he pointed out that they survived as independent economic entities because they practiced swadeshi. Indeed, every nation that was independent followed swadeshi in its own way. Switzerland and Denmark, for instance, achieved this by maintaining manufactures and trades that were suited to their own needs and were free from outside interference. Swadeshi and swaraj, in Gandhi's opinion, were thus inexhorably interdependent—if not actually synonymous. The reign of foreign domination would easily come to an end once the country ceased to be dependent for its material requirements on others and became instead capable of meeting its needs from its own resources.

The sword will be sheathed as soon as Manchester calico ceases to be saleable in India. It is much more economical, expeditious and possible to give up the use of Manchester and, therefore, foreign calico than to blunt the edge of Sir William's sword. The process will multiply the number of swords and, therefore, also miseries in the world.

Like opium production, the world manufacture of swords needs to be restricted. The sword is probably responsible for more misery in the world than opium.

Hence do I say that, if India takes to the spinning-wheel, she will contribute to the restriction of armament and peace of the world as no other country and nothing else can.[13]

A fuller appreciation of Gandhi's position here calls for some explanation. Clothing is one of our basic necessities. Before the advent of colonialism in India, the economy of the country was flourishing enough to meet the basic needs of the people, leaving enough surpluses for export. That is what had drawn the foreigner to India in the first place. The village at that time was virtually a self-contained economic unit that satisfied all the basic needs, and more, of its inhabitants. Handicrafts and cottage industry flourished, and agriculture supported a satisfying quality of life of the people in India.

Colonialism destroyed all that by policies coercively enforced to pursue its own interests. The compulsions and requirements of industrialization at home obliged the colonial rulers to supplant the prevailing economic system by a pattern that not only met their own needs but also aimed at strengthening the shackles of the subject people by making them dependent upon the metropolitan country, in this case, England. As industrialization there grew, so did the dependence of India and its people on England.

The spinning jenny revolutionized weaving and cloth making. Soon the textile mills of Manchester and Lancashire were producing huge quantities of cloth that duly swamped India, impoverishing in the process the craft-workers and weavers in the villages along with the others. In reviving and rejuvenating these sources, basic to the life and economy of the village, Gandhi saw the only hope for the salvation of the people of India. Hence, his insistence on swadeshi, which included not only cloth but all those items that could be—and not long ago were—produced in the small, self-reliant Indian village.

Gandhi thus argued that India's independence would be hollow as long as it remained dependent for its basic needs upon England. The industrial and corresponding technological development of over a century in that country had increased the gap tremendously with regard to India. Only an India relying upon its own resources and strength could possibly reduce or bridge that gap. Promoting and using swadeshi was the obvious first step India must take for its independence and giving meaning and substance to that independence.

This explains his call for stopping all imports from England so that India could regenerate its economy by its own efforts. In his opinion, this would improve international relations, for India's relations then "will no longer be based on consideration of self-interest but will be inspired by concern for general welfare."

Gandhi's argument may not make much sense to many modern economists, also because trade and commerce are major contributory factors to international interdependence and seeming unification of the world. But due recognition of its merit is reflected in the growing clamor for a new international economic order, as also in many an aspect of the North-South dialogue, a discussion of which need not detain us here.

In any case, given the context of Gandhi's times, his economic philosophy, and, most important, his priorities, his argument for swadeshi and its integral component, self-reliance, are perfectly consistent and very relevant. For instance, often he declared:

> Under nay scheme . . . men incharge of machinery will think not of themselves or even of the nation to which they belong but of the whole human race. The Lancashire men will cease to use their machinery for exploiting India and other countries, but on the contrary they will devise means of enabling India to convert in her own villages her cotton into cloth. Nor will Americans, under my scheme, seek to enrich themselves by exploiting the other races of the earth through their inventive skill.[14]

The spinning-wheel (charkha), which he held to be a "sign of peace," was crucial to Gandhi's concept of swadeshi, for it was through revival and resort to it that the rural economy in the country could be oriented toward self-reliance and finally to world peace. It was this belief that made him claim that the spinning-wheel was the most appropriate and effective answer to the atomic bomb. Andrew Freeman of the New York Post asked him if the spinning-wheel had a cultural and therapeutic value for the malaise infecting the West, which had culminated in the atomic bomb, and if the wheel could serve as a counterweapon to the bomb. Gandhi responded that he did not have the "slightest doubt that the saving of India and of the world [lay] in the wheel."[15] He further argued that, in order to save the world from destruction, life had to be simplified; human dignity could be sustained only by serving everyone—even the last, the smallest, or seemingly most insignificant—on the earth: "We must do even unto this last [creature] as we would have the world do by us. All must have equal opportunity. Given the opportunity, every human being has the same possibility for spiritual growth. This is what the spinning-wheel symbolises."[16]

Apparently, Gandhi's seminal ideas in this regard have much more than meets the eye, and it would not be productive to interpret his statements literally. The charkha for him has both literal and symbolic significance. Literally, it meets the immediate basic needs of the individual by producing the cloth through a fruitful use of one's time, which in any case is plentiful in the rural milieu; it precludes dependence upon the mercy or charity of others and enables one to meet a basic need in the dignity of one's own labor. On a symbolical level, the wheel signifies the spirit of self-reliance that sustains life. A complete discussion of his views on the value of the charkha, which he spelled out in his writings, is beyond the scope of this work, however.

The essential point to bear in Timid here is that, by stressing the role of the charkha in the life of the individual, Gandhi is drawing attention to an honorable, dignified means of resisting exploitation and preventing alienation inherent in the entire system of industrial production. Industrialization in the world has occurred unevenly and at the cost of so much misery for the majority who feed the phenomenon by being merely suppliers of raw material and cheap or free labor. More often than not the industrial relations are marked by exploitation and consequent strife instead of equality and cooperation. Yet the charkha, Gandhi is absolutely certain, facilitates cooperation among millions in various ways. Through such cooperation "on the largest scale known to the world," he wants to teach "the uselessness, nay, the sinfulness of exploitation of those weaker than ourselves."[17]

Thus, he insists, a self-supporting, self-reliant India— chiefly through swadeshi, of course—would be a proof against the temptation to exploitation. This, in turn, will make India least attractive to the greed or caprice of any power, Western or Eastern, and would automatically make India secure without its having to carry the burden of expensive, wasteful armaments. "Her internal economy [of swadeshi] will be India's strongest bulwark against aggression."[18] In this way, a sturdy contribution to a durable peace would naturally have been made, for self-support and self-reliance were the very essence of a peaceful world order.

THE COMPROMISE OF A WORLD FEDERAL GOVERNMENT

Gandhi's belief in universal brotherhood, and his view of internationalism, quite logically led him to think in terms of and advocate a world government preceded, as a compromise, by a world federation based on non-violence:

Yes I claim to be a practical idealist. I believe in compromise so long as it does not involve the sacrifice of principles. I may not get a World Government that I want just now but if it is a government that would just touch my ideal I would accept it as a compromise.

Therefore, although I am not enamoured of a world federation I shall be prepared to accept it if it is built on essentially non-violent basis.[19]

Nations must eventually unite. Gandhi abhored "isolated independence," least of all of India; rather, he espoused "voluntary interdependence."[20] Whereas isolated independence could easily menace the world, a federation of friendly interdependent states the world over—for which India was always ready —would unite the world in lasting peace. And if by India's efforts such a world federation of independent states comes into being, the hope of the kingdom of God, otherwise described as Ramarajya, assured Gandhi, may legitimately be entertained.

Gandhi saw neither a contradiction between the freedom of India and a world federation brought about on a voluntary basis, nor a matter of choosing one to the rejection of the other. Shortly before his arrest in August 1942, Gandhi was asked, "Instead of striving for India's freedom why would you not strive for a far greater and nobler end—world federation? Surely that will automatically include India's freedom as the greater includes the less." Conceding that federation was "undoubtedly a greater and nobler end" than to be merely "self-centred, seeking only to preserve their own freedom," Gandhi pointed to the obvious fallacy implied in the question; namely, how could the subject nations be federated with the free as equals? So, clearly,

The very first step to a world federation is to recognise the freedom of conquered and exploited nations. Thus, India and Africa have to be freed.

The second step would be to announce to and assure the aggressor powers, in the present instance the Axis powers, that immediately [after] the war ends, they will be recognized as members of the world federation in the same sense as the Allies. This presupposes an agreement among the members of the world federation as to the irreducible fundamentals.[21]

The agreement on irreducible fundamentals was a necessity—otherwise, the federation would fall to pieces under the slightest strain—

and it must come voluntarily; non-violence is the basis of voluntariness. Since, of all the nations of the world, India was the only one with the message of non-violence, it must first have its immediate freedom to be able to play a constructive part in the creation of a world federation later on. According to Gandhi, India's freedom as a first step toward a world federation was necessary also because,

If I can get freedom for India through non-violent means, power of non-violence is firmly established, empire idea dissolves and the World State takes its place in which all the states of the world are free and equal, no state has its military.[22]

And, asserted Gandhi,

A free democratic India will gladly associate herself with other free nations for mutual defence against aggression and for economic co-operation. She will work for the establishment of a real world order based on freedom and democracy, utilising the world's knowledge and resources for the progress and advancement of humanity.[23]

More than "a world federation of free and independent states," Gandhi considered it to be vitally necessary for these states to unite under one central governing body composed of their representatives. Indeed, "that is the only condition on which the world can live," as he told the correspondent of the United Press of America in June 1947. He viewed the world as an organic whole: "God has so ordered this world that no one can keep his goodness or badness exclusively to himself. The whole world is like the human body with its various members. Pain in one part must inevitably poison the whole system."[24] But this one world, as he told George Catlin, had to be founded upon respect for truth.[25] There was too much deception and hypocrisy about contemporary international relations. People declared themselves to be righteous, even in the face of utterly unjustified facts of murder and sudden death in the world; one must not compromise or come to terms with these ugly facts. The brightest prospect of world unity, Gandhi assured Catlin, rested upon respect for truth and ahimsa; non-violence was the most appropriate and right course always, for non-violence had never done any harm to anybody.

True to his faith of a lifetime, Gandhi, accordingly, pleaded for the adoption of non-violence as a way of life by the nations of the world as "it will promote their happiness and peace," while, at the same time, being "their biggest contribution to the attainment of world peace after which we are all hankering."[26] As early as 1919, he had written in *Young India*,

It is [the] law of love which, silently but surely, governs the family for the most part throughout the civilised world.

I feel that nations cannot be one in reality, nor can there be activities conducive to the common good of the whole humanity, unless there is this definition and acceptance of the law of the family in national and international affairs, in other words, on the political platform. Nations can be called civilised only to the extent they obey this law.

Thus, a world state based on and permeated with non-violence constitutes a prominent feature in Gandhi's blueprint for permanent peace. But he was realistic enough not to anticipate "a time in India or the world when all will be followers of ahimsa," though he did "contemplate a time when in India we shall rely less on brute force and more on soul force."[27]

A state without police was very much in his scheme of things, of course, and its attainment quite feasible too, but Gandhi also conceded that it requires a higher degree of courage and unity than is ordinarily available. Therefore, "whilst I can invite all states to do without police or army," he candidly admitted, "I have not yet been able to bring myself to believe that you can preserve a society without police. " . . . You can thus say that my toleration of police is a limitation of non-violence." [28] And "police there will be even in satyayuga [the age of truth and perfection]," he felt.

Accordingly, Gandhi envisaged that as a transitory measure there "may be a world police to keep order in the absence of universal belief in non-violence."[29] He would allow "an armed police to enforce the lightest terms of peace. Even this retention of an international police," said Gandhi ruefully, "will be a concession of human weakness not by any means an emblem of peace."[30]

But never for a moment did Gandhi see any need for an army for, in his opinion, an army was "opposed to non-violence." Whatever tolerance or sympathy he might have had for it in his early days in South Africa for its virtues of discipline and devotion to duty had dwindled drastically, if not completely evaporated. He is frank, however, in acknowledging.

If is my inability to convince my people to do without army. I have not mustered sufficient strength to pit non-violence against thieves and scoundrels and cut-throats but I can ask people to pit non-violence against hordes of the army.

If perchance India wins her deliverance through non-violence we may perhaps show to the world that it is not necessary to have an army state.

I do not regard it utopian to think of a state without army, but it requires a higher degree of courage and purity.[31]

He might well have added that, until humanity regenerates the high moral fiber appropriate to such a transformation, an army would be necessary.

The nearest Gandhi gets to the idea of an army is that of a non-violent "army," which differed fundamentally from the usual violence-oriented organization. The difference lay in the nature of the discipline his non-violent army would observe and emulate: the discipline would come from within the "soldier" rather than from without. The soldier of the usual army "yields obedience whilst at war, but will yield to wild licence when free from it. But a non-violent soldier carries discipline in his heart and will carry an atmosphere of restraint in every walk of life."[32]

It appears that for establishing peace Gandhi had far greater hope in the British Commonwealth of Nations than in the United Nations. But the Commonwealth must first be transformed into "a fellowship of free nations joined together by the 'silver cords of love'. ... I would have India enter freely into such a fellowship and with the same rights of equality for Indians as for other members of the Commonwealth." He explained that my ambition is much higher than independence. Through the deliverance of India I seek to deliver the so-called [weak and backward] races of the earth from the crushing heels of western exploitation in which England can have the privilege of becoming a partner if she chooses.[33]

He elaborated the thought by reiterating what he had always maintained:

Puma Swaraj [complete independence] does not exclude association with any nation—much less with England. But it can only mean association for mutual benefit and at will. Thus, there are countries which are said to be independent but which have no Purna Swaraj, for example Nepal.[34]

To that example he could have added the countries of central and southern America, where the type of independence Gandhi visualized was far from being a reality or even an aspiration. Anyway, when eventually India became a full-fledged and equal member of the transformed Commonwealth of its own volition, Gandhi considered it to be an event of great importance, for the members had willingly launched a multi-racial Commonwealth. This, in his opinion, augured well for the forces of peace in the world, for justice had at last been done to a people who had long clamored and struggled for it.

THE DECEPTION OF DISARMAMENT

For years, Gandhi campaigned for the view that peace was a matter of justice rather than of strength: "all the world over a true peace depends not upon gun powder but upon pure justice." Unless nations learned to be just by renouncing exploitation and their total reliance on force, there could never be peace on the earth. Armaments were both a symptom of force and a temptation to use force. Thus, instead of talking of a mere restriction of armaments, their quantity and quality, Gandhi pleaded passionately for complete, universal disarmament.

Apparently in thorough approval, he published in the columns of *Young India*, which he edited, an excerpt from a monthly called International Sunbeam:

Total world disarmament, the only material safeguard for peace, should be the outward and visible sign of that inward mental disarmament on which alone outward peace can secure. So long, however, as one people is actually subjecting another to itself by superior military might even the very first step toward this inward mental disarmament has not been taken.[35]

Europe should take this first step, held Gandhi, "unless Europe is to commit suicide." The tendency to outdo one another in building up armaments would subside once that steps were taken.

By the same token, it would be equally disastrous if India, after attaining its freedom, were to join the arms race: "For India to enter into the arms race is to court suicide. With the loss of India to non-violence the last hope of the world will be gone. ..." Gandhi hoped "that India will make non-violence her creed, preserve man's dignity, and prevent him from reverting to the type from which he is supposed to have raised himself."[36]

The bloodshed of the Hindus and Muslims in the wake of partition and independence of India greatly distressed Gandhi, of course, but what exasperated him even more was the country swearing by the military and all that naked physical force implies. Our statesmen have for over two generations declaimed against the heavy expenditure on armaments under the British regime, but now that freedom from political serfdom has come, our military expenditure has increased and still threatens to increase and of this we are proud!

However . . . the hope lingers in me and many others that India shall survive this death dance and occupy the moral height that should belong to her after the training, however imperfect, in non-violence for an unbroken period of thirty-two years since 1915 [the year Congress accepted the method of non-violent struggle for the country's freedom].[37]

Gandhi never reconciled himself to the partition of India. Its aftermath of communal massacres in the Panjab and Bengal saddened him further. Talk of strengthening and relying upon the military as a means of meeting the situation, which was surcharged with suspicion, anger, and frustration, grieved him greatly.

He saw little sense in India after attaining its freedom incurring a heavy defense budget and felt that the country was groaning under this unnecessary and unsupportable burden: "We are convinced that we do not need the arms that India is carrying."[38] He stuck to his oft-repeated position that nothing could be more disastrous than India trying to imitate or rival the Western powers, including the United States, in their defense strategy based on military capability.

Gandhi unequivocally advocated that India—even Asia—take a lead with regard to disarmament. At the concluding session of the Asian Relations Conference at Delhi on April 2, 1947, he declared that the West is despairing of a multiplication of the atom bomb, because atom bombs mean utter destruction not merely of the West but of the whole world, as if the prophesy of the bible is going to be fulfilled and there is to be a perfect deluge.

It is up to you to tell the world of its wickedness and sin that is the heritage your teachers and my teachers have taught Asia.[39]

His anguish at the talk in India of continuing with the military, in fact strengthening it, is therefore in character.

Gandhi was certainly opposed, however, to the forced disarmament of a nation. For instance, referring to the disarming of India during World War I, Gandhi declared with vehemence:

Much as I abhor the possession or the use of arms, I cannot reconcile myself to forcible prohibition.

As I said three years ago, this forcible disarmament of a people will be regarded by history as one of the blackest sins committed by the British Government against India. If people want to possess arms they ought to have them without ado. . . . We cannot learn discipline by compulsion. We must learn not to use arms or to use them with responsibility and self-restraint, notwithstanding the right to possess them.[40]

In the same spirit, he condemned the disarming of the vanquished as a punitive measure. This was not merely due to compassion; Gandhi believed that guilt of war was so pervasive that it was virtually impossible, and wrong, to apportion all the blame for it to just one of the parties at the expense of the other.[41]

If the great powers disarmed themselves, felt Gandhi, they would not only escape the ravages of war but also cover themselves in glory, restore sanity to the world, and earn the eternal gratitude of posterity. These powers would, at the same time, have to give up their imperialistic designs and exploitation of the weak and hapless, while revising their own way of life. All this, evidently, amounts virtually to a total revolution, the only alternative to which, in Gandhi's opinion, was absolute disaster. The great powers could not be expected to move in the direction of total revolution—contrary to what lifestyle they had thus far been used to—spontaneously, of course.[42]

Nor could disarmament be worked out overnight; it would take time. The one thing Gandhi was absolutely certain of was that it would come only through the adoption of non-violence by a nation—indeed, by all the nations of the world. The evils of armaments can be cured, held Gandhi, by non-violence, which will eventually be the weapon of all nations. I say 'eventually' deliberately, because we shall have war and armaments for a very long time. It is two thousand years since Christ preached his "Sermon on the Mount" and the world has adopted only a fragment of the imperishable lofty precepts therein enunciated for the conduct of man toward man. Until we take all Christ's principles to our hearts, war, hatred and violence will continue.[43]

It was wrong to think that armaments implied or imparted strength, for real strength, according to Gandhi, came by self-sacrifice, from within and not through physical force. He pointed out that the rishis (sages) of yore, themselves great warriors, realized the utter uselessness of force and "taught a weary world that its salvation lay not through violence but through non-violence."

Gandhi was emphatic that nations should strengthen themselves spiritually, for "Internal spiritual forces are stronger and induce a more certain and lasting life. It is not by arming yourself that you will guarantee peace to the world. External arms, guns, cannons and gas have only evil and passing results."[44] To say that one is arming oneself for self-defense was, he said, "a wretched plea ... a bad thing," for, in effect, the result invariably was that you organized yourself to "prey upon ill organized communities and nations." The crux of the matter was that real disarmament could come only when "the nations of world cease to exploit one another."[45]

Gandhi would not accept the proposition that, since disarmament chiefly depended upon the great powers, small, neutral and non-aggressive countries like Switzerland, for instance, should be forced to disarm. Gandhi asserted that the very fact of neutrality and nonaggressiveness of Switzerland rendered the army there completely redundant. Indeed, it would be a far superior thing for Switzerland to give the world a lesson in disarmament and establish that the Swiss are brave enough to live without an army. Nor was he willing to accept the proposition that the mere presence of the Swiss army had saved that country from being overrun by foreign armies. Rejecting both the deterrent role of the Swiss military forces as well as the value of military development, Gandhi astutely pointed out the fallacies involved:

Will the questioner forgive me if I say that a double ignorance underlies this question?

He deplores the fact that, if you give up the profession of soldiering, you will miss the education you receive in service and sacrifice.

None need run away with the idea that because you avoid military conscription you are not in for a conscription of a severer and nobler type. When I spoke to you about labour, I told you that labour ought to assimilate all the noble qualities of soldiering: endurance and defiance of death and sacrifice. When you disarm yourself, it does not mean that you will have a merry time. It is not that you are absolved from the duty of serving your homes when you give up soldiering; on the contrary, your women and children would be taking part in defending your homes.

Again I am not talking to you without experience. In the little institution [sic] that we are conducting, we are teaching our women and children also how to save that institution—as we are living among thieves and robbers.

Everything becomes simple and easy the moment you learn to give up your own life in order to save the life of others.

And lastly, it is really forgotten that safety which an individual derives from innocence is safety which no amount of arms will give you.

The second part of the ignorance lies in the second part of the question.

I must respectfully deny the truth of the statement that the presence of the Swiss army prevented the War from affecting Switzerland. Although Belgium had its own army, it was not saved and if the rival armies had wanted a passage through Switzerland, believe me, they would have fought you also. You might have fought in turn, but you would have fought much better non-violently.[46]

Gandhi was also not deluded by the description of an arms race among the powers of Europe, and elsewhere, as a manifestation of their desire to eliminate war. This was a misconception at best and plain hypocrisy at worst for the noble ideal of peace could not possibly be achieved by the disastrous means of war. And where was even the slightest indication that in acquiring more and more weapons the concerned nation had abjured the motive of being dominant and jockeying for the position of strength? In his message editor of a U.S. magazine. The Cosmopolitan, Gandhi wrote:

If recognised leaders of mankind who have control over engines of destruction were wholly to renounce their use with full knowledge of implications, permanent peace can be obtained.

This is clearly impossible without the great powers of the earth renouncing their imperialistic designs. This again seems impossible without these great nations ceasing to believe in soul destroying competition and the desire to multiply wants and therefore increase their material possessions.[47]

With regard to nuclear weapons, Gandhi thought it quite futile merely to restrict them; he seriously doubted that the nations possessing them would remain content merely with their possession. Dismissing the efficacy or permanence of "balance of terror" or "balance of nonuse" and the supposition that their "overkill" capacity by itself would induce and enforce non-violence in the world, he emphasized that so long as the thinking in these quarters remained rooted in violence we will continue heading toward disaster and self-destruction. Indeed, "the violent man's eyes would [be] lit up with the prospect of much greater amount of destruction and death which he could now wreak," Gandhi said. At best the destructive capability of these weapons may temporarily postpone the outbreak of war. "Like a man gutting himself with dainties to the point of nausea and turning away from them only to return with redoubled zeal after the effect of nausea is well over. Precisely in the same manner will the world return to violence with renewed zeal after the effect of disgust is worn out."[48] Gandhi quite frankly considered the "balance of terror" to be nothing more than the "preparations for a third World War." He was willing to concede that atomic energy "may be utilised . . . for humanitarian purposes" but was sure that it would not be confined to that alone.

According to Gandhi, nations armed themselves out of fear of each other and to guard their imperialist possessions. Quite early in his life, echoing the philosophy of the Gita, Gandhi in his *Hind Swaraj* asserted that nations armed themselves because they were filled with the fear that others may take away their possessions; force was used when people were under the spell of fear, and "what is gained through fear is retained only for as long as fear is present."[49] At the same time, fear breeds hatred. Apparently then, the very first step that nations must take toward ensuring peace was to dispel fear and, along with it, mistrust. Gandhi said his instincts told him that if you do not intend violence to anyone, no one will use it against you either: "It is only when we are afraid of our opponent, we employ unclean strength like his that we learn unclean ways and so become weak. ... If we meet uncleanliness with cleanliness, the total result would be less of uncleanliness and the people, the world, would be happier for this."[50]

Gandhi put it succinctly and without any equivocation when he declared:

Peace will never come until the Great Powers courageously decide to disarm themselves. . . .

I have an implicit faith—a faith that today burns brighter than ever, after half a century's experience of unbroken practice of non-violence—that mankind can only be saved through non-violence.[51]

Speaking about Britain, before World War II broke out, Gandhi stated:

Someone has to rise in England, with the living faith to say that

England, whatever happens, shall not use arms. They are a nation fully armed, and if they having the power fully deliberately refuse to use arms, theirs will be the first example of Christianity in active practice on a mass scale. That will be a real miracle.[52]

He thus called upon the greatest nation of its times to make the noble beginning.

A realist and ever a man of action, Gandhi fully realized that, before general disarmament prevailed, a beginning had to be made somewhere.

Some nation will have to dare disarm herself and take large risks. The level of non-violence in that nation, if that event happily comes to pass, will naturally have risen so high as to command universal respect. Her judgment will be unerring, her decisions will be firm, her capacity for heroic self-sacrifice will be great, and she will want to live as much for other nations as for herself.[53]

In calling upon Britain to take the initiative in unilaterally disarming itself, Gandhi seemed to be saying that a voluntary renunciation of its formidable military capability would make a tremendous and multifaceted impact on the nations of the world. His invitation also implied in a way the great faith he had in the people of that country—once they decided to do something, they could and did it well. And would it not be some atonement for their past sins?

All good things, Gandhi believed, began always with one single person. Thus, he urged that an initiative toward disarmament be taken soon by some country. To one of his biographers, Frederick B. Fisher (author of The Strange Little Brown Man Gandhi), Gandhi sent a message on September 31, 1931, for American Christians on World Peace and Disarmament in which he unambiguously stressed that Peace and disarmament are not a matter of reciprocity.

When real Peace and Disarmament come, they will be initiated by a strong nation like America irrespective of the consent and co-operation of other nations. . . .

As Thoreau has said so well, "all reform all the world over always began with one person taking it up." . . .[54]

Here is the very kernel of Gandhi's entire thinking and campaign with regard to disarmament. Having concluded that disarmament was moral, eminently desirable, and urgent in a world quickly moving toward self-annihilation, the karmayogi in Gandhi was moved to seek courses of action. In unilateral disarmament he saw a bold but perfectly feasible course of action in concrete terms. And he pressed for it whenever he could relax the focus of his campaign for non-violence and rampant international exploitation, particularly in the colonial world.

For much of his later life, Gandhi was preoccupied with the

particular issues raised by India's freedom struggle. Since he had been thoroughly disillusioned about the intentions of the British Empire, he could now more easily explore the implications of a total rejection of war. World War II reinforced this position both because of the urgent need to consider what action to take if the Japanese invaded and because of the awareness that war was now something that involved a new level of destructiveness. As a result, what emerges is a crystallized conviction of war as an evil that must be prevented by eliminating its root causes and resorting to moral means in preference to arms or their regulated use.

Asserting that "physical possession of arms is the least necessity of the brave," Gandhi stated that non-violence requires the strength and courage to suffer without retaliation, to receive blows without returning any. Non-violence, the surest means of ushering in permanent peace, becomes futile "unless the root cause is dealt with, and the root cause is the greed of nations. If there were no greed, there would be no occasion for armaments: the principle of non-violence necessitates complete abstention from exploitation in any form. Immediately the spirit of exploitation is gone, armaments will be felt as an unbearable burden." He declared, "I have no doubt that unless big nations shed their desire of exploitation and the spirit of which war is the natural expression and atom bomb the inevitable consequence, there is no hope for peace in the world."[55] In sum, an eternally peaceful world federation could be raised only on the sturdy and deep foundations of non-violence; violence will have to be given up in all shape and form in world affairs; and disarmament—a contributory condition of such peace—will come only when nations shed their exploitation and the fetish for arms.

Certain that maneuvers like those of President Wilson would not bear the fruit of peace expected of them since they were rooted in deep hypocrisy, Gandhi ceaselessly endeavuored to break a new path. Wilson had remarked, "After all, if this endeavour of ours to arrive at peace fails, we have got our armaments to fall back upon." Gandhi's rejoinder to such an attitude was: "I want to reverse that position and say our armaments have failed already. Let us now be in search of something new, and let us try the force of love and God which is Truth."[56] He wanted to show that physical force "is nothing compared to the moral force and that moral force never fails."[57] Moreover, not for a moment did he think that peace could ever be attained in a piecemeal manner: "Peace is unattainable by part performances of conditions even as chemical combination is impossible without complete fulfilment of conditions of attainment thereof."[58]

Real, effective, lasting peace, Gandhi reiterated, could only be attained through the rule of the "law of love" saturating the life and style of nations the world over. Love for one's own nation is not enough, for "such love is an armed peace." War will only be eliminated when the conscience of humanity becomes elevated enough to recognize the undisputed supremacy of the law of love in all walks of life.[59] This was not all that Utopian, or beyond the reach humanity, as might be imagined; Gandhi was absolutely confident that all this will come to pass here and perhaps in not too distant a future. So the columns of *Young India* articulated: Till a new energy is harnessed and put on wheels, the captains of older energies will treat the innovation as theoretical, impractical, idealistic and so on. It may take long to lay the wires of international love, but the sanction of international non-co-operation in preference to continued physical compulsion ... is a distinct progress towards the ultimate and real solution.[60]

Gandhi maintains, "perfect peace comes when mind and heart are pure."[61] All his life, he bent the entire energies of his being in purifying the heart and elevating the mind of his countrymen with the contagion of his tireless pursuit of truth—concretized in non-violence, fearlessness, sense of responsibility and duty, and a loving concern for his fellow beings. Congenital optimist perhaps, but certainly one who had implicit, unbounded, and a proud faith in his country and countrymen, Gandhi seemed to expect unilateral disarmament in India. Perception by a newly independent India may be blunted for a time with the euphoria of emancipation. But Gandhi was confident that "even in my absence my influence for peace will last; though I may be far away, my spirit will remain behind."[62]

Mahatma Gandhi stood for a simple and, more or less, self-sufficient living in the rural surroundings mainly because he could foresee that a highly sophisticated and centralised life in the cities would inescapably lead to the organisation of inhuman violences and aggressive nationalism resulting in international tensions and wars of unprecedented devastation. Gandhiji therefore advocated the establishment of ideal villages where the people could pursue the ideal of "simple living and high thinking." But this ideal has been criticised, ridiculed and even denounced as an opiate to keep the poor quiet and help the present social order to go on.

Dennish Meadow's is of the opinion that human environment is a shocking way and there is limit to the world material growth and the world economy faces a very gloomy picture in the new millennium if we do not change radically our present policies. The indiscriminate use of technology and the pursuance of industrialisation on competitive basis have led to serve economic and social consequences of new and different nature. The ever widening gap between rich and poor, worsening economic and political relations, economic imperialism, multinationals and techno-structure are among the more important problems at both the internal and international levels, the solution of which is not becoming possible through the traditional and conventional methods of modern world. With reference to these problems the relevance of Gandhian ideas are very much emphasised by Tinbergin in the following words—the rich of the earth should prepare themselves for the simpler life in future. The leading philosophy of the present day society which always asks for more material goods and does not attach much value at simplicity of life or modesty in claims has to be replaced by alternative philosophies and surely much could be learned from Mahatma Gandhi's words and example. The real values of life do contain a sufficient quantity of goods and shelter, but it is not necessary to have the luxuries now aimed at. Cultural values will have to be upgraded again."[63]

According to Gandhiji advancement, is not only economic or industrial it is the ethical and spiritual progress of man's nobler pursuits for a higher and sublimer goal of life. Gandhiji says, "Civilisation in the real sense of the term consists not m the multiplication, but in the deliberate and voluntary restriction of wants."[64] Even the Laws of diminishing utility and the law of insatiable wants clearly indicate that the more a man has the less he is able to derive pleasure from the articles of consumption.... "The end consists in the total elimination of all the wants, existing at the moment." Just a few months before his death Gandhiji wrote to Mr. Nehru: "The New Social Order that we envisage should not be judged by the quantity of material comforts and luxuries that we are able to accumulate, by the high standard of moral and ethical values that govern the life of a nation."[65] He advised simplification of the standards of living and that one should place voluntary limits on his property and practice self-renunciation. Gandhiji held that "many of the so called comforts of life are not only indispensable but positive hinderances to the elevation of mankind."[66] Having correctly diagnosed the disease, he called for the revival of village economy with indigenous industries so that the people could have enough to eat and keep the wolf off their doors.

Chesterton's article was an attack on the so called Indian awakening. His objection was not against Indians asking for independence or preserving their cultural heritage. His objection was against Indians asking for Western political system, education, philosophy, etc. He wrote: "The right of the people to express itself to be itself in action, was a genuine right. Indians have a right to be and live as Indians. But Herbert Spencer is not an Indian, his philosophy is not Indian philosophy; all his clatter about the science of education and other things is not Indian .... But this is our first difficulty that Indian nationalist is not national.[67] As Bell rang an alarm on an earlier occasion, Chesterton's words acted as red signal. These words told Gandhiji where to stop and how to proceed. These words were ringing in his mind when he embarked the Kildonan castle on November 13, 1909. Though cool winds were cooling his body, the five of patriotism was smouldering within. There was the clash of ideas and ideals within. There was also the clash between the biting cold, literally and figuratively, outside and the burning five inside. This dialectical conflict brought about an awakening. Indian Home Rule or *Hind Swaraj* was Gandhi's answer to Chesterton. Dr. Chandran Devanesan calls it the "Manifesto of Gandhian Revolution."[68] No one could now say that Indian nationalist were not national enough.

Indian Home Rule or "*Hind Swaraj*"[69] was the product of Gandhiji's profound concern for the welfare of all. It was this concerned that prompted him to wage a relentless non-violent war in South Africa against racial discrimination and resultant injustice. Though Gandhiji's immediate aim was the attainment of true Swaraj for India his ultimate goal was the Swaraj of all mankind. Through the service of India, Gandhiji wanted to serve the whole mankind. By the establishment of Swaraj Gandhiji envisaged the possibility of a new world order, where Truth, Non-violence and Love would be the guiding principles in the relation between man and man and between State and State. Gandhiji wanted India to the lead to the world in this matter.

According to Gandhiji the root meaning of Swaraj being self-mode, it may be rendered as disciplined rule from within, and purna swaraj means completely disciplined Self-rule.[70] He makes a fine distinction between Swaraj and independence. Independence may mean Licence to do as you like.[71] Swaraj is positive, independence is negative.[72] The word Swaraj is a sacred word, a vedic word, meaning self-rule and self-restraint and not freedom from all, restraint which independence often means.[73]

Gandhiji often interchanges the words Swaraj and Ramarajya. Of course, Swaraj is the basis of Ramarajya. Ramarajya is the harmonious co-existence of persons who have attained self-control or Swaraj. Ramarajya is not possible without Swaraj. If true Swaraj or Purna Swaraj is attained by all, then Ramarajya will be its natural consequence. Gandhiji says: "Self-Government entirely depends upon our internal strength, upon our ability to fight against the heaviest odds. Indeed Self-Government which does not require that continuous striving to attain it and to sustain it, is not worth the name. I have therefore, endeavoured to show both in words and indeed that political Self-Government—that is Self-Government for a large number of men and women—is no better than individual Self-Government and therefore, it is to be attained by precisely the same means that are required for individual self-Government or Self-rule."[74] Again Gandhiji says that "real Swaraj will come out by the acquisition of authority by a few but by the acquisition of the capacity by all to resist authority when abused. In other words Swaraj is to be attained by educating the masses to a sense of their capacity to regulate and control authority."[75] The Swaraj of Gandhiji's dream recognised no racial or religious distinction. It was to be for all. A state where non-violence and love reign supreme, where everyone works according to one's capacity and consumes according to one's needs keeping in mind the welfare of all, would have attained Swaraj for the individuals and Ramarajya for all. This is what the Westerners call the Kingdom of God on earth. Gandhiji preferred to use the words Ramarajya probably because his "Swadeshism" or because the words of Chesterton were still ringing in his mind.

Ramarajya in the narrow Hindu context could mean the rule of Rama, the divine King. But it was not in this sense that Ramarajya was significant. For Gandhiji Rama was not merely a king. He is simply God. Ramarajya then means the Kingdom of God. Ramarajya is significant in another sense also. Rama's rule was an enlightened one. It was true Swaraj when true democracy prevailed, though it was in the fomm of a monarchy. Gandhiji calls Ramarajya as the dharmarajya, the rule of dharma. It is also called People's Raj or democracy. As all are children of God, it is only natural that everyone should receive a fair deal.

Gandhiji knew that the welfare of all, which was the ideal of Ramarajya depended on the moral conviction of the members of Ramarajya, depended on the moral conviction of the members of Ramarajya. This is why he insisted that moral values should guide all our actions. Gandhiji never wanted economics, or politics of religion or morality or any other worthwhile human concern to be kept apart from the other. All have to be mutually supporting and enhancing the value of life. For him politics bereft of religion is absolute dirt, ever to be shunned.[76] "That economics is untrue which ignores or disregards moral values."[77] True economics never militates against the highest ethical standard, just all true ethics to be worth the name must at the same time be also good economics.[78] His Ramarajya is a moral Kingdom where truth, love and respect for everything being are of supreme importance.

Eventhough Gandhiji insisted on the importance of moral principles in his Ramarajya, he was not unaware of the importance other factors in the attainment of human welfare. He also knew at man being physical, spiritual and social being all his needs responding to these natures should be satisfied atleast in reasonable measure before he could be asked to be happy and rontented. Ignoring any one in favour of the others not only does not lead to human welfare and social harmony but leads to political disharmony and distrust. He realised that a "Starving man thinks first of satisfying his hunger than anything else. We will sell his liberty and all for the sake of getting a morsel of food. For them liberty, God and all such words are merely letters but ether without the slightest meaning. They jar upon them. If want to give these people a sense of freedom, we shall have provide them with work which they can easily do in their desolate homes and which would give them a bare living."[79] "Gandhiji understood that economic equality is the master key to non-violent independence"[80] and hence a very important aspect of his Ramarajya. He thought that by a few simple principles some kind of practicable economic equality would be achieved.

Gandhiji favoured "production by the masses" opposed to "mass production." But it is significant that he never opposed machinery as such; What he opposed was craze for machinery. Gandhiji was realist; he knew that every country needs certain large-scale industries to cater to vital needs—steel, cement and so on. He knew that even millions of blacksmiths cannot replace a steel plant. But according to him, such industries should be controlled and managed by the State and should occupy the least part of the vast national activities which will mainly be in the villages."[81]

Gandhijis plan of production by the masses also has other distinct advantages over mass production. As Dr. Schumacher wrote, "The system of mass production, based on sophisticated, highly capital intensive, high energy-input dependent, and human labour-saving technology presupposes that you are already rich, for a great deal of capital investment, is needed to establish one single work place. The system of production by the masses mobilises the priceless resources which are possessed by all human-beings, their clever brains and skilful hands, and supports them with first-class tools. The technology of mass production is inherently violent, ecologically damaging, self-defeating in terms of non-renewable resources, and stultifying for the human person. The technology of mass production by the masses, making use of the best of modern knowledge and experience is conducive to decentralisation, compatible with the laws of ecology, gentle in its use of scarce resources, and designed to serve the human person instead of making him the servant of machines."[82]

For a moment, let us take it for granted that the total output under mass production is larger than that under the system of production by the masses; even the latter should be preferred over the former from the view point of distributional aspect. Gandhiji remarked, "Granting for the moment that machinery may supply all needs of humanity, still it would concentrate production in particular areas, so that you have to go in a round-about way to regulate distribution both in the respective areas where things are required, it is automatically regulated and there is less chance for fraud and none for speculation." It is worth nothing that vast organisations like the General Motors Corporation of the United States and the British National Coal Board have been decentralised to improve efficiency and promote employee's welfare and job satisfaction. Gandhiji's view on the social responsibility of business and his trusteeship theory constitute a revolutionary step in the field of socio-economic reform.

Absence of peace is both the cause and effect of tension in the social, national and international spheres. It frustrates all attempts at economic development/social progress and human solidarity. Inspite of several efforts made by League of Nations and U.N.O. for co-operation and goodwill in the world, the battles have still been going on and a wave of cold war has swept over the world which has created a suffocating atmosphere.

Recently, on 24th December 1999 at Kandahar, Indian Airlines Air Bus was hijacked and 187 passengers were made as hostages. After the information, the U.N.O. officials rushed to Kandahar, Afghanistan and they had a talk with hijackers and at last the U.N.O. talk was failed. The hijackers never accepted the demand made by the U.N.O. officials.

No where peace is found. The race for armament is still going on. The U.N.O. recognises that the Government of almost all the countries of the world are not prepared to renounce war for one reason or the other. War cannot produce peace. It produces only war. One cannot expect peace from the balance of power since it nourishes mutual hatred, struggle for widening the sphere of influence, fear and suspicion, which may be the elements of generating wars. Hence, some new and basic thought will have to be adopted for permanent and long lasting world peace.

Gandhiji an apostal of non-violent action never approved war—a violent action. He rejected outright and condemned war as a means of resolving a conflict. According to Gandhi the problem of peace was not just a political problem involving the adjustment or rectification of relations between armed nations. It was the problem of mankind, posing a challenge not only to states but also to every individual human being and human group. He, therefore, endeavoured to established peace between man and man, group and group and nation and nation.

It was a life long conviction with Gandhiji that mankind and its civilisation can be saved from destruction only through non-violence. The individual as well as his environment — local, national and international have to be purged of violence. If the individual regenerates himself—through strict self-discipline, and if the nations of the world reconstruct themselves along non-violent lines, the emerging international order will naturally be peaceful and co-operative. The great fear of a war and destruction could at once disappear. Indeed the adoption and practice of such an idea at global level is an urgent need of the day. Such a condition could avert the modern wars which have the potentiality to cause unimaginable horrors and destruction not once to the present generation but also to the coming generations. At the very outset one finds that his approach to the problem of world peace was overloaded with moral philosophy of life. It is for this reason that the Mahatma had been scoffed at by many of his critics as an Utopian, blind to the facts of the grim world of real politics. At the same time one has to be cautious while challenging Gandhian philosophy of life and his techniques of action. Gandhiji's main aim was the "moral regeneration of human society" in which peace can be obtained. One has to take into account that moral philosophy does play an important role in the relation of human behaviour. In the same way the application of moral values in regulating the behaviour of nations is also possible. George Caltin, one of the important political scientists, is of the opinion that "the mission of Mahatma Gandhi was to be our educator, and to call the world's attention on the need for an education in the beauties of Ahimsa."[83]

Gandhiji advised us to mobilise millions of people for non-violent resolution of conflicts and for the proper achievement and establishment of world peace. This would mean the adoption of the following ways:

(a) "Starting a non-violent movement on the international level. Peace workers all over the world must unite.

(b) Through peace education workers should bring a change in mentality of the masses and infuse the feeling of unity."

Peace workers of each nation should press their government for total disarmament which requires a strong public opinion. So long as total disarmament is not accepted atleast nations should not join military pacts.

It would not be out of place to mention that apart from his own philosophy of peace, Gandhiji also advocated certain other measures such as disarmament, world peace organisation and world police to secure peace. Gandhiji suggested disarmament. In his own words Gandhiji says that "real disarmament cannot come unless the nations of the world cease to exploit one another. If the mad race for armaments continues, it is bound to result in a slaughter such as has never occurred in the history."

Gandhiji further said that, "absence of fundamental sincerity makes all talk about the limitation of armament meaningless. Not disarmament—whether partial or total in respect of nuclear weapons, but renunciation of all force is the answer to the problem of international peace."[84]

Gandhiji suggested that only a world organisation backed by a moral or non-violent sanction can guarantee international peace. He had given his own view regarding the nature of this world organisation different from the nature of the present day U.N.O.

According to Gandhiji this world peace organisation must have the following characteristics:

1. The individuals and the nations composing the world should be predominantly non-violent.
2. All the nations of the world should be fully independent. There can be no place in such a world for colonialism, imperialism and race hatred.
3. The distinction of big and small should be obliterated and every nation should feel as tall as the tallest. Each and every nation must be represented in the International organisation.
4. It should be based on general disarmament. Failing that some one nation, at least, should take the initiative and give a lead to the rest of the world. Its example may become infections in course of time, even as the example of the non-violent individual become infectious.
5. The International Society should be a voluntary organisation of States for the common good, in which every nation should be willing to sacrifice itself for all.
6. All disputes between nations should be settled peacefully and amicably by such methods as negotiation, mediation and arbitration.

As a realist Gandhiji was prepared to concede that "there might be a world police in the absence of universal belief in non-violence."[85] But this force would be, "a concession to human weakness, not...an emblem of peace."[86] This would function more as a SHANTI SENA or a PEACE BRIGADE than a modern fighting force. The successful implementation of the Gandhian technique depends on the willingness of the individual to commit himself for the chosen ideal with the attitude of "one step is enough to me." His manner of living will indicate his commitment. What he is and does is not without significance. The way to peace lies through peace.

Gandhiji's passion for Truth, found in every person a divine fire, with a diamond-sharp sincerity, opposed every force which enslaved man, woman or child. The central conviction of man's dignity and divinity flamed forth in many revolutionary articles of faith and spread over the whole spectrum of celestial and terrestrial being in the advaitic spirit. This became his God, that is Truth, his human divine conception, his spiritual orientation, secular toleration and belief in the moral order of mankind his conviction that higher values are basic to politics, economics and other material pursuits, his fascination for Sarvodaya and abjuration of violence his communism without cruelty and government without coercion and his creed that there is innate goodness in every man. And this is the secret of his merger with the hungry, the poor, the sick and the downtrodden. He was a Mahatma because he realised that regardless of station, colour, creed or skin, everyone was at man and any system that dimished or denied this truth was unjust, asuric and *ultra-vires*.

The social philosophy that sustained his life-work and life style was a eclectic and open-minded as Gandhi himself. An open-minded system of social philosophy has one essential characteristic unity of thought and practice. The primacy of this unity was recognised by Gandhi.

Gandhi who did not claim adherence to any set ideology, described his continuing quest in the realms of thought and action as "Experiment with Truth." The thought and practice of Gandhi provides a fruitful area for rethinking, Gandhian ideas present a complete, even if not fully articulated, basis of an entire socio-ethical system. The dynamics of the relationship between Maxim and Truth and the "Welfare of all" and the operational role of non-violence will progressively bring into realisation the commodities of Gandhi's utility function. In short, Gandhi achieved a great change in history, through the application of the principle of Satyagraha. He turned the historic process into a supra-personal fact. Gandhiji presents ethical significance in terms of man's social responsibilities.

Gandhiji's speculative wisdom includes an enquiry into power structure, institutional frameworks, balance between technical skills and spiritual culture, ends and means to deal with human and historical situation, moral facts in new economic order and a synthesis of individual and Social attitudes. Thus, Gandhi drew all human activities into the widening not of philosophy. By asserting its centrality in all levels of thought and action, Gandhi stirs philosophy from its apathy of irrelevance.

Gandhiji was a revolutionary thinker. He revolted wherever the *status quo* offered a challenge to his conscience. His acceptance of spiritual determinism gave him supreme faith in the inevitable emergence of the non-violent society in the future. The emphasis on spontaneity, faith and devotion, the acceptance of love as the supreme value, the demand for service and sacrifice, the insistence on the dignity of Truth—all these find full manifestation in the life and teachings of Gandhi. He was sanguine that political action would be made to conform to the ultimate values of the spirit.

Gandhij showed to the whole world the efficacy of the principle of live and peace as instrument of social change. His undying faith in the goodness of man and the efficacy of non-violence is beyond doubt. Since the individual is the basis of all social progress, one should place greater reliance on the development of the individual than of any intellectual device. Man is not a "lost" creature. He is ever capable of self-development. The fundamental Gandhian means for bringing about social change rests on the reformation of the individual "internally, morally and spiritually." If all individuals practised self-control, a control over all senses, followed the principles of truth and non-violence in their daily dealings and tried to incorporate these principles in their thoughts and attitudes, society would gradually gravitate towards the ideal he cherished. Essentially, all the teachings of Gandhi were entirely based on the concept of individual perfection by a strict adherence to Truth and Non-violence.

Gandhiji's devotion to individual rights made him a fighter for democratic freedom. He stressed communal unity and the absolute elimination of untouchability among the foundations of political freedom. Only a community constituted by persons imbued with a sense of deep social cohesiveness can attain the benefit of Swaraj. Hence, it is essential to combine the quest for political individuality with the voluntary acceptance of social and political discipline which is the basis of social solidarity and cohesiveness.

According to Gandhiji, moral and spiritual freedom depend on the effective cultivation of the two ancient virtues of truth and non-violence. He never accepted the view of freedom as arbitrariness or licence. Genuine Swaraj is a function of the development of inner sources of power.[87]

Ideally, Gandhiji visualised a stateless society and repudiated the authority of the state at every level and in every form. Gandhiji as convinced that mere constitutional structures will not suffice for the concrete realisation of rights and hence he postulated the ideal of "Rama Rajya" which means the kingdom of love, justice and righteousness. This amounts to the synthesis of the Augustian conception of the kingdom of God on earth with the democratic ideal of the sovereignity of the people. Gandhiji believed in "Sovereignty of the people based on pure moral authority."

Traditional deprivation of the backward sanctions based on

ascription was shifted to relative deprivation based on the new values of freedom and equality—Exploitation, suppression illiteracy, poverty and host of other malpractices prevalent in the structure were opposed by Candhiji. Gandhiji championed the concept of equality on metaphysical grounds. Everyman is equal in the eyes of God as the Bhagavad Gita points out. Hence, every man should be legally, politically and socially equal. This presupposes his faith in justice. Gandhiji observes: "the first condition of non-violence is justice in every department of life."[88] The chief evils against which Gandhiji fought were racialism, imperialism, communalism and untouchability. His crusade for the liberation of the suppressed lower classes in India shows his deep attachment to the concept of Social and economic justice.[89]

THE DECEPTION OF DISARMAMENT

For years, Gandhi campaigned for the view that peace was a matter of justice rather than of strength: "all the world over a true peace depends not upon gun powder but upon pure justice." Unless nations learned to be just by renouncing exploitation and their total reliance on force, there could never be peace on the earth. Armaments were both a symptom of force and a temptation to use force. Thus, instead of talking of a mere restriction of armaments, their quantity and quality, Gandhi pleaded passionately for complete, universal disarmament.

Apparently in thorough approval, he published in the columns of *Young India*, which he edited, an excerpt from a monthly called International Sunbeam: Total world disarmament, the only material safeguard for peace, should be the outward and visible sign of that inward mental disarmament on which alone outward peace can secure. So long, however, as one people is actually subjecting another to itself by superior military might even the very first step toward this inward mental disarmament has not been taken.[90]

Europe should take this first step, held Gandhi, "unless Europe is to commit suicide." The tendency to outdo one another in building up armaments would subside once that steps were taken.

By the same token, it would be equally disastrous if India, after attaining its freedom, were to join the arms race: "For India to enter into the arms race is to court suicide. With the loss of India to non-violence the last hope of the world will be gone. ..." Gandhi hoped "that India will make non-violence her creed, preserve man's dignity, and prevent him from reverting to the type from which he is supposed to have raised himself."[91]

The bloodshed of the Hindus and Muslims in the wake of partition and independence of India greatly distressed Gandhi, of course, but what exasperated him even more was the country swearing by the military and all that naked physical force implies. He said: our statesmen have for over two generations declaimed against the heavy expenditure on armaments under the British regime, but now that freedom from political serfdom has come, our military expenditure has increased and still threatens to increase and of this we are proud! However . . . the hope lingers in me and many others that India shall survive this death dance and occupy the moral height that should belong to her after the training, however imperfect, in non-violence for an unbroken period of thirty-two years since 1915 [the year Congress accepted the method of non-violent struggle for the country's freedom].[92]

He saw little sense in India after attaining its freedom incurring a heavy defense budget and felt that the country was groaning under this unnecessary and unsupportable burden: "We are convinced that we do not need the arms that India is carrying."[93] He stuck to his oft-repeated position that nothing could be more disastrous than India trying to imitate or rival the Western powers, including the United States, in their defense strategy based on military capability.

Gandhi unequivocally advocated that India—even Asia—take a lead with regard to disarmament. At the concluding session of the Asian Relations Conference at Delhi on April 2, 1947, he declared that the West is despairing of a multiplication of the atom bomb, because atom bombs mean utter destruction not merely of the West but of the whole world, as if the prophesy of the bible is going to be fulfilled and there is to be a perfect deluge. It is up to you to tell the world of its wickedness and sin that is the heritage your teachers and my teachers have taught Asia.[94]

Gandhi was certainly opposed, however, to the forced disarmament of a nation. For instance, referring to the disarming of India during World War I, Gandhi declared with vehemence: Much as I abhor the possession or the use of arms, I cannot reconcile myself to forcible prohibition. As I said three years ago, this forcible disarmament of a people will be regarded by history as one of the blackest sins committed by the British Government against India. If people want to possess arms they ought to have them without ado. . . . We cannot learn discipline by compulsion. We must learn not to use arms or to use them with responsibility and self-restraint, notwithstanding the right to possess them.[95]

In the same spirit, he condemned the disarming of the vanquished as a punitive measure. This was not merely due to compassion; Gandhi believed that guilt of war was so pervasive that it was virtually impossible, and wrong, to apportion all the blame for it to just one of the parties at the expense of the other.[96]

If the great powers disarmed themselves, felt Gandhi, they would not only escape the ravages of war but also cover themselves in glory, restore sanity to the world, and earn the eternal gratitude of posterity. These powers would, at the same time, have to give up their imperialistic designs and exploitation of the weak and hapless, while revising their own way of life. All this, evidently, amounts virtually to a total revolution, the only alternative to which, in Gandhi's opinion, was absolute disaster. The great powers could not be expected to move in the direction of total revolution—contrary to what lifestyle they had thus far been used to—spontaneously, of course.[97]

Nor could disarmament be worked out overnight; it would take time. The one thing Gandhi was absolutely certain of was that it would come only through the adoption of non-violence by a nation—indeed, by all the nations of the world. The evils of armaments can be cured, held Gandhi, by non-violence, which will eventually be the weapon of all nations. I say 'eventually' deliberately, because we shall have war and armaments for a very long time. It is two thousand years since Christ preached his "Sermon on the Mount" and the world has adopted only a fragment of the imperishable lofty precepts therein enunciated for the conduct of man toward man. Until we take all Christ's principles to our hearts, war, hatred and violence will continue.[98]

It was wrong to think that armaments implied or imparted strength, for real strength, according to Gandhi, came by self-sacrifice, from within and not through physical force. He pointed out that the rishis (sages) of yore, themselves great warriors, realized the utter uselessness of force and "taught a weary world that its salvation lay not through violence but through non-violence."

Gandhi was emphatic that nations should strengthen themselves spiritually, for "Internal spiritual forces are stronger and induce a more certain and lasting life. It is not by arming yourself that you will guarantee peace to the world. External arms, guns, cannons and gas have only evil and passing results."[99] To say that one is arming oneself for self-defense was, he said, "a wretched plea ... a bad thing," for, in effect, the result invariably was that you organized yourself to "prey upon ill organized communities and nations." The crux of the matter was that real disarmament could come only when "the nations of world cease to exploit one another."[100]

Gandhi would not accept the proposition that, since disarmament chiefly depended upon the great powers, small, neutral and nonaggressive countries like Switzerland, for instance, should be forced to disarm. Gandhi asserted that the very fact of neutrality and non-aggressiveness of Switzerland rendered the army there completely redundant. Indeed, it would be a far superior thing for Switzerland to give the world a lesson in disarmament and establish that the Swiss are brave enough to live without an army. Nor was he willing to accept the proposition that the mere presence of the Swiss army had saved that country from being overrun by foreign armies. Rejecting both the deterrent role of the Swiss military forces as well as the value of military development, Gandhi astutely pointed out the fallacies involved: Will the questioner forgive me if I say that a double ignorance underlies this question? He deplores the fact that, if you give up the profession of soldiering, you will miss the education you receive in service and sacrifice. None need run away with the idea that because you avoid military conscription you are not in for a conscription of a severer and nobler type. When I spoke to you about labour, I told you that labour ought to assimilate all the noble qualities of soldiering: endurance and defiance of death and sacrifice. When you disarm yourself, it does not mean that you will have a merry time. It is not that you are absolved from the duty of serving your homes when you give up soldiering; on the contrary, your women and children would be taking part in defending your homes.

He wrote: Again I am not talking to you without experience. In the little institution [sic] that we are conducting, we are teaching our women and children also how to save that institution —as we are living among thieves and robbers. Everything becomes simple and easy the moment you learn to give up your own life in order to save the life of others. And lastly, it is really forgotten that safety which an individual derives from innocence is safety which no amount of arms will give you. The second part of the ignorance lies in the second part of the question. I must respectfully deny the truth of the statement that the presence of the Swiss army prevented the War from affecting Switzerland. Although Belgium had its own army, it was not saved and if the rival armies had wanted a passage through Switzerland, believe me, they would have fought you also. You might have fought in turn, but you would have fought much better non-violently.[101]

With regard to nuclear weapons, Gandhi thought it quite futile merely to restrict them; he seriously doubted that the nations possessing them would remain content merely with their possession. Dismissing the efficacy or permanence of "balance of terror" or "balance of nonuse" and the supposition that their "overkill" capacity by itself would induce and enforce non-violence in the world, he emphasized that so long as the thinking in these quarters remained rooted in violence we will continue heading toward disaster and self-destruction. Indeed, "the violent man's eyes would [be] lit up with the prospect of much greater amount of destruction and death which he could now wreak," Gandhi said. At best the destructive capability of these weapons may temporarily postpone the outbreak of war. "Like a man gutting himself with dainties to the point of nausea and turning away from them only to return with redoubled zeal after the effect of nausea is well over. Precisely in the same manner will the world return to violence with renewed zeal after the effect of disgust is worn out."[102] Gandhi quite frankly considered the "balance of terror" to be nothing more than the "preparations for a third World War." He was willing to concede that atomic energy "may be utilised . . . for humanitarian purposes" but was sure that it would not be confined to that alone.

According to Gandhi, nations armed themselves out of fear of each other and to guard their imperialist possessions. Quite early in his life, echoing the philosophy of the Gita, Gandhi in his *Hind Swaraj* asserted that nations armed themselves because they were filled with the fear that others may take away their possessions; force was used when people were under the spell of fear, and "what is gained through fear is retained only for as long as fear is present."[103] At the same time, fear breeds hatred. Apparently then, the very first step that nations must take toward ensuring peace was to dispel fear and, along with it, mistrust. Gandhi said his instincts told him that if you do not intend violence to anyone, no one will use it against you either: "It is only when we are afraid of our opponent, we employ unclean strength like his that we learn unclean ways and so become weak. ... If we meet uncleanliness with cleanliness, the total result would be less of uncleanliness and the people, the world, would be happier for this."[104]

Gandhi put it succinctly and without any equivocation when he declared: Peace will never come until the Great Powers courageously decide to disarm themselves. . . .I have an implicit faith—a faith that today burns brighter than ever, after half a century's experience of unbroken practice of non-violence—that mankind can only be saved through non-violence.[105]

And here, Gandhi saw an independent India in the role of a catalyst. In an interview for the News Chronicle, soon after his release from prison in 1944, he observed: I am a lover of peace through and through. After independence was assured, I would probably cease to function as adviser to the Congress and as an all war resister I would have to stand aside, but I shall not offer any resistance against the national Government or the Congress [if they decided to support the war effort]. My co-operation [to the war effort] will be abstention from interfering with even tenor of life in India. I shall work with the hope that my influence will be felt to keep India peace minded and so affect the world policy towards real peace and brotherhood among all without the distinction of race and colour.[106]

Gandhi maintains, "perfect peace comes when mind and heart are pure."[107] All his life, he bent the entire energies of his being in purifying the heart and elevating the mind of his countrymen with the contagion of his tireless pursuit of truth—concretized in non-violence, fearlessness, sense of responsibility and duty, and a loving concern for his fellow beings. Congenital optimist perhaps, but certainly one who had implicit, unbounded, and a proud faith in his country and countrymen, Gandhi seemed to expect unilateral disarmament in India. Perception by a newly independent India may be blunted for a time with the euphoria of emancipation. But Gandhi was confident that "even in my absence my influence for peace will last; though I may be far away, my spirit will remain behind."[108]

The Central Principles of Gandhian Thought on economics, politics, social reform and prove their relevance to "THE NEW WORLD ORDER." The relevance of Gandhian ideas, and their universal applicability is precisely because of the fact that his ideas and thoughts are not based on colonial dominations and exploitative attitudes, cut throat competition, and some other material and worldly values. As against these they are based on strong human values with moral and spiritual touching. He wanted to give a spiritual touch to all economic, social, political and other problems which he thought as the root cause of all prosperity and happiness. His ideas were always to the best interests and to the real solution of the problems of mankind.

One may argue that the Gandhian declarations on peace contain some practical difficulties for them to be implemented in the present day world. But Gandhi himself would not countenance such a "practical" difficulty. He would counterpoise by saying: "If an individual can practice non-violence, why not whole groups of individuals and whole nations? He believed that one must make a beginning and the rest would follow. The Gandhian concept of world peace should be viewed as in integral part of his philosophy of life and one should try to appreciate his attitude within the general framework of philosophy of ahimsa. Good means alone can lead us to ever lasting peace. If peace is established by violence it will be of no use. Now-a-days quite often we read in the newspapers that police, in some places army, marching into an agitating place and peace being established. But that peace is undoubtedly that of the graveyard." But when the non-violent person wins, he wins the heart of the foe.

Peace is a relationship between people and between certain kinds of people. Peace begins with a harmony between individuals. Gandhiji lived and worked for the establishment of such relationship among individuals and groups. His is an unique contribution to peace in the modern context. Gandhiji's style of life and the techniques he propounded deserve to be studied and applied so that the world may be a safe place to live. Gandhian ideas were relevant during his life-time, continue to be relevant in the New Millennium and shall remain so for many decades to follow.

Albert Einstein rightly declared that Gandhi showed how someone could win allegiance, "not merely by the winning game of political fraud and trickery, but through the living example of a morally exalted way of life." Einstein considered Gandhi to be the most enlightened statesman of their time, and he predicted. The problem of bringing peace to world on a supranational basis will be solved only by employing Gandhi's methods on a large scale.

Notes and References

1. *The Collected Works of Mahatma Gandhi* (Delhi: Publications Division, Ministry of Information and Broadcasting, Government of India), Vol. 30, p. 50.
2. Pyarelal, *The Last Phase*, Vol. I (Ahmedabad: Navajivan Press), 1956, p. 119.
3. *The collected Works of Mahatma Gandhi* (Delhi: Publications Division, Ministry of Information and Broadcasting, Government of India), Vol. 62, p. 285.
4. *Ibid.*, Vol. 27, pp. 255-56.
5. *Ibid.*, Vol. 28, pp. 126-27.
6. *Ibid.*, Vol. 31, p. 181.
7. *Ibid.*, Vol. 45, p. 319.
8. *Young India*, 18-6-1925, p. 211.
9. *The Collected Works of Mahatma Gandhi*, *op. cit.*, Vol. 55, pp. 426-30.
10. *Harijan*, Vol. 6, p. 404.
11. Pyarelal, *The Last Phase*, *op. cit.*, Vol. 1, p. 30.
12. *Harijan*, Vol. 7, p. 8.
13. *The Collected Works of Mahatma Gandhi*, *op. cit.*, Vol. 28, p. 454
14. *Ibid.*, Vol. 28, p. 189.
15. *Harijan*, Vol. 10, p. 404.
16. *The Collected Works of Mahatma Gandhi*, *op. cit.*, Vol. 21, p. 161.
17. *Harijan*, Vol. 7, p. 304.
18. Pyarelal, *The Last Phase*, *op. cit.*, Vol. 1, p. 120.
19. *Ibid.*, p. 126.
20. *The Collected Works of Mahatma Gandhi*, *op. cit.*, Vol. 24, p. 395
21. *Harijan*, Vol. 9, p. 265.
22. Pyarelal, *The Last Phase*, *op. cit.*, Vol. 1, p. 120.
23. *Harijan*, Vol. 7, p. 278.
24. *Ibid.*, Vol. II, p. 184.
25. Catlin George, *In the Path of the Mahatma* (London: MacDonald), 1998, p. 281.
26. *The Collected Works of Mahatma Gandhi*, *op. cit.*, Vol. 62, p. 174.
27. *Ibid.*, Vol. 48, p. 158.
28. *Ibid.*, Vol. 2, p. 130.
29. Pyarelal, *The Last Phase*, *op. cit.*, Vol. 1, p. 120.
30. Tendulkar, D.G., *Mahatma*, Vol. 7, (New Delhi: Publication Division, Ministry of Information and Broadcasting, Government of India), 1960, p. 3.

31. *The Collected Works of Mahatma Gandhi*, *op. cit.*, Vol. 48, p. 158.
32. *Ibid.*, Vol. 19, p. 444.
33. *Ibid.*, Vol. 35, p. 457.
34. *Ibid.*, Vol. 45, p. 264.
35. *Ibid.*, Vol. 38, pp. 160-61.
36. *Harijan*, Vol. 7, p. 305.
37. *Ibid.*, Vol. 11, p. 453.
38. *The Collected Works of Mahatma Gandhi*, *op. cit.*, Vol. 48, pp. 200-01.
39. *Harijan*, Vol. 11, p. 117.
40. *The Collected Works of Mahatma Gandhi*, *op. cit.*, Vol. 20, p. 406.
41. Pyarelal, *The Last Phase*, Vol. 1, p. 114.
42. *Harijan*, Vol. 6, p. 328.
43. *The Collected Works of Mahatma Gandhi*, *op. cit.*, Vol. 45, p. 319.
44. *Ibid.*, Vol. 46, pp. 402-03.
45. *Ibid.*, p. 441.
46. *The Collected Works of Mahatma Gandhi*, *op. cit.*, pp. 419-20.
47. *Harijan*, Vol. 4, p. 109.
48. *Ibid.*, Vol. 10, pp. 212-17.
49. Gandhi, Mahatma, *Hind Swaraj* (Ahmedabad: Navajivan Publishing House), 1962, p. 16.
50. *The Collected Works of Mahatma Gandhi*, *op. cit.*, Vol. 19, p. 10.
51. *Harijan*, Vol. 6, p. 395.
52. *The Collected Works of Mahatma Gandhi*, *op. cit.*, Vol. 67, p. 76.
53. *Ibid.*, Vol. 48, p. 85.
54. *Ibid.*, Vol. 54, p. 335.
55. *Harijan*, Vol. 3, p. 276.
56. *The Collected Works of Mahatma Gandhi*, *op. cit.*, Vol. 28, p. 23.
57. *Ibid.*, Vol. 15, p. 142.
58. *Ibid.*, Vol. 62, p. 175.
59. *Ibid.*, Vol. 31, p. 143.
60. *Young India*, June 23, 1919, p. 51.
61. *The Collected Works of Mahatma Gandhi*, *op. cit.*, Vol. 19, p. 10.
62. *Ibid.*, Vol. 48, p. 353.
63. Tinbergin, Jan, "Limit to Growth", *The Economic Times*, 1972.
64. Mathur, J.S. (ed.), *Economic Thought of Mahatma Gandhi* (Allahabad: Kitab Mahal), 1971, p. 200.
65. *Journal of Gandhian Studies*, University of Allahabad, p. 103.
66. *Ibid.*
67. *The Collected Works of Mahatma Gandhi*, *op. cit.*, Vol. IX, pp. 426-27.
68. Devanesan, C., *The Making of the Mahatma* (Madras: Orient Longmans), 1969, p. 56.
69. *The Collected Works of Mahatma Gandhi*, *op. cit.*, X, pp. 66-68.
70. *Ibid.*, Vol. XIV, p. 263.
71. *Ibid.*
72. *Ibid.*, p. 204.
73. *Ibid.*
74. Bose, N.K., *Selections from Gandhi* (Ahmedabad: Navajivan Publishing House), 1948, p. 35.

75. *Ibid.*, p. 475.
76. Krishnakripala (ed.), *All Men are Brothers* (Ahmedabad: Navajivan Publishing House), 1950, p. 69.
77. *The Collected Works of Mahatma Gandhi, op. cit.*, Vol. X, p. 476.
78. Bose, N.K., *Selection from Gandhi, op. cit.*, p. 40.
79. *The Collected Works of Mahatma Gandhi, op. cit.*, XXX, p. 133.
80. *Journal of Gandhian Studies, op. cit.*, p. 95.
81. *Ibid.*
82. *Ibid.*, p. 96.
83. *Ibid.*, p. 105.
84. *Ibid.*, p. 106.
85. *Ibid.*, p. 107.
86. *Ibid.*
87. Devadoss, T.S., *Sarvodeya and the Problem of Political Sovereignty* (Madras: University of Madras), 1974, p. 453.
88. Gandhi, M.K., *Economic and Industrial Life and Reflections* (Ahmedabad: Navajivan Publishing House), Vol. III, p. 123.
89. Devadoss, T.S., *Hindu Family and Marriage* (Madras: University of Madras, 1979, p. 2).
90. *The Collected Works of Mahatma Gandhi, op. cit.*, Vol. 38, pp. 160-61.
91. *Harijan*, Vol. 7, p. 305.
92. *Ibid.*, Vol. 11, p. 453.
93. *The Collected Works of Mahatma Gandhi, op. cit.*, Vol. 41, p. 310.
94. *Harijan*, Vol. 11, p. 117.
95. *The Collected Works of Mahatma Gandhi, op. cit.*, Vol. 20, p. 406.
96. Pyarelal, *The Last Phase*, Vol. 1, p. 114.
97. *Harijan*, Vol. 6, p. 320.
98. *The Collected Works of Mahatma Gandhi*, Vol. 45, p. 319.
99. *Ibid.*, Vol. 48, p. 393.
100. *Ibid.*, pp. 402-03.
101. *Ibid.*, pp. 419-20.
102. *Harijan*, Vol. 10, p. 197.
103. Gandhi, M.K. *Hindi Swaraj, op. cit.*, p. 16.
104. *The Collected Works of Mahatma Gandhi, op. cit.*, Vol. 19, p. 10.
105. *Harijan*, Vol. 6, p. 395.
106. Tendulkar, *Mahatma, op. cit.*, Vol. 6, p. 256.
107. *The Collected Works of Mahatma Gandhi, op. cit.*, Vol. 19, p. 10.
108. *Ibid.*, Vol. 48, p. 353.

United Nations: Challenges, Constraints and Gandhian Alternatives

The United Nations came into existence in 1945 on conclusion of World War II in which the world witnessed unprecedented death and destruction, made possible by the harnessing of advanced technologies in the instruments of war. The United States use of atomic bombs against Japan at Hiroshima and Nagasaki and the massive destruction in its wake vividly illustrated how horrific future wars could be.

Gripped with this fear and horror, the victorious nations and other nations got together and established the United Nations Organisation. The Charter of the United Nations spelt out that the primary objective was "to save succeeding generations from the scourge of war.

In the last sixty years of its existence, the United Nations had to manage and cope with security conflicts ranging from the Cold War era to post-Cold War and now the abominable spectacle of global terrorism of the Islamic Jehad variety as exemplified by the Al Qaeda, Taliban and Pakistan state-sponsored terrorism against India in Jammu and Kashmir, more specifically.

The traditional model of UN peace-keeping developed during the Cold War era as a means of resolving conflicts between States and involved the deployment of unarmed or lightly armed military personnel between belligerent parties. The rise in the number of intra-state conflicts, following the fall of the Berlin Wall, has resulted in a shift towards multidimensional peace-keeping operations that are often mandated to support the implementation of a comprehensive peace agreement between parties to a civil war. This has, in turn, led to an expansion of the non-military component of peace-keeping operations whose success is increasingly dependent on the work of civilian experts in key areas such as the rule of law, human rights, gender, child protection, and elections.

The difficult experiences of the mid-1990's in countries such as Bosnia-Herzegovina and Rwanda prompted the UN to reassess its approach to peace-keeping. In March 2000, a Panel on United Nations Peace Operations issued a report that has come to be known as the "Brahimi Report" *(A/55/305-S/2000/809)*, named after the Panel's chairperson, Under-Secretary-General Lakhdar Brahimi. The report offered an in-depth critique of the conduct of UN peace operations and made specific recommendations for change. The report also underlined consent by the warring parties, a clear and specific mandate and adequate resources as minimum requirements for a successful UN mission.[1] Consequently, the UN and Member-States initiated a number of reforms aimed at improving UN peace-keeping, such as the establishment of a pre-mandate financing mechanism to ensure that adequate resources are available for new mission start-ups.

The United Nations has largely failed to maintain international peace and security, promote self-determination and basic human rights, and protect fundamental freedoms. While the conflicting interests of member-states have led to many of these failures, the U.N. system itself is partly to blame. The U.N. and its affiliated organizations are plagued by outdated and redundant missions and mandates, poor management, ineffectual oversight, and a general lack of accountability. In recent years, the U.S. Congress itself has neglected its responsibility to exercise proper oversight. Congress should press for U.N. reform and withhold funding when necessary to encourage reform. The working of UN in the direction of its main objective is not an easy task. There are so many challenges and constraints in achieving the desired goals. Some of the challenges are listed below:

CHALLENGES

Prevention of Conflict and Conflict Resolution

If the primary aim and role as envisaged by its founders was to spare humanity from the "scourge of war" then it would not be wrong to argue that the United Nations has failed, as the following brief examination would indicate.

The United Nations in the last sixty years, as the record would show, was unable to prevent conflicts and wars breaking out all over the world, e.g. Korean War, Vietnam War, Soviet military occupation of Afghanistan, the United States sponsored Islamic Jehad via Pakistan on Afghanistan against the Soviets, the three Gulf Wars and the wars leading to the break-up of Yugoslavia.

Unable to deter conflict, the United Nations has been a failure in conflict resolution also. In fact, it seems that over the years, vested interests have impeded conflict resolution as it served the purpose of keeping in being a large number of United Nations missions, observer groups and 'Advisers' to the United Nations Secretary General. Cambodia seems to be the only exception.

The United Nations was created to maintain international peace and security, promote self-determination and basic human rights, and protect fundamental freedoms. Regrettably, the past 65 years have yielded more disappointment than success in realizing these high aspirations. A great deal of the blame for this failure is due to divergent interests among the member-states that have prevented the organization from taking decisive, timely action.

However, the U.N. system itself is partly to blame. The U.N. and many of its affiliated organizations are beset by outdated or duplicative missions and mandates, poor management practices, ineffectual oversight, and a general lack of accountability. As former U.N. Deputy Secretary-General Mark Malloch Brown recently stated to *The New York Times*, "There's a huge redundancy and lack of efficiency" in the U.N. system, and the budget is "utterly opaque, untransparent and completely in shadow."[2]

These problems waste resources and undermine the U.N.'s ability to discharge its responsibilities effectively. The past six decades have seen dozens of initiatives from governments, think tanks, foundations, and panels of experts aimed at reforming the U.N. to make it more effective in meeting its responsibilities.[3] Although these reform efforts have seen rare success, for the most part they have failed due to opposition from the majority of the U.N. member-states. Indeed, the U.S. almost always finds itself on the losing side in U.N. debates and votes when it proposes reforms to improve U.N. management, oversight, and accountability.

This happens because the bulk of the U.N. member-states simply do not pay enough to the U.N. for inefficiency, waste, or corruption to trouble them. For instance, Sierra Leone is assessed 0.001 percent of the U.N.'s regular budget and 0.0001 percent of the peace-keeping budget. In contrast, the U.S. is assessed 22 percent and 27.1 percent, respectively. Therefore, while Sierra Leone and the dozens of other countries with the same assessments pay less than $35,000 per year to these budgets, the

U.S. pays billions.[4] With this in mind, is it surprising that the U.S. cares about how the U.N. is managed and how the funding is used, while most countries do not?

Yet these are the countries that control most of the votes. The combined assessment of the 128 least-assessed countries—two-thirds of the General Assembly—totals less than 1 percent of the U.N.'s regular budget and less than one-third of 1 percent of the peace-keeping budget, even though that group alone can, according to U.N. rules, pass the budget. These countries, combined with influential voting blocs in the U.N., can and do block U.S. attempts to implement reforms and curtail budgets.[5]

There is another problem. American administrations are often interested in pressing for reform, but frequently that long-term agenda is abandoned in favour of achieving more immediate political objectives. Pressing for reform ruffles feathers at the U.N. When the U.S. is lobbying for votes on a resolution, the last thing U.S. diplomats want to do is anger a mission by pressing for budgetary cuts or other reforms.

The U.S. should support U.N. peace-keeping operations when they further America's national interests. Legitimate questions must be asked as to whether the U.N. should be engaging in the current number of missions and whether these situations are best addressed through the U.N. or through regional, multilateral, or *ad hoc* efforts.

U.N. peace-keeping operations can be useful and successful if employed with an awareness of their limitations and weaknesses. This awareness is crucial because the demand for U.N. peace-keeping shows little indication of declining in the foreseeable future. This requires the General Assembly to press for substantial changes to address serious problems with U.N. peace-keeping. Without fundamental reform, serious problems will likely continue and expand, undermining the U.N.'s credibility and ability to accomplish the key mission of helping to maintain international peace and security. The General Assembly should re-evaluate all U.N. operations that date back to the early 1990s or earlier—some date back to the 1940s—to determine whether each U.N. mission is contributing to resolving the situation or retarding that process. If an operation is not demonstrably facilitating resolution of the situation, the U.N. should emulate the U.N. Peace-keeping Force in Cyprus (UNFICYP) model in which Greece and Cyprus pay for over 40 percent of the mission's cost. Stakeholders wishing to continue U.N. peace-keeping operations that have not resolved the conflicts despite being in place for decades should be asked to assume the financial burden of the continued operation. These missions are generally small and among the least costly, but such a re-evaluation would help to reduce the enormous peace-keeping budget and send a welcome message of accountability and assessment that too often has been lacking in the rubber-stamp process of reauthorizing peace-keeping operations. Together, five of the older U.N. missions (MINURSO, UNFICYP, UNDOF, UNMOGIP, and UNTSO) cost nearly $243 million. If the U.N. could shift these missions to voluntary funding, the U.N. could save more than $54 million per year and perhaps focus the most affected parties on resolving these outstanding disputes.

The U.N. has no standing armed forces and is entirely dependent on member-states to donate troops and other personnel to fulfil peace operation mandates. This is appropriate. Nations should maintain control of their armed forces and refuse to support the establishment of armed forces outside of direct national oversight and responsibility. However, the current arrangement results in an *ad hoc* system plagued by delays and other shortfalls. The member-states should support increasing peace-keeping resources under its Global Peace Operations Initiative, which has significantly bolstered the capacity and capabilities of regional troops, particularly in Africa, to serve as peace-keepers for the U.N., the African Union, or other coalitions.

The members states needs to consider carefully any U.N. requests for additional funding for a system in which procurement problems have wasted millions of dollars and sexual abuse by peace-keepers is still unacceptably high and often goes unpunished. Indeed, the decision by the Administration and Congress of U.S. to pay U.S. arrears to U.N. peace-keeping without demanding reforms sent entirely the wrong message and removed a powerful leverage point for encouraging reform. Without fundamental reform, these problems will likely continue and expand, undermining the U.N.'s credibility and ability to maintain international peace and security.

Mismanagement and Corruption

Audits and investigations over the past few years have revealed substantial mismanagement, fraud, and corruption in procurement for U.N. peace-keeping. An OIOS (Office of Internal Oversight Services) audit of $1 billion in U.N. peace-keeping procurement contracts over a six-year period found that at least $265 million was subject to waste, fraud, or abuse.[6] According to a 2007 OIOS report, an examination of $1.4 billion of peace-keeping contracts turned up "significant" corruption schemes that tainted $619 million (over 40 percent) of the contracts.[7] An audit of the U.N. mission in Sudan revealed tens of millions of dollars lost to mismanagement and waste and exposed substantial indications of fraud and corruption.[8] Moreover, the OIOS revealed in 2008 that it was investigating approximately 250 instances of wrongdoing ranging from sexual abuse by peace-keepers to financial irregularities. According to Ahlenius, "We can say that we found mismanagement and fraud and corruption to an extent we didn't really expect."[9]

Incidents of sexual exploitation and abuse by U.N. peace-keepers and civilian personnel are widespread and often go unpunished. There have been numerous reports of U.N. personnel committing serious crimes and sexual misconduct, from rape to the forced prostitution of women and young girls. U.N. personnel have also been accused of sexual exploitation and abuse in Bosnia, Burundi, Cambodia, Congo, the Democratic Republic of Congo, Guinea, Haiti, Kosovo, Liberia, Sierra Leone, and Sudan.[10] The U.S. and other member-states successfully pressured the U.N. to adopt stricter requirements for peace-keeping troops and their contributing countries. Contact and discipline teams are now present in most U.N. peace-keeping missions, and troops are now required to undergo briefing and training on behaviour and conduct.[11] However, these crimes continue, and the U.N. reported that allegations of sexual exploitation and abuse by U.N. civilian and uniformed personnel totalled 106 in 2009 and 83 in 2010.[12]

The U.N. is to end sexual exploitation, abuse, and other misconduct by peace-keepers, it must do more than adopt a U.N. code of conduct, issue manuals, and send abusers home.[13] The abusers and their governments must face real consequences to create incentives for effective enforcement. Member-states must commit to investigate, try, and punish their personnel in cases of misconduct. U.N. investigatory units need to be independent, quick to deploy, and possess ample capabilities and authority to investigate situations, including full cooperation by mission personnel and access to witnesses, records, and sites where crimes occurred so that trials can have sufficient evidence to proceed. Equally important, the U.N. needs to be stricter in holding member-countries to these standards. States that fail to fulfil their commitments to discipline their troops should be barred from providing troops for peace operations.

The end of the Cold War did not ease, but rather probably intensified, human insecurity. The UN recognizes that dangers to international peace and security now equate less with inter-state military violence, and more with other threats, varied and multiple, to local, regional or global survival. The priority reaction to these altered threats must be changes and flexibility in human response. Human perceptions, priorities and institutions must adapt to situations. The necessary process of reaction is so grave, urgent and universal that it must be addressed collectively, as at the UN World Summits.

Since the end of the Cold War, while conflict between states has become rare, intra-state violence has increased. Self-determination, ethnic and religious differences have replaced resource gain and even ideology as reasons for inter-human combat. The proliferation and lethality of new weapons alone demands the reduction and eventual elimination of mass conflict. There is a continuum of things the UN can and must do. Through prevention and mediation, varied military or other sanctions, peace-keeping, and other intervention or assistance designed to stabilize or defuse situations, the UN must act as it was designed to do —further the building of global peace. A shrinking world makes peacemaking everywhere enlightened self-interest for all.

Terrorism

The subject of "terrorism" seized the world's attention in late 2001 as a result of one fairly brief, yet highly dramatic and destructive, attack on two of the core symbols of the world's most powerful political actor, the United States of America. The targeting of the World Trade Center in New York City, the symbol of the United States' enormous global economic power, and the Pentagon Building in Washington, DC, the symbol of the United States' overarching military superiority, was well planned, coordinated, and executed. The attack itself attained symbolic stature as an affront to the established global order, a challenge to the world's dominant power, and an announcement that the prevailing US-led global order was not viewed, or valued, equally by all those whose daily lives are increasingly caught in the vortex of post-Cold War change.

Of course, the problem of terrorism was already well-known when the planes struck their targets in full view of a vast, global, tele-connected audience and created their indelible psychic images of sophisticated savagery. The politics of terror, and the overpowering fear that terror produces in its wake, lay at the very foundation of the evolution of social order. And it is the ultimate irony of societal development that modern acts of savagery have attained such high levels of sophistication. In its most simple terms, terror has stood as the stark alternative to civility in social relations from the time of humankind's earliest recorded reflections. As Hobbes explained in his 17th century treatise, "Out of civil states, there is always war of every one against every one…the nature of war, consists not in actual fighting; but in the known disposition thereto…and which is worst of all, continual fear and danger of violent death; the life of man [*sic*], solitary, poor, nasty, brutish, and short." At their roots, terror, force, and violence are integral and, as such, terrorism as a course of action is hardly distinguishable from coercion as a strategy or violence as a tactic.

Contemporary analyses of the problem of terrorism have usually foundered between the perceptual extremes that are inherent in the amorphous ideas of terror: conceptualizations of terrorism are either too broad to be analytically useful, too narrow to be analytically meaningful, or too complex to be applied systematically. The conceptualizations themselves are all too often politically motivated as the analyst attempts to rationalize a distinction between civil and uncivil applications of violence: (useless) terror and (useful) enforcement, (undisciplined) terrorism and (disciplined) war, and (dishonorable) terrorists and (honorable) "freedom fighters." Conceptual confusion is further exacerbated by the often cavalier usage of the pejorative term "terrorist" to refer to any political opponent, much as "communist" was used for political effect in the West during the Cold War. Hoffman offers an example of a broad definition, "[Terrorism is] the deliberate creation and exploitation of fear through violence or the threat of violence in the pursuit of political change."

The organizations of the UN system mobilized immediately in their respective spheres to step up action against terrorism. On 28 September, the *Security Council* adopted *resolution 1373*, under the enforcement provisions of the UN Charter, to prevent the financing of terrorism, criminalize the collection of funds for such purposes, and immediately freeze terrorist financial assets. It also established a *Counter-Terrorism Committee* to oversee the resolution's implementation.

The tragic events of 11 September also underlined the potential danger of weapons of mass destruction falling into the hands of non-state actors. That attack could have been even more devastating had the terrorists had access to chemical, biological or nuclear weapons. Reflecting these concerns, the *General Assembly*, in 2002, adopted *resolution 57/83*, a first-time-ever text on measures to prevent terrorists from acquiring such weapons and their means of delivery.[14]

In 2004, the Security Council took its first formal decision on the danger of the proliferation of weapons of mass destruction, particularly to non-state actors. Acting under the enforcement provisions of the Charter, the Council unanimously adopted *resolution 1540*,[15] obliging states to refrain from any support for non-state actors in the development, acquisition, manufacture, possession, transport, transfer or use of nuclear, chemical and biological weapons and their means of delivery. Subsequently, the Assembly adopted the *International Convention for the Suppression of Acts of Nuclear Terrorism*,[16] which was opened for signature in September 2005.

The Vienna-based United Nations Office on Drugs and Crime (*UNODC*) leads the international effort to combat drug trafficking and abuse, organized crime and international terrorism. It analyses emerging trends in crime and justice, develops databases, issues global surveys issued, gathers and disseminates information, and undertakes country-specific needs assessments and early warning measures—for example, on the escalation of terrorism.

In 2002, UNODC launched its *Global Project against Terrorism* with the provision of legal technical assistance to countries on becoming party to and implementing the 12 universal *anti-terrorism instruments.* In January 2003, UNODC expanded its technical cooperation activities to strengthen the legal regime against terrorism, providing legal technical assistance to countries on becoming party to and implementing the universal anti-terrorism instruments.[17]

In the legal sphere, the UN and its related bodies — such as the International Civil Aviation Organization (*ICAO*), the International Maritime Organization (*IMO*) and the International Atomic Energy Agency (*IAEA*)—have developed a network of international agreements that constitute the basic legal instruments against terrorism.[18]

These include conventions on offences committed on board aircraft; unlawful seizure of aircraft; acts against the safety of civil aviation; crimes against internationally protected persons, including diplomatic agents; the physical protection of nuclear material; acts against the safety of maritime navigation; and the marking of plastic explosives for the purpose of detection. In addition, they include protocols on acts of violence at airports serving international civil aviation; and on acts against the safety of fixed platforms located on the continental shelf.

The General Assembly has also concluded the following five conventions: the *International Convention against the Taking of Hostages*; the *Convention on the Safety of United Nations and Associated Personnel*; the *International Convention for the Suppression of Terrorist Bombings*; the *International Convention for the Suppression of the Financing of Terrorism*; and the *International Convention for the Suppression of Acts of Nuclear Terrorism.*[19]

Sadly, major terrorist assaults have continued over the years since 9-11—including attacks on *UN headquarters in Baghdad*[20] (August 2003), on four commuter trains in Madrid[21] (March 2004), on an office and an apartment block used by Westerners in al-Khobar, Saudi Arabia (May 2004), the London Underground[22] (July 2005), a seaside area and shopping hub in Bali[23] (October 2005), multiple sites in Mumbai (November 2008), the Marriott and Ritz-Carlton hotels in Jakarta (July 2009), and the Moscow Metro (March 2010), to name only a few.

As part of the international effort to stem this deadly tide, the General Assembly, in September 2006, unanimously adopted and launched the *UN Global Counter-Terrorism Strategy.* Based on the fundamental conviction that terrorism in all its forms is unacceptable and can never be justified, the Strategy outlines a range of specific measures to address terrorism in all its aspects, at the national, regional and international levels.

Nuclear Proliferation and Disarmament

In 2009, world military expenditures exceeded some $1.5 trillion. The need for a culture of peace and for significant arms reduction worldwide has never been greater. And this applies to all classes of weapons.

On the danger of nuclear weapons, Albert Einstein reportedly said: "I do not know with what weapons World War III will be fought, but World War IV will be fought with sticks and stones."[24] But the human and material cost of conventional weapons is also extreme. Of at least 640 million licensed firearms worldwide, roughly two-thirds are in the hands of civil society. The legal trade in small arms and weapons exceeds $4 billion a year. The illicit trade is estimated at $1 billion. And such conventional weapons as landmines take a toll on life and limb that continues for years after the conflicts that spawned them are finished.

And yet, beyond the obvious effects of these weapons is their deeper cost — a cost that stems from misplaced priorities and an absence of vision.

Former United States President Dwight D. Eisenhower (1952-60) and General Commander of the Allied Forces during World War II, put it this way. Speaking early in his term as President, he said: "Every gun that is made, every warship launched, every rocket fired signifies, in the final sense, a theft from those who hunger and are not fed, those who are cold and are not clothed. The cost of one modern heavy bomber is this: a modern brick school in more than 30 cities."

Since the birth of the United Nations, the goals of multilateral disarmament and arms limitation have been deemed central to the maintenance of international peace and security. These goals range from reducing and eventually eliminating nuclear weapons, destroying chemical weapons and strengthening the prohibition against biological weapons, to halting the proliferation of landmines, small arms and light weapons.

These efforts are supported by a number of key UN instruments. The *Treaty on the Non-Proliferation of Nuclear Weapons (NPT)*, the most universal of all multilateral disarmament treaties, came into force in 1970. The *Chemical Weapons Convention* entered into force in 1997, the *Biological Weapons Convention* in 1975. The *Comprehensive Nuclear-Test-Ban Treaty* was adopted in 1996. The 1997 *Mine-Ban Convention* came into force in 1999.

UN-supported regional treaties ban nuclear weapons in Antarctica, Latin America and the Caribbean, the South Pacific, South-East Asia, Africa and Central Asia. Other instruments adopted through the UN ban nuclear weapons in outer space in the sea-bed.

Responding to the rise of international terrorism, the General Assembly adopted resolution *57/83* aimed at preventing terrorists from acquiring weapons of mass destruction and their means of delivery. In 2004, the Security Council adopted *resolution 1540*, banning state support for such efforts. The Assembly's *International Convention for the Suppression of Acts of Nuclear Terrorism* was opened for signature in September 2005 and entered into force in July 2007.

The *General Assembly* and the Security Council address disarmament-related issues on a continuing basis. The Assembly also held special sessions on disarmament in 1978 and 1988. Some UN bodies are dedicated *exclusively* to disarmament. Among them is the Conference on Disarmament. As the international community's sole multilateral negotiating forum for disarmament agreements, the Conference successfully negotiated both the *Chemical Weapons Convention* and the *Comprehensive Nuclear-Test-Ban Treaty.*

At the local level, UN peace-keepers often work to implement specific disarmament agreements between warring parties. This approach has been used successfully in West Africa, for example, where the *Office of the Special Representative* of the Secretary-General has organized regional meetings to harmonize programmes for the disarmament, demobilization and reintegration of former combatants. The situation in Liberia provides a good example of how this works.

Established in September 2003, the United Nations Mission in Liberia (*UNMIL*) was charged with assisting in the disarmament, demobilization, reintegration and repatriation of all armed parties. The process was launched in December. Within 12 months, nearly 100,000 Liberians had turned in guns, ammunition, rocket-propelled grenades and other weapons. On 3 November 2004, Liberia's warring militias, formally disbanded in a ceremony at UNMIL headquarters in Monrovia. By the end of February 2006, more than 300,000 internally displaced Liberians had been returned to their home villages. After 15 years of conflict, the people turned out in massive numbers for UN-assisted elections in 2005.[25]

The situation following Iraq's 1990 invasion of Kuwait and the conclusion of the first Gulf War is a unique example of a UN ceasefire agreement requiring enforced disarmament. When the war ended, the Council adopted its resolution 687 of 8 April 1991, setting the terms of the ceasefire. Among them: the elimination of Iraq's weapons of mass destruction (WMDs).[26]

To that end, the Council established the United Nations Special Commission (*UNSCOM*) on the disarmament of Iraq, with powers of no-notice inspection. It entrusted the International Atomic Energy Agency (*IAEA*) with similar verification tasks in the nuclear sphere, with UNSCOM assistance. Over the ensuing 12 years, this process succeeded in reducing Iraq's WMD stash considerably. Unfortunately, the inability to certify that all of those weapons and systems had been destroyed led, in part, to the second Iraq war in 2003.[27]

UN Peace-keeping also employs the strategy of preventive disarmament, which seeks to reduce the number of small arms in conflict-prone regions. In El Salvador, Sierra Leone, Liberia and elsewhere, this has entailed demobilizing combat forces as well as collecting and destroying their weapons as part of an overall peace agreement. And in keeping with the sentiment expressed by General Eisenhower, the UN is also supremely mindful, in all these efforts, of the direct relationship between disarmament and development.

The prevention of Nuclear Proliferation should have been accorded top-most priority along with nuclear disarmament. Here again the record of United Nations agencies charged with this task has been deplorable. The United Nations did not focus, highlight or condemn any of the following developments:

- China's assistance to Pakistan in development of nuclear weapons.
- China's supply of nuclear capable missiles and missile technology to Pakistan.
- China's assistance in building up of North Korea's long-range and nuclear capable missiles.
- Pakistan's supply of nuclear weapons technology to North Korea.
- United States permissiveness in tolerating all of the above developments. Inaction despite CIA evidence was sought to be justified by the United States on grounds of lack of "actionable intelligence."

Obviously, structural inadequacies of the United Nations, the resolve and political inclinations of the United Nations Secretary General and the strategic interests and preferences of the United Nations Security Council permanent members were at play.

The end of the Cold War brought new hope for peace dividends, but left a world awash in arms, surplus arms-making capacity, and unemployed arms professionals. Traffic increased in both scale and recipients, as prices fell. Control over the development, manufacture and deployment of lethal weapons and substances, particularly nuclear, biological and chemical, has become no longer the preserve of the superpowers and their allies. UN concern and activity has grown, but will be constrained by: continued weapons research, driven by fear, greed and curiosity; global diffusion of both weapons and relevant knowledge; the increasing difficulty of verification; and the vulnerability of complex modern society to disruption. All demand global reaction.

The collapse of major institutions, both national and international, including numerous failed states, is foreseen as a delicate predicament for the international community. The UN may be the only acceptable resident physician in many cases. Two problems inevitably arise: the degree of global control and help that is tolerable yet sufficient, and the enormous cost and possibly time-scale involved. For many reasons, however, a political-security black hole can no longer be left unattended by an interdependent community.

The influence, wealth and activities of many non-state trans-national organizations (NGOs, corporations, ideological movements, media, etc.) is approaching or exceeding that of sovereign states. The international rules in regard to such bodies remain very limited. One reason is that they may have no genuine nationality and/or can play one state off against another. Somehow such organizations must be persuaded to respect a minimal system of supranational norms, or jurisdiction if necessary. Only the UN system has any hope of accomplishing this.

Human Resource

Behind most sources of global instability lie two inter-related factors. First, in many places and ways, humanity already exceeds the carrying capacity of both its biosphere and institutions. Its rapidly increasing capabilities have enabled it to expand its global impact and numbers much faster, and to conduct activities more destabilizing, than either the ecosystem or existing social arrangements can handle. Second, the global order, while knowledge-based, wastes most of the vast pool of human intelligence that might remedy or constrain these human numbers and profligate activities. Only a tiny handful of the humans now alive will ever approach their full potential. Billions live marginal lives; 30% of the world's labour force are not productively employed; 1.5 billion are condemned to the strait-jacket of illiteracy. Moreover, 80 million are added annually to human numbers—and to growing pressures on institutions and resources. Any alleviation of expanding human pressures and wasted human capacities—through responsible development and fertility, accelerated education and competence—is the most truly global challenge facing the international community, and UN.

Of course, the work of the UN for promotion of Human Rights is largely impeded by certain built-in limitations. There is in the first place the domestic jurisdiction clause in the principles of the UN, which acts as a double-edged sword. On the one hand it prevents even minimal interference of the world body in the domestic situation of the state accused of consistent human rights violations. On the other, it provides an easy defence of Governments for doing little about human rights.

Secondly, because of widespread differences in the social system and their sustaining ideologies, disagreements among governments at to which rights should get what priority often become irreconcilable. Liberal democracies of the west would mostly uphold political civil liberties such as freedom of speech, freedom of assembly and movement, competitive political campaigns and so on, so as to treat economic rights like the right to work, unemployment relief and other social security measures as secondary. The emphasis is reversed in the case of socialist states who attach greater importance to social, economic and cultural rights. Workers' security, rather than political freedom in the abstract. Certain rights like equal rights for women may challenge the conservative order in many societies, especially in the Islamic world. Also the capacities of states to uphold different types of rights vary considerably. Economic backwardness may prevent with a well-intentioned elite from implementing fundamental economic rights.

Two trends cause increasing health concerns. First is the rapid and relentless escalation in the global movement of both people and things. Every conscious transfer also carries the threat of transmitting human, plant or animal disease, and inevitably raises the likelihood of pandemics. Second, the very widespread (over)use of antibiotics, etc. has produced more resistant mutations, and a global race to keep ahead. All this calls for tighter global biological preventive and control measures. Fortunately many can be integrated to a degree with other security screening, and control of toxic goods movements. Again, any impervious system demands all-inclusive global coverage.

The formation and acceptance of universal human rights and democratic norms raises questions. While some governments argue that human rights are culturally based, in practice the body of those globally accepted is expanding. In any event, any universal code must be developed through the gradual build-up of norms. The process of formulation and acceptance is constantly underway in various UN fora, and has been for many years. Movement, though slow, is clearly forward and increasingly intrusive within states.

Humans now move in unprecedented numbers, not simply because there are more people, but because both the need and opportunity have grown: both push and pull forces are powerful. The UN officially recognizes well over 20 million refugees forced unwillingly out of their own country. Globally, about one person in a hundred is either a refugee or displaced, i.e. forced unwillingly to move within their country.[28] Other mass migrations are more ambiguous, particularly the uncontrolled flows in poorer countries from country to city. When either or both the migrant and the place of immigration is unwilling, problems are bound to arise beyond mere acculturation. These truly global issues can best be dealt with at the global level.

In a knowledge-driven world, the maximum and most rapid exploitation of accurate information and essential technology should be facilitated, if only to the general welfare. Assisting in raising global access to information is a challenge so big and beneficial that it falls on the UN. Third World states can be assisted electronically in gaining entry to the most essential pools of knowledge, particularly to exploit modern technology for rapid and general education. The distortions and instability that accompany the global revolution can thus be absorbed as quickly and painlessly as possible, and the Third World make a major contribution to global sustainable development.

The avoidable frustration, hopelessness and anguish of billions of humans, brought about by absolute privation, and extreme and growing income divergence, both within and between states, must be addressed—if only for enlightened self-interest in global stability. The international community through the United Nations has a unique capacity, and so responsibility. We must try; there is no rational excuse.

Natural Resources

Humanity's fixed global heritage is being destroyed or exploited at an accelerating rate, a process ultimately unsustainable. This applies to both renewable and non-renewable resources; to those claimed by individuals or organizations and those seen as humanity's common heritage and/or as valueless externalities. From now on, all exploitable reserves must be at least roughly calculated, valued, and used on a broadly sustainable basis. If these difficult aims are to have meaning and some hope of success, global accords and close cooperation are essential; the UN is already taking the lead.

Since the scientific revolution, and particularly since the population and technological explosions, certain human activities have done such dangerous and costly damage to the biosphere that *Homo sapiens* has no choice but to try to make corrections. At minimum, widespread and/or trans-boundary biospheric disruptions (e.g. air pollution; soil erosion, pollution and depletion; desertification; water misuse; deforestation) must be controlled or reversed. The scale and wide-spread nature of most of these problems, and the limited financial and technical ability of many of those worst affected, require that most can best or only be addressed collectively on a worldwide basis.[29]

We confront or create serious physical phenomena of global impact, many caused by forces that can only be indirectly influenced, or even understood. These may or may not be avoidable, but many can now at least be predicted, or reduced in force or effect. Examples may be climatic (global warming, ozone depletion); geological (earthquakes, volcanic eruptions, tsunami); meteorological (floods, storms, droughts);

or space-originated (asteroids). Almost any human counter-action can only or best be undertaken collectively by the global community.

Almost all the challenges identified raise the possibility of catastrophe, however prescient the UN's efforts. World interdependence increases chances that local events have global effects; the colossal and ever-growing scale of human intrusions on the biosphere make catastrophes both more likely and serious; and the omnipresent media, combined with the appalling discrepancies in wealth, make assistance politically unavoidable. Geography, resources and technology alone make UN-coordinated action preferable.

With the proliferation of weapons comes the profusion of those who could and might use them. The desperation of unemployment, the anger of those masses who perceive themselves deprived in a grossly unequal but more-informed world, and the boldness of ethnic and religious certainties, sows contagious seeds of terrorism, fanaticism and martyrdom. Arming and financing extremists are *inter alia* the growing numbers and wealth of drug dealers and other international criminals, and new thousands of well-trained and armed international mercenaries and activists. Miniaturization, the diffusion of lethal knowledge and components, and multi-use equipment and substances, impede surveillance, while the vulnerability of energy—and information—dependent society makes it more susceptible to focussed attack and blackmail. Counter-action must therefore involve all governments to eliminate sanctuary and safe transit. Counter-intelligence must become as airtight and coordinated as possible. Only global coverage is truly effective.

One major aspect of globalization is the interdependence of national finances. This reflects the vast, expanding scale and global nature of: international trade (goods; services; technology), investment (short-term; direct), migration (personal assets; remittances), and the related or speculative financial transfers (now worth about $1.5 trillion daily). This reality limits all governments' control over national fiscal policies, exchange rates, economic success, and debts, and can threaten national stability—increasingly through external financial developments. Resulting world-wide issues include: the need for terms of global financial rules and assistance; the nature, control and value of (national) currencies; the optimum rules for foreign trade, investment and migration; the damping of irrational confidence, price, stock-exchange frenzies; the elimination of tax havens and money laundering. All involve the UN system (particularly the IMF-World Bank).

As the volume and value of international trade grows, it raises new problems of negotiation, regulation and adjustment. The World Trade Organization will have a key role in dealing with the rapidly growing trade in services, chronic problems with agriculture, the issues of international investment and corruption, environmental and labour standards, and the taxing of international trade between parts of supra-national corporations. Many economic agreements are already global. They will inevitably grow in number and complexity as trade blocs form.

Structure of UN

All Member-states are represented in the General Assembly. Yet its decision is not binding on anyone. The Security Council consists of the representatives of only a few states. Yet its decision is binding. If a single permanent member vetoes, all other members cannot pass any resolution. Thus through the Security Council a permanent member like the USA may use the entire United Nations for its imperialistic and hegemonic designs. Yet they are not satisfied. At the time of his address in the United Nations on 12 September 2002, before launching his attack on Iraq, US President Bush asked, "Will the United Nations serve the purpose of its founding, or will it be irrelevant?" As if the United Nations is relevant only if it enacts the wishes of the US President. If it fails to do so, it is irrelevant. He really proved the United Nations irrelevant by launching a unilateral, unjust attack on "sovereign" Iraq without any authorisation from the United Nations on the false plea that Iraq under Saddam Hussein had Weapons of Mass Destruction and Saddam had connection with Osama bin Laden. The Coalition Force under the USA attacked and occupied Iraq, killed more than 2,00,000[30] Iraqis, and installed its puppet government there so that they might control the Iraqi natural resources like oil. Even after two years of occupation of Iraq, Bush could not find even a single WMD. The Commission appointed by him also could not find any proof of Saddam's connection with Osama.

Before that on 24 March 1999 NATO started an air campaign[31] on Kosovo to bring President Slobodan Milosevic to terms. It also clearly revealed the helplessness of the United Nations. Incidents like these tarnished the image of the Organisation to a great extent.

On this background, "in his address to the General Assembly in September 2003 United Nations Secretary General Kofi Annan warned Member-states that the United Nations had reached a fork in the road. It could rise to the challenge of meeting new threats or it could risk erosion in the face of mounting discord between States and unilateral action by them.[32] To enable the United Nations "to rise to the challenge of meeting new threats" he appointed a 16-member "High-Level Panel." They submitted the report entitled "A More Secure World: Our Shared Responsibility." After that, the Secretary General himself submitted his report "In Larger Freedom; Towards Development, Security and Human

Rights for All" on 21 March 2005. Introducing this report to the General Assembly, United Nations Secretary General Kofi Annan urged Member-states to adopt this year a package of specific, concrete proposals to tackle global problems and enable the Organisation to better respond to current challenges. What are the proposals for changing the composition for Security Council? No proposal for abolishing veto power. No proposal for extending the veto power. The proposal is simply to increase the number of some members without any veto power. The Secretary General himself and the members of the High-Level Panel appointed by him knew it well that the permanent members would not agree to give up the undemocratic, autocratic, tyrannical power of veto and permanent membership of the Security Council. So they did not to dare recommend so. They recommended either the introduction of six new permanent members without veto power and three two-year term non-permanent members (Model A) or eight four-year term renewable non-permanent members and one two-year term non-renewable non-permanent member (Model B).[33] What they have recommended will in no way alter the basic undemocratic, partial character of the United Nations. They are not bothered about it. The permanent members are only interested to polish the image of the United Nations, which had faded considerably by their misdeeds. They did the same thing with the League of Nations. They increased the non-permanent members of the Council of the League of Nations from four in 1920 to six in 1922 and nine in 1926. This increase in no way salvaged the League of Nations and, when the permanent members like Japan and Italy began to invade other countries in defiance of the League, the League became irrelevant. The League was dissolved in 1946. But it became non-existent long before that. It did not meet again after December 1939.[34] Similarly, the United Nations will remain intact as long as the permanent members do not defy it and the other members digest the unjust activities of the powerful permanent members. If the permanent members defy it or others oppose their misdeeds, the United Nations is destined to collapse. The Coalition attack on Iraq is an indication of that collapse.

The powerful permanent members will not allow United Nations to be just and democratic. They will bypass the United Nations when it suits them. But they expect others to honour it. Hence, arises the need of breaking it. All other nations should boycott the unjust United Nations and create one new World Organisation, on the principle of sovereignty equality and impartiality, and compel the permanent members to join the new just organisation, or face isolation.

The Charter established six principal organs of the United Nations:

- the General Assembly,
- the Security Council,
- the Economic and Social Council,
- the Trusteeship Council,
- the International Court of Justice, and
- the Secretariat.

The United Nations family, however, is much larger, encompassing 15 agencies and several programmes and bodies.

The General Assembly

The General Assembly consists of the representatives of all the Member-states, each of which has only one vote. It can deliberate on any matter subject to the limitation imposed by Article 12 of the Charter. The regular session of the Assembly generally begins in the month of September each year. In addition, the Assembly may meet on special sessions. Resolution on peace and security, admission of new members and budgetary matter requires two-third majority. Resolution on other matters requires only simple majority. Though consisting of all the Member-states, the decision of the General Assembly is not binding on anyone.

Security Council

Were the United Nations a just, impartial and democratic organisation for preserving world peace in the true sense, the General Assembly should have been the most powerful organ and all other organs must have been subordinate to it! But the Allied Powers had no such intention. They wanted to safeguard their own interest, sometimes their unjust greed, at the expense of weaker nations. So they drafted the Charter in such a way that the Security Council is the repository of the real power of the United Nations and no "substantive" resolution in the Security Council can be passed without their consent. Here lies the greatest malady of the United Nations.

Money Power

Money power is a big power. Naturally the Member-state which contributes more enjoys more clout in the UN.

Each Member-state contributes the amount assessed on a scale approved by the General Assembly on the recommendation of the Committee on Contribution. "The fundamental criterion on which the scale of assessments is based is the capacity of the country to pay. This is determined by considering their relative shares of total gross national product, adjusted to take into account a number of factors, including their per capita income."[35]

The scale of assessment (that is contribution in percentage) for 2004 is that USA alone contributes 22%, the maximum for any one contributor. The five permanent members (USA 22%, UK 6.127%, France 6.030%, Russian Federation 1.100% and China 2.053%) together contribute 37.310%. And along with other four developed countries (Japan 19.468%, Germany 6.662%, Italy 4.885%, and Spain 2.520%), nine countries contribute more than 70% (70.845%) and the remaining 182 countries contribute only 29.165%. USA contributes 22%. But there are as many as 48 countries which contribute only 0.001%. Each of the poorest 48 countries contributes only one-twenty-two thousandth part of what USA contributes. That is, USA contributes 22000 times that of the contribution of each country, and 466.667 times that of all the 48 countries together.[36] Naturally the UN is more dependent on US contribution than that of any other country. Withholding of contribution by USA will affect the UN more. Naturally, the USA commands more respect and power in the UN than any other country. But the power emanating from the Structure of the UN has got precedence over the money power also.

If money power was the only criterion, then Japan with contribution of 19.468% should have been the most powerful Member-state in UN, second only to USA, and its clout should have been more than the joint clout of other four permanent members together. But that is not the case. Everyone knows that UK, France, Russia, or even its immediate neighbour China holds more power and prestige in UN circle than Japan. This is because being the permanent members of the Security Council they possess veto power.

The USA is so powerful because veto power has given leverage to money power. It can buy with money and cut with veto.

Misuse of Veto Power

The veto is of course only a sympton of Great Power disagreement. The veto was introduced because the idea was that the Great Powers had the responsibility of enforcing peace and as such there should be unanimity among Great Powers on any issue affecting world peace. The United States was the first to propose the introduction of veto in the Security Council. There is great possibility of veto being misused by the permanent members of 'Security Council'. The entire UN-machinery is paralysed if any permanent member of Security Council exercises veto against any resolution. In case any resolution defeated in the Security Council due to exercise of veto, there is remote possibility of its being adopted by 2/3 majority of the members of the General Assembly because of the manoeuvres of the Great Power exercising veto. On certain occasions the permanent members of the

Security Council have tried to pursue their national interests and exercise the veto to achieve them. Under President Truman the American government had announced that it would veto all candidates for the post of Secretary General except Trygve Tylie, President Eisenhower also announced that the United States would use the veto to prevent the admission of People's Republic of China in the United Nations. By the end of 1960 out of the total number of 99 vetoes which had been mast the Soviet Union exercised veto for 92 times. On certain occasions the Great Powers have adopted partisan approach. For instance, in case of Kashmir issue the United States, Britain and France had unduly supported Pakistan's position and failed to realise the legality of India's stand on Kashmir. Similarly, these Western countries have not exercised veto on various proposals demanding imposition of comprehensive mandatory sanctions on the government of Union of South Africa which is practising the policy of apartheid to the detriment of the coloured people. If any of the five permanent members is an aggressor or decides to favour or help an aggressor state no action can be taken by the United Nations. Commenting on the privileged position of the permanent members of the Security Council, Lord Winster has aptly remarked thus, "This organisation will be one for keeping small boys in order by prebects-who are themselves exempt from the rules they administer." Commenting on the hegemony of Great Powers in the World body Dr. Murray has said, I strongly suspect that the first real strain on the new league will come when it attempts to give orders to some nation accustomed to freedom. It is a new provision that the Security Council should have the power to issue orders, while the fact that the Great Powers need not obey such order will great weaken such moral authority as they might have had.

Equal Weightage to All States

Taking advantage of the arbitrary, undemocratic and unjust nature of the Charter, the imperialist powers like the USA and UK have been using the United Nations since its inception as an instrument of oppression of the weaker states. On the one hand, they are using United Nations for the justification of their misdeeds, even wanton aggression for their imperialist interest. In the name of United Nations, time and again, they are waging wars against the weaker nations, who are slowly trying to get out of the imperialistic hegemony of the big powers. If you are weak and no veto-wielding power is behind you, then you may be condemned, sanction may be imposed against you to cripple you, even military force may be used against you, for bringing you in their line. Any attempt to get justice against these big powers or their allies, is ruthlessly frustrated by the veto power. On the other hand, if you are a big power with permanent membership in the Security Council or at least you enjoy the blessing of one such power, you can go on doing anything you like, even you can trample the Security Council Resolutions which are binding on all Member-states including the permanent members of the Security Council; nobody can touch you. You may blatantly violate the Resolutions of the Security Council, but any punishment against you may be imposed only through the Resolution of the Security Council, and if you have a veto power on your side, you can equally blatantly block that resolution. Yes, the General Assembly may consider the matter, and there you can give vent to your grievances. But nobody is bothered about that. Security Council is there as a shield to protect the offender. Such is the greatness of the present United Nations. A few examples will make the point clearer.

Libya in the African continent was an Italian colony since 1911 till it was captured by Franco-British Allied Forces during the Second World War. It attained independence in 1951. In 1959 oil reserves were discovered. So the big powers like the USA, UK and France were interested in controlling it in the form of neo-colonialism. In the 1970s and 1980s the Libyan leaders were not blindly obeying their dictates. For that, they had to pay a very high price. United Nations could not give any relief to them against the veto-wielding powers and their allies.

On 4 February 1986, two Israeli fighter aircraft, in gross violation of the international law forcefully intercepted, diverted and detained a private Libyan civilian G-2 type aircraft, while flying over the international airspace over the Mediterranean. Syria brought this flagrant violation of international law to the Security Council. At the 2655th meeting of the Security Council, USA vetoed the revised draft resolution submitted by Congo, Ghana, Madagascar, Trinidad and Tobago and the United Arab Emirates. The resolution wanted to condemn Israel for "its forcible interception of the Libyan civilian aircraft in international airspace and its subsequent detention of the same aircraft" and call upon "Israel to desist from" such act. The US representative stated that "although the United States opposed Israel's action in this case, it would not accept the said draft resolution as it did not take into sufficient account the need to address practically and appropriately the overriding issue of terrorism."[37]

On 15 April 1986, the United States aircraft bombed targets in the Libyan capital Tripoli and its second largest city Benghazi. The same day Libya requested for an immediate meeting of the Security Council. At its 2682nd meeting, on 21 April 1986, USA, UK and France vetoed the revised draft resolution submitted by Congo, Ghana, Madagascar, Trinidad and Tobago and the United Arab Emirates. The resolution, *inter alia*, wanted to condemn "the armed attack by United States in violation of the Charter of the United Nations and the norms of international conduct" and call upon "the United States to refrain forthwith from any attacks or threat thereof." "The United States representative rejected the said draft resolution as totally unacceptable."[38]

In its letter dated 4 January Libya requested the President of the Security Council for an immediate meeting of the Council to consider the drowning of two reconnaissance aircrafts by the United States Armed Forces. At the 2841st meeting on 11 January 1989, USA, UK and France vetoed the draft resolution submitted by Algeria, Columbia, Ethiopia, Malaysia, Nepal, Senegal and Yugoslavia. The resolution wanted to "deplore the drowning of the two Libyan reconnaissance planes by the armed forces of the United States" and "call upon the United States to suspend its military manoeuvres off the Libyan coast in order to contribute to the reduction of tension in the area." The US representative claimed that "the two Libyan aircrafts in question had not flown in routine observation pattern. They flew flight patterns consistent with aggressive, hostile intent and when the United States pilots attempted to evade them the Libyan pilots pursued them repeatedly."[39]

The list is long. The cases of Iraq and Palestine are more revealing.

Rule of Law

A final challenge explored by participants was the UN's ability to engage in comprehensive peace-building efforts through the establishment of post-conflict rule of law. This issue was found to be extremely pertinent to the future of peace operations, considering the increasing scope of UN peace-keeping missions in aspects relevant to the rule of law. According to Gantz, the immediate priority when first deploying a peace-keeping mission must continue to focus on ensuring a basic level of security, without which daily activities cannot commence. In the longer-term, however, he advised that the priority should shift to enhancing local institutional capabilities while simultaneously devolving authority to local establishments and actors. The challenge in establishing this local rule of law, Gantz argued, rests in the multiple issues at play, including the types of rules and laws that must be implemented, and the model (if any) to follow in doing so. The process requires, among other things, the elaboration of a constitution and the implementation of transparency mechanisms. It also requires training professionals, government officials, and a judiciary, including police, prisons and court officials, all of which demand special skills and special guidance. Gantz used the example of Haiti to demonstrate how the accomplishments of the international community can be as easily reversed if all factors for good governance are not in place before UN forces are withdrawn. He explained that while the police were fairly effective, the courts and prisons were not, causing an increase in extra-judicial responses to crimes and offenses. In the end, the lack of institutional capabilities was a major factor in the reversal of the situation in Haiti, and resulted in the efforts of the international community being compromised.

Every (binding) inter-state agreement constrains sovereignty, and every resolution passed in a universal forum contributes to creating global standards/norms. The general trend is thus for the body of international practice, precedent and law to grow at an unequalled rate. The reason is practical. A world whose international inter-connections grow exponentially must establish and maintain relevant rules, controls and principles. The development of international law and tribunals must keep pace with interdependence. If global, the UN is involved.

CONSTRAINTS

Political Will

The political will of western nations to engage in peace-keeping missions was a point of interest throughout the conference. Although participants acknowledged a decline in political will of developed nations to contribute larger contingents to UN peace-keeping missions, there was some disagreement over the extent of the phenomenon. Several participants pointed to a growing aversion on the part of developed countries to troop casualties and reluctance to deploy large contingents under UN command. These reasons, along with the increasing engagement of many western nations in Iraq and Afghanistan, led Ray Crabbe to suggest the future involvement of western states in peace-keeping to be questionable at best.

While agreeing with Crabbe on the importance of the West's strategic leadership, Jeremy Kinsman noted that perhaps the apparent waning willingness of western nations to commit forces to peace-keeping is overstated. While he admitted that there has been a decline in western troop contributions to UN missions relative to the contributions of developing nations, he argued that other factors are also responsible for this decline. In his view, the case for humanitarian intervention was stained by its use as an excuse for the United States (US) to enter Iraq. While he acquiesced that public opinion is beginning to regain confidence in the international system, electorates throughout the developed world remain split on the question of humanitarian intervention and governments remain risk averse in their foreign policy. Despite this setback to the case for humanitarian intervention, Kinsman sees a chance for progress on the horizon. As the Security Council is no longer paralyzed by Cold War politics, and as the setbacks of the 1990s and beginning of the 21st century are slowly dissipating, he saw a reason to be cautiously optimistic about the future of UN peace-keeping. Russia and China are showing a new willingness to cooperate and the US is learning the inadequacy of unilateralism.

In light of the weakening political will on the part of developed countries, participants discussed the growing willingness of developing countries to get involved in UN peace-keeping. The last five years have seen an unprecedented growth in UN peace-keeping, contributing to a considerable increase in the demand for peace-keepers. As a result, developing countries have stepped up and are now assuming the burden by contributing the majority of peace-keepers.[40] Once again, however, opinions varied widely as to the underlying reasons for such an increase.

Crabbe, for example, suggested that the increase in the contributions of developing countries partly reflects the desire of African states to assume greater responsibility in the area of peace and security. He questioned the motivation of some UN peace-keeping contingents, by pointing to the monetary incentives for countries to contribute troops, which can add up to a significant windfall for a developing economy. Skeptical of the phenomenon, he further noted that the growing involvement of developing countries in peace-keeping has created the negative perception that "developing country soldiers are being sent to keep western soldiers safe." Kinsman offered a different view, suggesting instead that it is simply a division of labour according to capacity, as many of the developed states are operating at close to full capacity in Iraq, Afghanistan, and elsewhere.

Financial Constraints

Closely related to political will are the challenges posed by troop and financial constraints. Troop and financial support are crucial elements of a peace-keeping deployment, without which a peace-keeping mission cannot assume its full range of capabilities. Within this theme, participants addressed the challenges that an increase in the number of peace-keepers coming from developing countries poses to peace-keeping.

Most participants agreed that many of the concerns surrounding the increasing role of developing countries in peace-keeping stem from their lack of capacity. While it was acknowledged that there have been many good contingents from developing countries, several participants pointed to the fact that many of these contingents are under-funded and lack training and/or equipment. This view was echoed by Pierre Kyer, who stated that many of the developing country contingents he saw while working in the Democratic Republic of Congo (DRC) were much less efficient. While on location in the field, he witnessed troops with little preparation (e.g. lacking a driver's license) and with limited knowledge of the local culture and language.

With these examples in mind, Greg Cran noted that the absence of developed nations poses new challenges to peace-keeping operations. Wider and more challenging mandates not only require more money, but also more specialized capacities (i.e. army engineers and logisticians, heavy-lift aircraft, proper command-and-control and intelligence gathering, etc.).[41] As Crabbe explained, peace-keeping missions rely on the command and control, logistics, as well as leadership strategies offered by western militaries and in the absence of this expertise, peace-keeping becomes much more challenging. This is an operational challenge which must be addressed, as specialized armies and capacities are in short supply.[42] While the capacity exists, it is mostly concentrated in western countries with established militaries, and it requires each member-state to voluntary contribute their capacity and equipment to a UN mission. In response to this challenge, Cran remarked that the focus should be on improving the capacity of developing contingents.

An increase in peace-keeping operations also translates into financial implications for the UN system and its member-states. The surge in operations witnessed in the pass few years has not only raised the demand for peace-keepers, but also caused the annual budget of UN peace-keeping to triple from its level ten years ago, putting more pressure on member-states. The annual budget is currently in the range of $6 billion.[43]

Manpower for Peace-keeping Operations

A third issue under discussion was that of rapid deployment and the possibility of building a standing capacity under UN auspices. Rapid response to crises and post-conflict areas remain difficult to achieve, and as such, constitute a considerable obstacle to the effectiveness of UN peace-keeping. It is increasingly recognized that to respond to the challenges posed by contemporary conflicts, forces must be mobile, flexible, effective, and sustainable. As the UN does not have a standing peace-keeping capacity, it must rely on voluntary contributions from member-states, causing the process of planning, authorizing and deploying a peace-keeping operation to be extremely complex.[44]

Crabbe noted that according to the Brahimi Report, soldiers must be on the ground within six weeks for most peace-keeping missions to be successful and the majority of missions to date have failed to respond in a timely manner. He described organizations that study the UN structure as well as those conducting country background studies as absolutely invaluable for mission success. In his view, it is crucial to have an understanding of the multifaceted approaches to peace-keeping and to have command and control headquarters that possess regional knowledge. He suggested that there is a need for more multinational regional headquarters around the world if the UN is to create the ability for rapid deployment. He further explained that there is a need for greater flexibility in UN deployment requirements. Instead of reinventing the wheel for every mission and counting individual soldiers and equipment based on the monetary will of contributing nations, he advocated for working with set peace-keeping "packages" that can be deployed much faster. Examples of such 'force packages' include SHIRBRIG, the NATO Response Force (NRF), the EU Rapid Reaction Force (ERRF), the EU Battlegroups, and the African Standby Force (ASF). Crabbe also recognized that the UN has collected rosters of military and civilian personnel; however, these rosters, in his opinion, are largely unmonitored and have not worked in the past.

Regarding the issue of standing capacity, Gantz argued that a significant standing capacity for UN peace-keeping would not be created any time soon. He did note, however, that there is a small standing police capacity of about fifteen police officers in the UN system. The UN Standing Police Capacity (SPC) is a new UN mechanism to help establish police components in new UN peace operations. The SPC can also support ongoing operations. Although few in number, Gantz sees the initiative as a foot in the door for those advocating a permanent military and police force that could rapidly deploy to conflict situations as the need arises. In his view, while the will to create a standing capacity for UN peace-keeping forces remains elusive, it is difficult to overstate the value of having core staff in place to ensure that each mission builds on previous experiences. This would allow for continuous improvement in the speed and efficiency of future UN missions.

Participants discussed rules of engagement and the use of force. The fundamental principles of UN peace-keeping—consent, impartiality, and the non-use of force except in self-defence—have, in specific cases, become obstacles to the deployment and success of UN peace-keeping missions. In particular, respect for the non-use of force has, in many cases, proven to be impractical in the face of large-scale massacres and detrimental to the mission both morally and physically. Rwanda, Bosnia, Somalia, and East Timor are stark examples of the consequences of the non-use of force. In response to the new strategic environment, today's missions are for the most part deployed under Chapter VII of the UN Charter, authorizing peace-keepers to use "all necessary means" to protect themselves and threatened civilians. For example, the missions in the DRC, Sierra Leone, Côte d'Ivoire and Haiti have, as part of their mandate, the explicit authorization to use force to protect civilians. However, this use of force raises a number of questions, such as the level of force at which it becomes too much and the extent to which peace-keepers should protect civilians if such protection can jeopardize a mission's objectives.

Kinsman noted the need for military peace-keepers to have clear rules of engagement that are suited to the particular mission to avoid repeating situations where peace-keepers lacked in both capacity and mandate. Indeed, it is crucial that when a force is deployed, the mandate under which it will operate matches the needs on the ground. Boutilier agreed that there is a need for a much stronger UN in current missions and that this must start with robust rules of engagement. Crabbe, on the other hand, argued that mandates have improved in strength and clarity since the early days of peace-keeping, and rules of engagement are now very detailed. In Afghanistan, for example, he claimed that soldiers know exactly what they can and cannot do. In his view, the real issue with rules of engagement is the need for UN forces to develop a credible deterrent capability. According to him, the major mistake made in the Balkans was to offer no assurances as to the consequences of breaking the ceasefire. As a result, he argued that the UN must act as a greater deterrent by creating a fourth principle of "credibility of force" to compliment the three principles already in place. One aspect of this credibility would be to force the UN to be clear about the consequences of violating cease-fires.

While all participants agreed that the UN has made progress on rules of engagement, the problem, according to Gantz, is that rules of engagement are still decided in an *ad hoc* way. In his view, the UN should develop a more professional approach to peace-keeping by developing doctrine. He argued that the UN should identify the desired outcome and identify how they are going to reach it. While Crabbe argued that UN peace-keeping operations already have an end-state in mind, he admitted that, since missions are often deployed hastily, defining an end-state can indeed be difficult. The process, he added, is further complicated by the need to draft rules of engagement appropriate for each national environment in which these missions operate.

Responding to Gantz' proposal for a peace-keeping doctrine, Kinsman stated that because the UN is made up of member-states, weaknesses in doctrine are simply a reflection of the inability of member-states to come to a consensus. He pointed out that general guidelines would likely be too difficult to sell and that perhaps *ad hoc* rules of engagement are better. He further suggested that a case-by-case approach offers material reasons to support *ad hoc* rules of engagement. More specifically, Kinsman expressed the need for the UN to create a case-by-case ability to employ strong Chapter VII mandates to make peace in conflict zones, and argued that Canada should be at the vanguard of this movement. While the UN used to be divided along East-West lines, the new divisions, he explained, are between the haves and have-nots, the democratic and non-democratic states, and those worried about sovereignty and those who feel this sovereignty should be broken in cases where humanitarian intervention appears necessary. Kinsman noted that in Rwanda the international community failed to see the aggressor, failed to authorize resistance, and ultimately failed to protect citizens at risk. In his opinion, there has been a paradigm shift from the security of states to human security that sometimes necessitates force by the international community. Building on previous points, Webb argued that perhaps the best option for addressing peace-keeping is to have a balance between a case-by-case approach of building precedents and having guidelines in place from which to work.

On the question of the protection of civilians, Gantz recognized the need for a strong mandate to use force in order to offer security for civilians, but suggested that we need to be careful that this does not derail the larger mission. To clarify his point, he used the example of Darfur where both the Government of Sudan and the rebel groups are attacking civilians. If UN forces abide by the principles of consent and impartiality, both the Government and rebel groups become partners in peace. If, on the other hand, UN forces are forced into combat with members from either group in order to protect members of the civilian population, they run the risk of driving a partner in peace out of the peace process.

Overall, participants stressed the need to ensure that UN forces receive mandates appropriate for each mission, including a credible deterrent capability when necessary. At the same time, the UN must study the effects of supplying a strong mandate to use force on the wider goals of the mission. When defining rules of engagement, the UN must strike a balance between an *ad hoc* approach specific to eachmission, and a general framework allowing for consistent and timely deployments.

Gandhian Alternatives

The context is the 'Global Peace' in the modern world and the text is Gandhian philosophy for its attainment. The broad hypothesis is: "World peace can only be realized through non-violence. There is no alternative to non-violence."

The modern world is facing a multi-dimensional crisis; a crisis that poses challenge to each and every aspect of our life. Among the outstanding aspects of this crisis are; over-militarization, nuclear proliferation and global reach of arms, overdevelopment and underdevelopment resulting in mal-development, a vast number of people suffering from poverty, hunger and marginalization. Added to these are environmental injustice, crisis in the field of energy, mounting insecurity and violence, terrorism, war and conflicts, drug trafficking, AIDs. Besides, there are corruption, communalism, unemployment, regionalism, problems of language, ethical and moral degradation in private and public life. All these together pose a grave challenge to the world. Peace is far away so long as these problems exist.

Among the various political ideologies, democratic governance appears to be best because it is this very system which provides maximum opportunities of public progress and development. People can themselves decide the mode of their welfare. But, is the democratic system of governance free from above problems? Therefore Gandhian Philosophy is very much contextual today on this accord.

Mahatma Gandhi treated his individual life in accordance with his ideas. He said, "my life is my message." Therefore, Gandhism is a mixture of Gandhi's concepts and practices. The basic groundship happens to be "Non-violence." He practiced and prescribed non-violence as a remedy against all social evils. It is the most ancient eternal values and culture of India. He said on this account, " I have nothing new to teach you Truth and non-violence are as old as hill." Non-violence and Truth are two sides of a same coin.

Total non-violence consists in not hurting some other one's intellect, speech or action per own thought, utterance or deeds and not to deprive some one of his life. In essence, abstinence in toto from violence is non-violence. In this context Gandhi clarified in an edition of *Young India.*

> "..... to hurt someone, to think of some evil unto some one or to snatch one's life under anger or selfishness, is violence. In contrast, purest non-violence is an epitome in having a tendency and presuming towards spiritual or physical benefit unto everyone without selfishness and with pure thought after cool and clear deliberations The ultimate yardstick of violence or non-violence is the spirit behind the action."[45]

From beginning unto now man has been ultimately treading path of non-violence. It came into existence along with man. It is co-terminus with life. In case, it has not with man from the very beginning, there might have been self-dom by man. Besides there has been gradual enhancement in development and proximity in spite of presence of various obstacles and hurdles.

Non-violence and Truth both are complementary to each other. It is more appropriate to say "Truth is God," rather than saying "God is Truth." He equated God with Absolute Truth as ultimate reality, Soul is the spark of this God of Truth. It is the moral, The spiritual force, the divine spirit which regulates our body and mind. It is the voice of God, the voice of Truth within us.

Both are two sides of the same coin. Both have same value. Difference consists in approach only. The derivation is that Truth stays with permanence and that Truth is permanent. Non-violence on account of being permanently present stays to be true. Non-violence is both a means and an end in itself.

It is not a weapon of the weak. It has no place for cowardice. It is an active force. Non-violence is impossible without bravery/courage/ fearlessness. Doing at any cost something that one ought to do. The courage of dying without killing. Having decided upon the rightness of a situation, Gandhi would not like one to be passive spectator to evil. This is the essence of Non-Alignments which is different from neutrality. When freedom is menaced or justice is threatened or where aggression takes place we can not and shall not be neutral.

Non-Violence has individual and social aspects too. It fosters co-operation and cooperative progress. Progress is difficult to achieve without co-operation. Co-operation is possible only when there is no violence. To him, regulation of mutual relations in society is through non-violence to considerable extent. He wished it to be developed on large scale. He called upon the people to continue to develop it in practice throughout life as the basis of life. It is all timely and all welfaristic. A non-violent is always ready to face punishment for the maximum benefit of all whereas a utilitarian is not.

Complete unity and integrity of body, mind and soul are in the individual human being. The body should be controlled by mind and the mind by the soul—a harmony among three. But this control is not to be achieved by despising or neglecting either the body or mind or soul.

Means are at least as important as, and often more important than, ends. It is, of course, desirable that ends should be good and reasonable. They give direction to life while the means adopted constitute life itself. The means confirm to the test of truth and no-violence, even mistakes, errors, and failures aid the growth of the individual. We can not get a rose by planting a noxious weed. There is an inviolable connection between the means and end as there is between the seed and tree. The relationship between the two is organic. There must be purity of means. Those who grow out of violence, they will end in violence. This is what makes Gandhi distinctly different from Kautilya, Machiavelli, Bentham, Karl Marx, Lenin, Trotsky and others.

Examination of Gandhi's view on State may, perhaps, lead to a better understanding of his vision of democracy. Sometimes a confusion is made between the acts of the individuals and those of the State, and it is expected that Gandhi's State is to be non-violent. But how is the State act non-violently, when it represents violence in a concentrated and organized form? Indeed a non-violent state is a contradiction in terms.

It could only be called a non-violent stateless society. This is the ideal for Gandhi. Non-existence of State as cherished by Gandhi is impossible instantly or in near future. At the level of imperfect nature of man, among the existing states, democratic governance appears to be best.

But the paradox is that being theoretically the best system of government, there is tidal waves of violence and other related problems sweeping across the world and seems to be having no respite.

Gandhi is certainly a staunch supporter of democracy. He believed that state is best which governs least and this is his second best ideal. He held the view that there are certain things which cannot be done without political powers, even though there are numerous other things which do not at all depend upon political power. While in ideal society, there is no room for the military and police, yet in the actual state there is provision for it according to the moral level of its citizens. Democracy should be intermingled with non-violence in even manner and governmental interference is minimum. The present democratic systems can overcome the problems most importantly "violence and terrorism" only when non-violence is accorded supreme status in practice as well as in principle and at social as well as individual plane. Only such a democracy can be successful in its real goal. The existing democratic deficit can be overcome by incorporating "Gandhism in democracy." Violence is not sacred, pure or welfaristic from any point of view. Whatever is gained on the basis of it is impure and temporary. Democracy and violence can never be mutual. The basis of democracy is non-violence in toto. In it, people will grow accustomed spontaneously to observe their social obligations without the operation of the State The more the individuals have imbibed the spirit of non-violence, the less the necessity of state. This is the implication of Gandhi's concept of Swaraj. The attempt to win Swaraj is Swaraj itself. It is a developing ideal and is "better than the best." Gandhi calls it "indefinable." Whatever political institutions Gandhi accepted, he did so as a transitional device, to be transcended by better ones. No institutional device is final. They must involve with the evolution of the individuals. The state should work in the direction of development of non-violence at individual, community, social and national levels. Gandhi believes that politics can remain pure and free of corruption only if and so far it is based on ethical principles—ethics which are common to all religions. He stands for the spiritualization and secularization of politics. Gandhi said: "If they are to be truly made democratic, they must be valiantly non-violent. In case of its absence, democracy shall be there for namesake only and it would be better for it clearly be supporter of dictatorship."[46] This democracy must be such that it should not warrant power of punishment. In it people will certainly be conscious of their duties. Peace requires peaceful method. There is no alternative to non-violence.

Gandhi's experiences in South Africa became his laboratory where he conducted experiments and formulated his worldview. The discovery was Satyagraha. The policy of apartheid by the white Minority Government made the lives of the millions of the coloured people deplorably miserable. Colonialism was legitimized. He valiantly fought against racialism, apartheid and colonialism. The historic challenge before him was whether the weak could fight the strong. Through his constant experimentation he realized that non-violence was the strongest weapon of the colonized masses and taught them to use it. He was able to induce courage and strength in the weakest of the weak and remorse in the hearts of the cruelest of the cruel and his belief that good exists in all humans, one only has to awaken that good within.

On his return from South Africa, Gandhi took the leadership of Indian National Congress and adopted a positive and dynamic stand on international affairs. He said: "My idea of nationalism is that my country may become free, that if need be the whole of the country may die so that human race may live. There is no room for race hatred here. Let that be our nationalism."[47]

He also said: "I do want to think in terms of the whole world. My patriotism includes the good of mankind in general. Therefore, my service of India includes the services of humanity isolated independence is not the goal of the world states. It is voluntary interdependence. The better mind of the world desires today not absolutely independent states warring one against another, but a federation of friendly, interdependent states. The consummation of that event may be far off. I want to make no grand claims for our country. But I see nothing grand or impossible about expressing our readiness for universal interdependence rather than independence. I desire the ability to be totally independent without asserting the independence."[48]

From the beginning of the Non-cooperation Movement, Mahatma Gandhi emphasized the view that free India would have friendly relations with other countries. In the issue of *Young India*, Gandhi wrote: "An India awakened and free has a message of peace and goodwill to a groaning world. Non-cooperation is designed to supply her with a platform from which she will preach the message."[49]

In November 1921 All India Congress Committee (AICC) passed a resolution, drafted by Gandhi, conveying to the neighbouring countries that the foreign policy of the then Government of India did not represent the Indian opinion and was formulated by the British Government for holding India in subjection rather than protect her border. Freedom movements in Asian countries drew inspiration, sympathy and support of the Congress.

Under his leadership the Congress did not want to limit its outlook to fighting against British imperialism in India and thought of combating imperialism elsewhere in the world. In 1927 at its Madras Session the Congress declared that India could not be a party to any imperialist war and in no case should India be made to join a war without the consent of its people. In September 1933 Mahamta Gandhi wrote to Pandit Nehru: "We must recognize that our nationalism must not be inconsistent with progressive internationalism I can, therefore, go to the whole length with you and say that we should range ourselves with the progressive forces of the world." Gandhi criticized the aggressive policies of Hitler and Mussolini. For India, it is one of complete opposition to Fascists; it is one of opposition to imperialism. All India Congress Committee reaffirmed its determination to oppose any attempt to involve India in the war without the consent of the Indian people.

After the outbreak of the Second World War, Gandhi supported the cause of Poland. Even despite British deception, Gandhi did not want to embarrass Britain when she was engaged in a life-and-death struggle with Nazi Germany.

It may be noted that after outbreak of the Second World War, Gandhi's insistence on the application of non-violence in the international arena led to his ideological break with the Congress organization. Realizing the futility of war in June 1940, Gandhi went to the extent of urging Congress to declare that free India would not use any armed force for its defence.

In September 1940 the AICC passed the resolution. The AICC stated its commitment to the policy and practice of non-violence, world disarmament and world peace. During the war, the nationalist movement in Afro-Asian Countries gained momentum. The end of the World War II was followed by the Cold War between the two Superpowers. In such a state of affairs, Mahatma Gandhi and Pandit Nehru propounded their doctrine of international amity and cooperation and resurgence of afro-Asian countries for the sake of liberation from colonial rule. India made it categorically clear to keep aloof from all alignments.

Asian Relations Conference was held from 23 March to 2 April 1947 in New Delhi. In this gathering both Gandhi and Nehru stressed the role of Asia and India in the promotion of world peace. Gandhi declared, "I would not like to see that dream realized in my life time." Gandhiji advocated "voluntary inter-dependence" of nations as against their "isolated independence", and "universal interdependence rather than independence." The AICC in its resolution 1942 under Gandhi subscribed to an idealistic approach to India's foreign policy. It expressed "the future" peace, security and ordered progress of the world demand a World Federation of free nations and on no other basis can the problems of the modern world be solved. Such a World Federation was advocated for the sake of the freedom of the member-nations, prevention of aggression and exploitation of one nation by another, protection of national minorities, advancement.

Gandhi advised the Asian delegates to convey to the whole world, particularly the west the message of Love and Truth. He said: "The west today is pining for wisdom. It is despairing of the multiplication of atom bombs, because the multiplication of atom bombs means utter destruction not merely of the west but of the whole world, as if the prophecy of the Bible is going to be fulfilled and there is to be, heaven forbid, a deluge. It is up to you to deliver the whole world, not merely Asia, from that sin. That is the precious heritage your teachers and my teachers have left us."[50]

Gandhi was in favour of building up of a "World Commonwealth." Gandhi in his speech on 15 September 1931 at the Round Table Conference (Second Session) said: "Time was when I prided myself on being, and being called, a British subject. I have ceased for many years to call myself a British subject, I would far rather be called a revel than a subject. But I have aspired—I still aspire to be citizen, not in the Empire, but in a Commonwealth; in a partnership if God wills it an indissoluble partnership but not a partnership superimposed upon one nation by another."[51]

Pandit Nehru formulated India's foreign policy adopting Gandhian prescription. It found its expression in the formulation of Panchasheel. Panchasheel are five principles of peaceful coexistence signed between India and China in April 1954. These are:

(i) Mutual respect for each other's territorial Integrity and sovereignty,
(ii) Mutual non-aggression,
(iii) Mutual non-interference in each other's internal affairs,
(iv) Equality and mutual benefit, and
(v) Peaceful coexistence.

The policy of Non-Alignment reflected the essence of Gandhian prescription and reiteration of 'Panchasheel'. It has grown into a gigantic movement having 118 countries as members and completing its 14th Summit. In fact, the Non-Aligned Movement (NAM) is rightly described "History's biggest peace movement", it stood for 'Atom for peace'. The only possible answer to the atom bomb is non-violence.

As Pandit Nehru used to say, "I would call ours the authentic Gandhian era and the policies and philosophy which seek to implement are the policy and philosophy taught to us by Gandhiji. There have been no break in the continuity of our thoughts before and after 1947."

Mahatma Gandhi is a practical idealist. He is not a pacifist. The impact of Gandhian message on Dr. Martin Luther King Jr. was so profound and electrifying that he practiced the message and techniques for the liberation of the black people in America. He also deserves to be considered as the first public figure who sensed and articulated the common concern in respect of environment. He taught "Earth is our mother and we are her children." A mother can satisfy the needs of her children but not greed, hence, limitation of human wants. He strongly pleaded for liberation and upliftment of women. If women are empowered and reign the world, it would be a peaceful world. Gandhi is a post-modernist in the sense that he has harmoniously balanced the multiple identities. There is no private Gandhi and public Gandhi. He has prescribed basic education for cultivating and nurturing moral life.

The ultimate ideal of 'Non-violence and Truth' is unrealized and unrealizable; its value consists in pointing out the direction, not in their realization. Striving after the ideal is the very essence of practicing Gandhi's philosophy. This consciousness should make one strive to overcome the imperfection. Mahatma Gandhi did not have a shadow of doubt that the world of tomorrow will be, must be, a society based on non-violence.

Mahatma Gandhi inspired the world with his faith in truth and justice for all Mankind. He was a great soul who loved even those who fought against his ideals to bring about peace with non-violence.

How could a meek and fragile person of small physical stature inspire millions to bring about a profound change in a way the mightiest had never achieved before? His achievements were nothing less than miracles — his creed was to bring peace to not only those who suffered injustice and sorrow but to espouse a new way of life for Mankind with peace and harmony. His life was a message — a message of peace over power, of finding ways to reconcile our differences, and of living in harmony with respect and love even for our enemy.

The force of power never wins against the power of love. At this hour of greatest unrest and turmoil in our world, the greatest force to be reckoned with lies within our hearts—a force of love and tolerance for all. Throughout his life, Mahatma Gandhi fought against the power of force during the heyday of British reign over the world. He transformed the minds of millions, including my father, to fight against injustice with peaceful means and non-violence. His message was as transparent to his enemy as it was to his followers. He believed that, if we fight for the cause of humanity and greater justice, it should include even those who do not conform to our cause. History attests to his power as he proved that we can bring about world peace by seeking and pursuing truth for the benefit of Mankind. We can resolve the greatest of our differences if we dare to have a constructive conversation with our enemy.

A war always inflicts pain and sorrow on everyone. History has witnessed countless examples of dictators, including Hitler, Mussolini, and Stalin to name but a few, who inflicted sorrow and destruction on our world. A world of peace can be achieved if we learn the power of non-violence, as shown by the life of Mahatma Gandhi.

Mahatma Gandhi has proven that we can achieve the noble causes of liberty, justice and democracy for Mankind without killing anyone, without making a child an orphan, and without making anyone homeless with the damage caused by war.

We live for our values and passion but at the core of our existence lies our innate desire to live a peaceful life. The greatest noble cause is to display our desire to bring about peace in this world by our own sacrifice and not that of those who oppose our views. The strength of cowardice is in using power to cause death and destruction for others. The strength of courage is in self-sacrifice for the benefit of all.

Mahatma Gandhi sacrificed his own lucrative law practice in Durban, South Africa to lead a simple life and to share the pain of the powerless and destitute. He won over the hearts of millions without ever reigning power over anyone — simply with the power of altruism. We too can bring peace to our world by showing our willingness to sacrifice our self-centered desires. Our utmost cause in life should be to win the hearts of others by showing our willingness to serve causes greater than ourselves.

History can attest to the fact that most human conflicts have been as a result of a stubborn approach by our leaders. Our history would turn out for the better if our leaders could just learn that most disputes can be resolved by showing a willingness to understand the issues of our opponents and by using diplomacy and compassion.

No matter where we live, what religion we practice or what culture we cultivate, at the heart of everything, we are all humans. We all have the same ambitions and aspirations to raise our family and to live life to its fullest. Our cultural, religious and political differences should not provide the backbone to invoke conflicts that can only bring sorrow and destruction to our world.

A great leader always leads with an exemplary life that echoes his ideals. Mahatma Gandhi sacrificed his thriving law practice and adopted a simple life to live among the millions who lived in poverty during his freedom struggle. Today, we see modern leaders cajoling the masses with promises that they never intend to keep – let alone practicing what they preach in their own lives. One cannot bring world peace to all unless a leader demonstrates peaceful acts of kindness daily. Mahatma Gandhi believed that we are all children of God. We should not discriminate amongst ourselves based on faith, caste, creed or any other differences.

An outstanding example of Mahatma Gandhi's leadership was his famous Salt March, which brought about a profound change. On March 2nd 1930, as a protest at tax on salt, Gandhi wrote a remarkable letter to Lord Irwin, the Viceroy of India. He wrote, "*Dear Friend, I cannot intentionally hurt anything that lives, much less fellow human-beings, even though they may do the greatest wrong to me and mine. Whilst, therefore, I hold the British rule to be a curse, I do not intend to harm to a single Englishman or to any legitimate interest he may have in India...*" With these words, he inspired millions to fight for this righteous cause and eventually forced the British to leave India without inflicting harm to any Englishman. Such were the quintessential qualities of justice and peace that made Mahatma Gandhi the man who changed our world for the better with his ideals of faith, love and tolerance.

Mahatma Gandhi taught us that we can bring harmony to our world by becoming champions of love and peace for all. The task is daunting, but he has shown that a fragile, meekly man of small physical stature can achieve feats of incredible magnitude with a staunch belief to practice peace through non-violence.

There has been no greater advocate of one humanity in One World, and no stronger opponent of violence and war than Gandhi, for, his faith in non-violence was absolute and he believed that peaceful means alone could lead to peaceful ends. Once Gandhi said: "My goal is friendship with the world and I can combine the greatest love with the greatest opposition to wrong...Through the realisation of freedom of India, I hope to realize and carry on the mission of the brotherhood of man."

The concept of One World is fascinating indeed. Behind every attempt at permanent world peace and even in the background of world organisations, snob as the League of Nations and the United Nations Organisation, there lurks the hope that one day there will be One World. Whatever the shape of that One World, we all hope that war as an instrument of solving conflicts of interests shall have no longer any place in human affairs. Instead, there will be peaceful ways of resolving conflicts through friendliness and mutual help and cooperation towards common ends. One World and World Peace are practically synonymous. Neither of them can exist without the other. The strong desire and the frequent attempts for both are rooted in the hunger of the human heart for peace and happiness.

How heartening it is to imagine that when there is One World, all the natural and human resources, all the sciences and technology which are today being marshalled and arrayed for destructive purposes will be used for the elimination of poverty, ill-health and ignorance. They shall be used for promoting goodwill and for creating better conditions of life for the whole of humanity. Though this rosy picture is today the privilege only of the poets and the dream of idealists, there is no doubt that this is the cherished hope of every one who strives for peace. It has been the living faith of persons like *Gandhi*. He once wrote: "*Not to believe in the possibility of permanent peace is to disbelieve in the godliness of human nature.*"

Both World Peace and One World are inherent in Gandhi's philosophy and the Gandhian way of life. He believed in Truth and for him *Truth was God*. Man may deny the existence of God. Very many have an agnostic attitude. But none dare deny Truth, though people may have different conceptions about particular truth. Truth is a matter of experience. To deny Truth would be to deny cue's own existence. But what was far more important in the case of Gandhi was his declaration that "There is no way to find Truth except the way of non-violence: "Non-violence was not merely an ethical principle nor a temporary policy. His non-violence was a positive principle, the principle of love which springs from the inner experience of the identity of interest with those whom we love.

He once declared, "All life is one"; for him life meant not only human-beings, but all sentient creatures. He said, "Non-violence is not a mechanical thing. You do not become non-violent by merely saying I shall not use force." It must be felt in the heart... When there is that feeling it will express itself through some action." That action, for Gandhi, was ceaseless service of mankind. His constructive approach to life, his whole constructive programme of action for the betterment of human life at all levels, arose out of him intense love, his deep sense of identity with all life and with the whole of humanity. "My constructive programme is rooted in non-violence", he said.

For Gandhi, man was the measure of all things. The basic purpose of human life was to reach higher levels of consciousness; man was *mind and consciousness* more than body and the senses. Therefore, Gandhi emphasised the spiritual progress of man. He carried on a relentless quest of Truth, of the Truth of life, of the law and discipline necessary for elevating the human soul. He came to the conclusion that love was the law of the human species and not violence which seemed to reign supreme in the animal kingdom. He saw that truthfulness and non-violent adherence to it through thick and thin strengthened the human soul. Purification of the mind by purging selfishness and strengthening of it by selfless service was a positive step in developing soul-power. It was this kind of developed soul-force which he hurled against all evil and injustice which he came across.

Gandhi realised that if the embodied human spirit was to progress, muffled as it was by selfish desire, man must be free, full of dignity, and earnest about his own advance. Socially, all men and women, irrespective of caste, creed, or sex must be equal and be given equal opportunities. Thus he conceived a world in which all would be equal and all would uphold the dignity of each and help achieve spiritual progress. Seemingly, his earlier life and youthful energy were devoted to the cause of equal rights for Indian residents in South Africa. After coming to India, he engaged himself mainly in the struggle for Indian independence.

But never for a moment was the cause of the whole of humanity or of world peace and harmony out of his mind. In fact, *Tolstoy*, in one of his letters to Gandhi while he was fighting for the rights of Indians in Transvaal, wrote that what Gandhi was doing in Transvaal was of world significance. He referred to the purity of the means which Gandhi adopted to fight evil which in South Africa had taken the form of racial injustice. Gandhi too was well aware of his mission in life, that of 'peace on earth and goodwill unto men.' He wrote in *Young India*, "My ambition is much higher than independence. Through the deliverance of India, I seek to deliver the so-called weaker races of the earth from the crushing heels of Western exploitation... India's coming into her own will mean every nation doing likewise."[52] This has proved prophetic.

He wrote more expressly on this subject many a time. He said, "Through the realisation of freedom of India, I hope to realize and carry on the mission of the brotherhood of man." There has been no greater advocate of one humanity in One World, and no stronger opponent of violence and war than Gandhi, for, his faith in non-violence was absolute and he believed that peaceful means alone could lead to peaceful ends.

Because Gandhi believed in non-violence, he did not look for just subduing violence. He wanted to conquer violence as far as he was concerned. His leadership turned any protest movement into a "peace with justice" movement showing equal concern for justice to the opponents.

In his concept, peace was something positive which included Sarvodaya (welfare of all, not just the greatest good of the greatest number), trusteeship, brotherhood of mankind. The means, Gandhi clearly stated to achieve any goal must be as noble as the end. The end cannot justify the means. And the man must always be non-violent.

Non-violence, according to Gandhi, offer meant conscious suffering—"it means the pitting one's whole soul against the will of the tyrant. Working under this law of our being it is possible for a single individual to defy the whole might of an unjust empire."[53]

Gandhi did not apologize for suffering that might come as one sticks steadfastly to peace and non-violence, because "Love ever suffers, never revenges itself. Love never claims, it gives.[54] This is a unique characteristic which Gandhian approach to peace added to the practice of non-violence. It underscored that non-violence is not a substitute for inability to use violent means. "Self-suffering is the essence of non-violence and is the chosen substitute for violence to others."[55] For that, fear must be conquered when one acts. One must act when conscience stirs, and the consequence thereof must be accepted.

In an age of utmost violence (1861-1948), stood Gandhi the fearless and did demonstrate to the world that "there can be a strength far greater than that of armaments and that a struggle can be fought, and indeed should be fought without bitterness and hatred."[56]

In India's peace movement in Gandhi's time, he was the wave and the people of India were on the crest of that wave during 1939-45 and later, until 1948. Gandhi said and wrote much about the use of non-violence in preventing external aggression besides using it for the liberation of the oppressed in his won country. The common statement from many scientists, leaders and even generals that can be heard today, in the eighties of the 20th century, is the conviction that Gandhi a technique alone can redeem today's world threatened by the nuclear weapons. As Gandhi said: "unfortunately for us, we are strangers to the non-violence of the brave on a mass scale — I hold that non-violence is not merely a personal virtue. It is also social virtue to be cultivated like the other virtues. Surely, society is largely regulated by the expression of non-violence in its mutual dealings. What I ask for is an extension of it on a larger national and international scale."[57]

The secret of the unbelievable success of the peace move-meat in India, perhaps lay in the fact that human-beings under Gandhi's leadership meant a great deal to him. He stopped at the threshold of the huts of the thousands of dispossessed, himself dressed like one of their own. He spoke in their language. Here was the living truth—not just quotations from books. Tagore sums up, "At Gandhi's call India blossomed forth to new greatness, just as once before, in earlier when Buddha proclaimed the truth of fellow feeling and compassion for all living creatures."[58]

In an age of conflict within a given nation and in the international world, the individual must rediscover the "right mind." Gandhiji worked for the rediscovery of the "right mind" which would reach out to unity, love and peace, emphasizing the fact that there are certain indisputable, eternal values ethical, universal, spiritual and philosophical—which man has needed everywhere, which he acquired in the past because these are values without which he cannot, live but which are now in large measure lost, to him because of his carelessness and insensitivity toward them. He is now, in a way, unequipped to face life in a fully human manner, and is inevitably heading toward destroying his own self. Bharata Kumarappa was underscoring this aspect of Gandhian thought, when he said: "While pacifism hopes to get rid of war chiefly by refusing to fight and by carrying on propaganda against war, Gandhiji goes much deeper and sees that war cannot be avoided so long as the seeds of it remain in man's breast and grow and develop in his social, political and economic life. Gandhiji's cure is, therefore, very radical and far reaching. It demands nothing less than rooting out violence from oneself and from one's environment."[59]

The "right mind" that Gandhiji envisioned is universal, inclusive, non-exclusive. It is not, a mind of intolerance, of accusation, of division. Rather, it is a mind of unity, understanding, and infinite love that works for harmony, for peace. It is a spirit that would heal division. Gandhiji knew, the reality of hatred and intolerance because he had experienced them in his own life in South Africa, in British dominated India, in the caste-ridden society of India of his time. Indeed, he succumbed to the reality of intolerance and hatred when his life was taken on January 30, 1948. No peace could be built on exclusivism, absolutism and hardness of hearts which must result if individuals made no efforts to rediscover the "right mind."

Peace cannot be built on vague slogans or pious programmes. There can be no peace on earth without, the kind of interchange that restores man's mind to the facts that all life is one emanating from one universal self—"What though we have many bodies? We have but one Soul. The ways of the sun are many through refraction. But they have the same source."[60] All forms of necessity can contribute to man's freedom—material and economic need, spiritual need. The greatest of man's spiritual needs is the need to be released from evil and untruth that are in himself and in Society. One important question in today's world is the crisis of sanity that surrounds us all in a fragmented society, in fragmented national structures, in schizoid military and business complexes. "We are at war with ourselves, and therefore at war with one another."[61]

Non-violent means were vital to Gandhi's peace-building efforts for several reasons. First, non-violence means not harming others either in thought or deed. Second, Gandhi viewed non-violence as also having more dynamic and positive state, i.e. love and compassion to the opponent. This love served as the means to get to the ends of truth. Gandhi held absolute Truth as God, and there was no difference between the absolute Truth and God in his belief. Since all human-beings belonged to God, each and every person had the property of Truth.

Further he held that the Truth known to human-beings was never absolute but relative and shared among them. Therefore, a seeker of Truth (God) had to adhere to the path of non-violence because unless he used the method of non-violence, he would not be ·able to be receptive to the notions of Truth held by others. For Gandhi, excluding the use of violence was the best, because humans are not capable of knowing the absolute truth and therefore not competent to punish.

Gandhi designed Satyagraha movement as an initiative in search of Truth by purifying self and the opponents. He did not inflict any violence rather than his soul force against the British during the Satyagraha movement. It later pricked the conscience of the British to rectify their errors. In short, Satyagraha became a Joint search for Truth by the conflicting parties. Gandhi held the view that change of mind would definitely bring peace in the World. Through the Satyagraha movement he was trying to change the mind of his opponents. Success of Indian independence proved the potential of Satyagraha as a positive peace-building strategy on a larger societal level. This later imparted an ideological capital to the civil disobedience and non-violent movements across the World. Non-violent movements led by Martin Luther King, Jr., Nelson Mandela, Vaclav Havel, and Aung San Suu Kyi come under this category.

The Satyagraha movement virtually was an effective peace-building tool through non-violent means. Gandhi developed Satyagraha as a moral equivalent to war and violent conflict. Both war and conflict are waging to conquer the opponents. They suppress human virtues of kindness, love, compassion and forgiveness as well as encourage the feelings of hatred, anger and hostility towards opponents. War and violent conflict do not respect the opponent. On the contrary, the Satyagrahi while resisting injustice, shows respect for his/her opponents and appeals him/her to be responsive. A Satyagrahi avoids the possibility of physical confrontation with the other side. A Satyagrahi leads opponents to the negotiation table by gaining their trust. Gandhi himself attended round table conferences with the British while he was leading the Satyagraha movement against the latter. Peace talks are always possible even during the course of Satyagraha. Since a Satyagrahi does not have any hatred to the opponent, an agreement can be easily achieved. Moreover, the very nature of Satyagraha itself is helpful to transform the milieu of the conflict affected area into a place of sustainable peace, because, more than concluding a peace agreement between the parties to conflict, Satyagraha is a reconciling process between the parties to conflict. Satyagraha is a struggle for winning the heart of the opponent, as well as a positive approach to vanish evil force, hatred and fault lines of the self and opponent. Such things are not possible between the parties to conflict during the course of violent confrontation.

Gandhi developed a participatory peace-building strategy by involving all parties to conflict. For instance, the partition of India witnessed communal riots, genocide and mass level displacement of people in various parts of the country. One of the crucial affected areas of violence was Noakhali in Bengal. Death toll figured double digits in a short span of time during the riots at Noakhali. Gandhi visited every nook and corner of Noakhali village and painstakingly did his best to cool down the tension there. He engaged in dialogue with various religious community leaders to end misunderstanding and hostility among them. In order to put an immediate end to violence, Gandhi started fasting on 2 September 1947. By the next day the parties involved in conflicts came to Gandhi and laid down their arms. Mixed processions for communal harmony took place in various parts of Noakhali. A delegation of prominent political and religious leaders visited and assured Gandhi that there would no communal violence in future.[62] Gandhi organized prayer meetings to facilitate inter-faith understanding and communal unity. By involving all parties to the conflict in peace process and cultivating inter-faith understanding. Gandhi could successfully build peace in the violent-torn areas.

Satyagraha in South Africa was to resolve ethnic question so that the interest of Indians were protected in the continent. Satyagraha movements at Champaran, Kheda and Bardoli had economic connotation, in the sense that these movements were trying to transform the economic reasons of conflicts and violence. More than protesting against the exploitative policies of the British, Gandhi set forth Swadeshi movement as a constructive and destructive strategy to heal root-cause of economic conflict. Swadeshi was constructive in the sense that, it was intended to create employment opportunities by adhering to indigenous and eco-friendly technology.

Swadeshi is not harmful to environment, less prone to resource depletion and in favour of creating more job opportunities and empowering the workforce in the country. Swadeshi is destructive in the sense that, it conduces to end dependency to the exploiter by boycotting their goods. Advocates of World System Theory and Dependency Theory hold the same notion on economic integration and growing inequalities. They argue that, dependency of the Periphery (people who have being exploited or the developing countries) over the Core (the exploiter or the developed countries) is the root cause behind the growing economic disparities between the developed and developing countries. The best way to avoid disparity, in their view, is to end economic relations with the core.[63]

Market integration at a global scale is transforming the World into a basket and waste box of the mass produced goods. It conduces to increase the number of unemployment, the pace of resource depletion and environmental degradation. The global economic meltdown that we have witnessed recently also raises doubts about the positive outcomes of neo-liberal programmes. At the same time, the World witnesses the massive protest against the neo-liberal programmes and rolling back of welfare measures by the governments. Today, protest is not confined to the four-borders of nation-states but it spills over to the international level. Global civil society movements such as World Social Forum gather together on the sidelines of WTO Ministerial Conferences and organize protests against the neo-liberal programmes. It is visible that the ongoing neo-liberal programmes and its development agenda marginalise the poor. Mass level displacement of people is also seen in the light of neo-liberal programmes. On such occasion, people are evacuated from their native land for two reasons: first, for the accomplishments of big development projects, second, as the result of environmental degradation. For instance, raising sea level compels people to leave their native places.[64] Mass level migration, their accommodation to new areas, growing number of unemployment followed by crimes lead to violent conflict. In the light of these developments, we have to understand Swadeshi movement as an effective method for peace-building.

Gandhi held a view that a struggle for noble cause need not use violence. Through employing non-violent means a Satyagrahi could attain his goal. Though the intention was noble, use of violence might create an opposite result. Gandhi set forth his concept of the purity of ends and means from this notion. He never resorted to violence in his Satyagraha against the British. There were numerous instances in the freedom struggle, for provocation to die use of violent force. The massacre in Jallianwala Bagh aggravated extremists to intensify armed conflict against the British. While blaming the British in committing such an extreme evil action against the Indians, Gandhi admonished his fellow people not to unleash counter-attack. Gandhi held that the socio-economic and political institutions established or restructured by the British had the genesis of violent conflicts. If the people in India were able to delink them from the British institutions by setting up their own institutions, then it would mark the end of British Raj. He wrote in the *Hind Swaraj* that, British rule sustained in India with the co-operation of Indians. Non-cooperation movement indeed was an initiative for Home Rule for Indians in all sense. Throughout the movement, Gandhi appealed people to set-up alternative mechanisms for dispute settlements, administration and education; because, the British courts, police force, law-making, educational and administrative systems were designed to exploit the people in India and lock them in perpetual dependence. If Indians follow the same system even after getting freedom, Gandhi commented in *Hind Swaraj* that it would be nothing more than a British rule in the absence of the British. As far as Gandhi was concerned, the non-cooperation movement was a preparatory step towards Swaraj by restructuring the Indian society. Gandhi felt it was necessary to sustain peace in the post-independent India. It is pertinent to discuss the relevance of the Gandhian concept of Square of Swaraj in ensuring sustainable peace in society. Like its equal measurement of each side of a square, each individual had to attain economic, social, educational, and political freedom in an equal volume. These four elements are major determinants of peace and conflict. Even though a human being was educated, lack of economic resources might throw him/her to perpetual dependency or conflict with other human-beings. The outcome would not be different in case of unequal distribution of other elements also. Having enlightened through attaining the Square of Swaraj, each and every person in society would be a responsible citizen to his fellow beings and society. Such a society would be a replicable model for sustainable peace and there was no room for violent conflict there. The alternative institutions were, therefore, entrusted the mission of building peace in the Indian society. The ashrams set-up by Gandhi were the effective institutions to attain that supreme goal.

Gandhi's relentless adherence to non-violence was clear with the call of non-cooperation movement and the strategies adopted in the Salt Satyagraha. It was the Chauri Chaura incident that compelled Gandhi to halt the non-cooperation movement.[65] Even though the number of people killed in the Chauri Chaura massacre was much lower than that was made by the British, Gandhi was not ready to justify that action. The Chauri Chaura incident convinced Gandhi about the need to train the Satyagrahis. In the following years, Gandhi was training each Ashramite to be able to acquire the qualities of true a Satyagraha. The Ashram life imparted the calibre to Satyagrahis to adhere to non-violence even though they had to submit their life before the brutal British force. In short, Gandhi was empowering Ashramites to be the agents for building peace. It is pertinent to state that Gandhi started Salt Satyagraha with a few selected Ashramites who had successfully proved their adherence to non-violence in any difficult situations. The success of Salt Satyagraha largely depended on its strict adherence to non-violence.

Gandhi was much concerned about the socio-economic and political elements as determinants of conflict. Through the Constructive Programmes, Gandhi set forth 18 points to tackle the root causes of violence in society. These Programmes were practical methods to build peace by facilitating inter-religious harmony, upliftment of poor and weaker sections, creating employment without harming environment, etc. In his famous book *Hind Swaraj,* Gandhi criticized the impact of Modern Civilization on humanity. For Gandhi, peace was not separated from justice, development and environment. The World had to take decades to conceive the message of the life and thought of Gandhi. Many of the social scientists today seriously study the influence of development programmes and environmental issues on conflict. For instance, Bjorn Hettne, whose study is focused on the relationship between models of development and peace, is largely indebted to Gandhi in shaping his perspective. Ame Naess, who coined the term deep ecology, also expressed the influence of Gandhi on his work. In the similar way Johan Galtung, a well known peace researcher, acknowledged Gandhi in the evolution of his concept of structural and cultural violence. His advocacy of ideas such as self-reliance and models of development focused on basic needs also have a strong Gandhian influence.

Violent conflict in a large-scale normally erupts, when a section of society deliberately marginalised by the dominant community or by the Government. Disparities created by the unequal distribution of resources are major determinants of conflict. The classical example in this regard is the Sri Lankan experience. Developments since the Official Language Act (1956), framing of new Constitution and the Land Colonization policy fuelled ethnic problem in Sri Lanka. The strategy to pacify Tamils' protest was the coercive apparatus of the Sri Lankan state, eventually transformed this island nation into the hot burner in South Asia. Equal distribution of resources and accommodation of all sections in society is vital to build peace in such condition. For this end, Gandhi set forth the ideals of Sarvodaya, Decentralization of Power, and wealth, Trusteeship, Social Harmony and communal unity, Economic equality, Sarva Dharma Samabhava, etc. His approach for peace-building had been always holistic as human being is a synthesis of a large variety of components, which cannot be divided into watertight compartments of social, religious and political life.[66]

The Gandhian way to understand conflicts and his methods for building peace has largely influenced the contemporary peace initiatives across the World. Observing Gandhi Jayanti as International Day of Non-violence is a real tribute to its mentor. Gandhi could successfully set forth an alternative framework to look into conflict. For him, violent conflict was not mere a state of the distortion of law and order. Rather, he considered it as the reflection of the socio-economic and political factors that existed in that area. Therefore, he appealed for a constructive approach to resolve conflicts rather than resort to physical force for the same purpose. He further held that such constructive approach should address the socio-economic and political factors that led to the outbreak of violent conflicts. In traditional approach peace was enforced above from a political authority. But Gandhi successfully proved that peace could be built from the bottom level by involving the parties to conflict in the peace initiatives.

Notes and References

1. http://www.un.org/brahimi_report.htm
2. Saltmarsh, Mathew, "A Bloated U.N. Bureaucracy Causes Bewilderment," *The New York Times*, January 5, 2011.
3. Schaeter, Brett, D., "A Progress Report on U.N. Reform," Heritage Foundation Backgrounder No. 1937, May 19, 2006.
4. http://www.un.org/budget.htm
5. Schaeter, Brett, D., "Who Leads the United Nations?" Heritage Foundation WebMemo No. 1054, December 4, 2007.
6. "Peace-keeping Procurement Audit Found Mismanagement, Risk of Financial Loss, Security Council Told in Briefing by Chief of Staff," UN Security Council, February 22, 2006, http://www.un.org/News/Press/docs/2006/sc8645.doc.htm
7. "Report of the Office of Internal Oversight Services on the Activities of the Procurement Task Force for the 18-Month Period Ended 30 June 2007,: A/62/272, October 5, 2007 at http://www.eyeontheun.org/assets/attachments/documents/5522_report_OIOS_activities_procurement_task_force_30_june_2007.doc
8. Lynch Colum, "Audit of UN's Sudan Mission Finds Tens of Millions in Waste," *The Washington Post*, February 10, 2008, p. A16.
9. Charbonneau, Louis, "UN Probes Allegations of Corruption, Fraud," *Reuters*, January 10, 2008.
10. Holt, Kate and Sarah Hughes, "UN Staff Accused of Raping Children in Sudan,' *The Telegraph*, January 4, 2007.
11. U.N. Contact and Discipline Unit, "About CDU: Conduct and Discipline Teams," at http://cdu.unbl.org/About CDU/ConductandDiscipline Teams.aspx, January 28, 2011.
12. Csaky, Corinna, "No One to Turn to: The Under-Reporting of Child Sexual Exploitation and Abuse by Aid Workers and Peace-keepers." Save the Children, 2008 at http://news.bbc.co.uk/2/shared/bsp/hi/pdfs/27_05_08_savechildren.pdf
13. U.N. Contact and Discipline Unit, "Statistics Allegations for All Categories of Personnel per Year (Sexual Exploitation and Abuse)," at http://cdu.unbl.org/Statistics/AllegationsbyCategoryofPersonnelSexualExploitationandAbuse, January 28, 2011.
14. http://www.un.org/general_assembly/resolutions.htm
15. http://www.un.org/security_council/resolution_1540.htm
16. http://www.un.org/security_council.htm
17. http://www.un.org/unodc.htm
18. http://www.un.org/agencies.htm
19. http://www.un.org/conventions_on_terrorism.htm
20. http://www.globalsecurity.org/miltiary/world/iraq/un_hq_baghdad_bombing.htm
21. http://www.globalsecurity.org/security/madrid.htm

22. http://www.news.bbc.co.uk/2/hi/in_depth/uk/2005/london_explosion/default.stm
23. http://articles.cnn.com/bali.blast/2005.10.01.htm
24. Einstein, Albert, Ideas & Opinions (New York: Bonaza Books), 1954, p. 7
25. http://www.un.org/en/peace-keeping/missions/unmil
26. http://www.politybooks.com/up2/casestudy/un_and_the_gulf_war_casestudy
27. http://www.un.org/en/peace-keeping/missions/unscom
28. http://www.un.org/refugee.htm
29. Earth Summit, Rio, 1992
30. Vikram Sood, "Clash of Ideas and Convictions", *The Hindustan Times*, Kolkata, 28 March 2005, p. 5.
31. Stephen Badsey and Paul Latawaski (eds.), Britain, NATO and the Lessons of the Balkan Conflict, 1991-99 (London: Frank Cass), 2004, pp. 39-63.
32. UN Department of Public Information, Executive Summary, A More Secure World: Our Shared Responsibility, 2004, p. 1.
33. *Ibid.*, p. 81.
34. Norman Lowe, Mastering Modern World History (New Delhi, Macmillan), 1997, p. 47.
35. Basic Facts about the United Nations (New York, UN Department of Public Information, 2004), p. 19.
36. *Ibid.*, p. 67.
37. Anjali V. Patil, The UN Veto in World Affairs, 1946-90 (Mansell, UNIFO, 1992), pp. 264-68.
38. *Ibid.*, pp. 268-71.
39. *Ibid*, pp. 272-74.
40. Schaeter, Brett, D., "Who Leads the United Nations Heritage Foundation Webmen, No. 1054, *op. cit.*
41. *The Economist*, "Call the Blue Helmets: Can the UN Cope with Increasing Demands for its Soldiers?", 4th January 2007.
42. Guehenno, Jean-Marie, Key Challenges in Today's UN Peace-keeping Operations (transcript) (Washington D. C.: Council on Foreign Relations), 2006.
43. The full deployment of the operation in Lebanon and the Mission in Darfur could raise the budget to S7 billion.
44. Challenges of Peace Operations: Into the 21st Century Project, Draft – UN Capstone Doctrine (Sweden: The Challenges Project/Folke Bernadotte Academy), 2006.
45. *Young India*, 23.02.1922, p. 113.
46. *Young India*, 09.03.1922, p. 150.
47. *Ibid.*, 18.06.1925, p. 210.
48. Desai, Mahadev, Gandhiji in Indian Village (Madras: S. Ganesan), 1927, p. 42.
49. *Young India*, 1 June, 1921, p. 120.
50. *Young India*, 31.12.1931, p. 421.
51. *Ibid.*, p. 465.
52. *Young India*, January 12, 1928, p. 360.
53. *Ibid.*, August 11, 1920, pp. 5-10.
54. *Ibid.*, July 9, 1928, 284.
55. Gandhi, M.K., Non-violence in Peace of War (Ahmedabad: Navajivan Publishing Press), n.d., p. 49.

56. By Jawaharlal Nehru, addressed to J. Bondurant in original ms, "Gandhian Satyagraha and Political Raj—An Interpretation", quoted in preface of Conquest of Violence by J. Bondurant, p. xvii.
57. Gandhi, M.K., Towards Lasting Peace (Ahmedabad: Navajivan Publishing House), 1999, p. 41.
58. Rabindranath Tagore: *The Call of Truth*, p. 1.
59. Kumarappa, B., Editor's note in Gandhi: For Pacifists (Ahmedabad: Navajivan Publishers), 949.
60. Bose, N.K., Selections from Gandhi (Ahmedabad: Navajivan Publishing House), 1957, p. 25.
61. Coomarswamy: Am I My Brother's Keeper (New York: W.W. Norton & Company Inc.), 1947, p. 67.
62. Guha, Ramachandra, India After Gandhi: The History of World's Largest Democracy (London: Macmillan), 2007, p. 17.
63. Shaw, Timonthy M., "The Semiperiphery in Africa and Latin America: Sub-imperialism and Semi-industrialism", *The Review of Lack Political Economy*, Vol. 19, No. 4, p. 350.
64. Doornkamp, J.C., "Coastal Flooding, Global Warming and Environmental Management", *Journal of Environmental Management*, Vol. 52, No. 2, p. 238.
65. Nishant, Batsha, "Gandhi and Chauri Chaura", *Intersections*, Vol. 10, No. 3, p. 28.
66. Chhaya Rai, "Gandhi's Role and Relevance in Conflict Resolution", International Seminar on Conflict Resolution, 15-17 February, 2003, available at http://igandhi.blogspot.com/2006_10_06_archive.html.

Conclusion

More than six decades ago the United Nations was born amidst great hopes and expectations of a generation, which had seen the most devastating war in human history. It was devised to "to save succeeding generations from the courage of war" and "ensure fundamental human right, dignity and worth of the human person" and equal rights for all nations, large and small. It was to usher in an area of peace and prosperity and provide machinery for the pacific settle temporarily as it now seems the capacity of the national politicians to turn each international problem into an international disaster. The framers of the charter were, however, shrewd politicians who circumscribed UN ideals in a structural design based on big-power politics. The big—USA, UK, France, Russia and China must share responsibility for the sandy foundation on which they built this impressive edifice. They made the Security Council the sole instrument of peace-keeping and made themselves its permanent members with the power of veto.

They had pledged to maintain unity in peace as they had done in war but it did not survive even a year. The General Assembly, where members are equal, was given few powers. It is now a truly universal representative body. Its membership has risen from 51 in 1945 to more than three times in 2004. It could play a significant role in achieving the purposes and objectives of the United Nations and assist in the realization of peace, disarmament and development but it has got enmeshed in cold war politics. All efforts of Non-Aligned Nations to rescue it from super-power diplomacy thus make little headway. Apartheid, racism, neo-colonialism, Zionism survives because some great powers are not willing to carry out the resolutions of the General Assembly in letter or spirit.

The Charter enjoins promotion of a "social progress and better standards of life in larger freedom" and devotes a Chapter on "International Economic and Social Cooperation." The resolution passed by the General Assembly in 1982 on the New International Economic Order remains inoperative because of the intransigence of the affluent North. Powerful nations have tried to bend the machinery of the United Nations to their own selfish interest. And if they do not succeed in it, they resort to other methods to paralyse United Nations action. Namibia, Palestine, South Africa and many other similar cases have become intractable despite UN resolutions because these powers are not yet interested in their solution.

Outside the domain of politics, the UN and its agencies like FAO, WHO, ILO, UNESCO and UNICEF have an impressive record of achievements to their credit. Their area ranges from deep oceans to the space and celestial bodies; environment, communication, transfer of technology, trans-nationals, copyright and many similar activities which vitally affect the lives of people all over the globe. Thanks to modern technology and economic organization, the world has become inter-dependent and it is as well that international mechanisms for its regulation are available and are being used in the interest of humanity.

There are people who say that the United Nations have had a chequered history since 1945. They tend to forget that the last forty years have been one of the most momentous in the history of mankind. Revolutionary changes have taken place in science, technology, industry, economic organization. Mighty empires have crumbled before our eyes and the political map of the world has entirely changed. New nations have burst upon the international scene, claiming their right to be heard, the super-power confrontation has led to the cold war and proxy wars are being arranged and fought. In such a tense and fast changing world, it is itself a 'wonder that the United Nations still exists and continues to provide a forum for the nations to talk and not resort to gun'.

The poor nations have been exploited by colonialism for too long and are now exposed to the exploitation of neo-colonialism. They now ask for their fair share for economic development. They insist on disarmament because there can be no peace without it and peace is a pre-condition for development. It is now for the rich nations of the North to show vision and help development processes of countries in the South.

There is an equal need for the powerful nations to positively respond to the call of United Nations for disarmament for their own sake. The next war will finish them as well. Disarmament will release billions of dollars being wasted on perfecting weapons of mass-destruction which could then, be recycled for mass development.

United Nations with all its weakness still remains the only glimmering hope for humanity. It was set-up for peace and conflict-resolution. It promised fair deal to the deprived peoples. It was expected to bring about a better world and free humanity of colonialism and racism. During these years of its existence, its achievements have by no means been inconsiderable but its failures have been dramatic in areas which vitally affect future peace. It however still remains the only world forum where glowering nations can still meet and talk and not cut each other's throat and in the process destroy humanity.

Yet in these years of its existence the UNO, more specifically the Security Council, has often failed to act efficiently. Drawn into the maelstrom of veto, it has been hypnotized into dull helplessness.

Thinkers in international law are divided between two extremes of opinion. One view is that the Security Council is inert. Unless veto is either abolished or circumvented it cannot function effectively. The other view is that the obligation of self-preservation supersedes all other obligations and therefore, if the Security Council fails to function effectively, other means must be used even if the UNO dies in the process.

There is no doubt in it that United Nations—like all human institutions, is far from perfect but its value to the governments and peoples of the world and the unique promise it holds for the future cannot be underestimated. To maintain peace and to build a better world-order are immensely ambitious tasks. Those who undertake them must be determined and dedicated. The UN was founded on the belief that human race is capable, by an effort of will, of improving its lot and fulfilling in a more satisfactory way its promises and genius. Unless one believes this, the work of UN has little or no meaning.

The world of 2004 is radically different from the world of 1945, and the organisation has also radically changed. With more than three times its original membership, it is active in a variety of new fields scarcely dreamt of by its founders. Admittedly its plan and objectives are sometimes more impressive than its practical performance but, that is not unusual for human institutions especially one reflecting a new world in the process of active evolution. As Dag Hammarskjold, the former UN Secretary General once remarked, "The UN reflects both aspirations and a falling short of aspirations, but the constant struggle to close the gap between aspirations and performances now, as always, makes the difference between civilization and chaos." The struggle to close the gap widened and diversified since Hammarskjold's time, but the task and rationale remain the same.

Underlying all the activities of the UN is the problem of balancing and reconciling national sovereignty and interests with international responsibilities and the long-term interests of the world community as a whole. Dr. Kurt Waldheim, Ex-UN Secretary General has discerned three main threats in the work of this organisation within this basic task.

The first of these is the maintenance of international peace and security, without which all other tasks would soon become meaningless. The shortcomings of the UN are nowhere clearer than in its efforts to maintain the peace and nowhere are the reasons for them more manifest.

The UN can only achieve what its sovereign members wish it, or are willing to allow it, to achieve. With their assent and co-operation it can do much to forestall conflict, to put an end to violence. On several occasions, the Security Council has provided the means and the pretext to retreat from a dangerous confrontation. But conflicting economic and political considerations crystallized around conflicting ideologies. Cold war saw cold-shouldering of erstwhile allies. The picture has even more blurred in the post-cold war era. Divided on their issues, the permanent members have remained united on one—they continue to use the right to veto. It is a prerequisite of victory, more than often the device was used and is being used by the permanent members to cover acts of aggression, committed by them or their protégées. It was used in Spanish, Albanian, Greek, Czech and several other cases. These developments created a virtual paralysis of the collective security system.

The second main threat in the work of the United Nations is its function as an agent of peaceful change. From its inception the organisation has played a crucial role in the great movement of decolonization. Without UN this process would have been far more bloody and disruptive, far more difficult for the former colonial powers, as well as for the newly independent nations, and, certainly far more protracted. On the political side the original mechanism of peace keeping has played an important role in maintaining quiet during periods of transition and, on occasion, in filling the vacuum created by the withdrawal of old colonial powers.

Meanwhile the political scene continues to charge. Almost all the emerging nations have joined the UNO. Simple majority in General Assembly has passed out of the hands of the permanent members and their associates. More than once the power to veto was used either to keep out of the UN certain nations or to make package deals on a *quid-pro-quo* basis. The spectre of challenge to the powers of permanent members has raised its head.

The world is now facing an even more fascinating change in the management of change; the effort to adjust the relationships of developed, and developing nations in the new world, North-South dialogue has replaced the East-West problem as dominating themes of UN activity. It has also to tackle the global problems that have arisen from technological change and the growing inter-dependence of nations, and in the current efforts to establish a new international economic order. The readjustment of the economic relationships of all nations and the groups of nations in the world is an immense challenge. I do not believe that it could be undertaken anywhere else, than in the United Nations, with its nearly universal membership.

The third threat in the world of United Nations is the attempt to plan in advance, on a co-operative global level, for the future. As in all political organisations, UN is also occupied with the problems and the concerns of the present but the pressing and immediate duties should not be allowed to exclude a vision of the future. Rather it is essential to have such a vision constantly in mind if UN is to maintain any equilibrium or sense of direction in the turbulent and confining world in which we live. Each task undertaken, each response to a particular situation should not only fulfil its immediate purpose, but should, if possible, carry a step further towards a more reliable, equitable and just world order. The UN must evolve a better system for managing the affairs of the world through the give and take of debate, facing dangers together, learning to co-operate and through the development of an overwhelmingly strong sense of common interest. There are already a number of areas—peace, disarmament, the environment and energy for example—where the world must co-operate or face the greatest risks of chaos and decline, if not destruction. No task of United Nations is more important than the steady expansion of the areas of common interest among nations and provisions of acceptable means by which governments will voluntarily limit their sovereign rights in the long-term common interests.

In the post-cold war era today some new and crucial developments have taken place in the international politics. After the collapse of Soviet Union, United States have assumed the self-styled role of the World Policeman. The outcomes were at least predictable in the cold war period. But how the things will shape today, nobody knows. The Super Cop (U.S.) wants all the rights but is not willing to fulfil its obligations. The unfortunate pressure tactics of the U.S. and its protégées have hit the United Nations hard. The world remained a silent spectator of how the UN was hijacked and used during the Iraq-Kuwait war by the US and its allies. Such happenings were out of question during cold war period.

Again, the budget of UN has multiplied. But some of the major powers are not fulfilling their obligations. The US and UK are applying pressure and have walked out of UNESCO and UNCTAD. From 1980s onward they are trying to blackmail UN by threatening substantial reduction in their contribution. The UN owes millions of dollars in arrears, instead of paying it US is continuously threatening further heavy cuts unless the UN toes it, line of thinking. The attitude of US on the issue of the re-election of Dr. Boutros-Boutros Ghali, which was all, set to block Ghali's appointment and is even prepared to use the veto in the Security Council. While almost whole of the world was supporting his re-election. The USA, for long, has been opposing the format of UN where even the poorest and weakest nations have the equal number of votes as the strongest ones in the General Assembly. There have been talks over changing the format to have a two or three-tier system under which the powerful nations will hold most of the aces. Luckily this has not found favour with most of the UN members—including US allies. The UN was created to rise above such vested and limited interests. The threat to UN is from the great powers and not from the developing world.

This does not, however, mean that the Organisation cannot be strengthened or made more responsive to changing international needs. The growing involvement of this body in international economic issues is itself a reflection of momentous change that has taken place in the consciousness of the world community, in seeking to strengthen the Organisation, increasing efforts have been directed at securing mechanism that would make its tasks in the political and economic fields more effective. Today, the UN represents a vast bureaucracy. Each year the documentation in the General Assembly increases by leaps and bounds and has reached almost unmanageable proportions. It has been said that if the documentation of the UN is placed end to end it would straddle the globe around the Equator one and a half times over!! Resolutions adopted tend to be repetitive, and in some respects even incomprehensible except to the jaded professional. Preventive diplomacy is rarely practised and the confidentiality of consultations rarely observed. All too often, the stress is on public diplomacy through a repetition of established positions and pre-occupation with polemical, sometimes sterile, debates. Isn't it time for us to take a fresh look at not so much the institutional set-up of the United Nations but the style of our multilateral diplomacy today? There is a strong case that can be made for bringing the UN Secretariat within more manageable limits and seeking a tighter control over the functioning. The volume of documentation can be rationalised and curtailed provided individual delegations practise greater self-discipline both in the tasks assigned to the Secretariat and even in the length and drafting of resolutions placed before the General Assembly. To some extent this will also involve giving a greater area of discretion to the Secretary General. In the Security

Council there is scope for greater informal consultation and the development of a collegial spirit as well as the preservation of confidentiality in negotiations and discussions particularly where disputes or conflicts simmer below the surface and call for preventive diplomacy. Several suggestions have already been made to the Secretary General regarding standby forces, fact finding missions, etc. all of which deserve careful scrutiny. The essential requirement, however, is a greater preparedness on the part of the individual states to deal with issues in substantive terms at the United Nations rather than utilize this Organization as a mere sounding board for the propagation of their own set positions.

We cannot afford a retreat from multilateralism. The attitude of some states in recent times has been clearly indicative of such a trend. The disregard of the role and contribution of the UN and the suspicion of multilateral approaches where they do not directly and measurably promote the immediate interests of states had become evident in the attitudes and statements of important leaders in the world. Ratings have been assigned to individual countries on the basis of their record of votes and where they coincide with the perceived interests of some countries. Clearly these actions are intended to change the attitudes of the smaller and more vulnerable states to suit the predispositions of powerful ones. Can we afford a situation where the UN is left to fend for itself without presence of even one of the permanent members of the Security Council? The answer to these dilemmas has to be found in introspection on the part of the smaller and medium states and a greater sense of responsibility on the part of the more powerful ones.

Under the scenario there is an urgent need for the democratization of working of UN especially of Security Council. More permanent members should be added to it. By its own merit the largest democracy in the world, India deserves a permanent place in it. If national sovereignty, national interest and world peace are still the primary motivations of governments, UN is still available as a unique mechanism for this purpose.

GANDHIAN PERSPECTIVE

The supreme tragedy of our time is that we are trying to fit old, habitual solutions to a problem of epic proportions, the like of which man had not faced since he first took to a gregarious life on earth. We have lost, or perhaps never achieved, the capacity for epic thinking. We seem unable to accustom ourselves to the bizarre challenges that face us. The revolutions in science have given us the power of quick and disastrous invention but not the power of dauntless thinking. Our machines increasingly resemble men and imitate their subtle ways—but alas, how near we ourselves are to the condition of a robot, tottering along set grooves of thought and action, afraid to venture out into new and unknown ways, and pathetically suspicious of anything that might upset our accustomed ways and valuations. History is full of examples of such persons who tried to use their original thinking (for the betterment of all) becomes the soothsayers of the time and society. Of course, Mohandas Karamchand Gandhi was one among those who left his imprint on each and every class and mass of the human society for his ideas and their pursuits.

Gandhi fervently hoped for "a world federation of free and independent state." His concept of World Government transcended the traditional thinking, "the pattern of conventional international organisations could not satisfy the condition, for bringing genuine peace. He held that peace could not be established through mere conferences." He was not optimistic about the League of Nations and the U.N. Since they lacked the spirit of non-violence and failed to serve as vehicles of peace in the absence of a force to enforce their decisions.

Gandhi believed that the doctrine of non-violence held 'good' in the matter of relationship between states and within states also. This conviction impelled him to unequivocally recommend total disarmament. He was optimistic enough to advocate unilateral disarmament. "If even one great nation agrees unconditionally to perform the supreme act of renunciation many of us would see in our life-time visible peace established on earth. His call for unilateral disarmament betrayed his idealism, while the realist Gandhi appreciated that with the establishment of a democratic world federation disarmament would be practicable in all countries.

We are living in fantastic times—let us face this fact—and only an act or acts of fantastic courage and daring can deflect us from the path of certain disaster. This is no time for lukewarm attitudes or a gradualist, empirical approach. Nor for leisurely feeling our way, one little step at a time. This is the time for a bold, reckless leap, even a leap into the unknown. This is the time for a revolution in our thinking; for an agonizing reappraisal of our basic concepts of peace and human brotherhood. This, in short, is the time for a new realism in international relations.

This realism is most in evidence in Gandhi's hitherto unheeded call for unilateral disarmament. In our current phantasmagoria of the megaton bomb, the Polaris missile and mega-death, the only step that makes many coherent sense is for each nation, big or small, nuclear or non-nuclear, to take the lone decision of scrapping its own armoury all on its own without waiting for others to make a start. A negotiated disarmament is a political fiction. We shall await till dooms-day and how near dooms-day is, if we hope that agreement will be reached on all the minutiae that have kept disarmament negotiations going endlessly for the best part of two generations.

Even a cursory study of the history of disarmament will reveal that every so-called disarmament proposal is a veiled move in the game of international hide-and-seek, an essential factor in the strategy of power. It would be the height of imagination that the ever-new disarmament proposals that often catch the headlines have been motivated by a genuine desire for peace. On the contrary, every one of them can be shown to be a sinister move to gain a strategic advantage over one's opponent. This being the case, it will be unpardonable folly to expect anything to come out of the present merry-go-round of disarmament talks. Multilateral disarmament is a contradiction in terms. Someone must lay down arms first. Disarmament will never get a start except unilaterally. It must begin with some one nation, big or small. There is no other way. And this is the only way to break the ice. Here lies the practical and functional approach of Gandhi. He believes very aptly what is the Goal and what is the realistic term to achieve it rather than to enter into the intellectual jugglery.

Disarmament is not a new problem. In the sense of a penal destruction or reduction of the armament of a defeated country, disarmament is perhaps as old as war itself. In the sense of a reduction and limitation of national armament by general international agreement—what now mostly goes by the vogue-word of Arms Control—it was first discussed in The Hague Conference of 1899 and is thus virtually a product of the twentieth century. In the more comprehensive sense of an abolition of all armament—the only sense that can have any meaning to us in the thermonuclear age disarmament came into the arena of international discussion only after the Great War and the founding of the League of Nations, and even then only in a lackadaisical, half-hearted way. It took Hitler, the World War and Hiroshima for nations to think of disarmament seriously.

But the disarmament issue that faces us today is of an entirely different complexion and magnitude. We have no longer the luxury of time at our disposal to weigh the pros and cons and to go into the political niceties of the available traditional approaches to disarmament. Failure to achieve a quick solution can have only one relentless result: disaster. The extraordinary urgency of our present situation is not one that could be argued about. Men who ought to know have told us in unmistakable terms what the consequences of our folly could be. Herman Kahn has categorically asserted that "one must eventually introduce a major change in the situation or expect to get into a war anyway." For, as he rightly argues, "it is most unlikely that the world can live with an uncontrolled arms race lasting for several decades." A recent report of the National Planning Association of America has this alarming conclusion: "Not only does the danger of war remain a possibility, but the probability totalled over time increases, becoming a certainty if sufficient time elapses without succeeding in finding alternatives."

What major change have we introduced into the present situation of bewilderment and drift? What alternatives have we found? None whatsoever. We are victims of our own clichés. We are a race of bewildered, impotent men trying to fit disarmament, in its nuclear overtones, into our frozen, pre-nuclear stereotypes and being rather dismayed at the result. For though it looks like an old problem, disarmament as we know it today is, in fact, a stark new problem and it can only be solved in a stark new way. Our crisis is thus essentially psychological; a crisis of failure to break away from habits of thought which have no relevance to the problems of our time. To ascribe it to the rapid advances in weapons technology or the misuse of scientific knowledge is to misunderstand the true implications of our problem.

The general objection against unilateral disarmament is that it is quixotic, unrealistic, and utopian. Maybe it is all these. But are we not living in a very quixotic age? What is realistic about the nightmare world that is unravelled, say, in the yearly proceedings of the Pugwash Conference? And why should any man be apologetic about being utopian when the only alternative to a Utopia is the extinction of man?

But, fortunately, unilateral disarmament is neither quixotic nor utopian. In fact, if there are any lessons to be learnt from the woeful history of disarmament, the unilateral approach is the only probable and realistic way to achieve disarmament in our time. For consider the conflict between national security and disarmament. Every government gives first precedence to its own security and will in no case agree to any change in the existing armament balance unless it is satisfied that such change will not endanger its security. Add to this the axiom that one nation's security is another's insecurity, and we at once see what a hopeless mess we would land ourselves in if we believed in the myth of negotiated, multilateral disarmament. The security demands of even two nations are hard to reconcile, not to speak of the security needs, whether real or imagined, of the five score nations which sit around the United Nations table.

No, we cannot have national security and international disarmament at one and the same time. One will eventually have to be sacrificed to the other and which shall that one be? The answer is clear. Unless we are either insane or inhuman, or both, there is no doubt we shall all opt for the saving of humanity and human civilization rather than the illusory pursuit of our own, private, national safety.

In the final analysis, the case for unilateral disarmament stands or falls by how we answer two simple questions:

(a) Is there any known method, other than a unilateral act of courage and sacrifice, by which the besetting fear of one nation for another can be rooted out? And

(b) Even if unilateral disarmament were to fail, will the failure be as catastrophic to humanity as the continuance of the arms race which is implicit in the never-ending process of negotiated disarmament?

We can improve upon many things that Gandhi taught us—his religion and philosophy, even his economics and politics—but we cannot improve upon this central theme—song of his whole life, this concept of daring, unilateral action Satyagraha which finds its culmination in his call for unilateral disarmament. Many of us swear by Satyagraha and some of its more fashionable modern variants, little realizing that unilateral disarmament, the phrase we shun like the plague is nothing other than Satyagraha in its international dimension. We are universal in our condemnation of armaments but we are blind to the logical corollary of our condemnation; that if we are genuine in our belief that all arms are evil the honest thing for us to do is to strip ourselves of the evil at once, regardless of whether others do likewise.

Gandhi believed that disarmament was possible only through "the matchless weapon of non-violence." And it was his hope that "India will ... prove herself worthy of being the first nation in the world to give lead to other nations for the delivery of earth from the burden of war. He wanted the great powers lead the rest by disarming themselves: they should give up ambitions and exploitation and revise their mode of life. Thus according to Gandhi, disarmament cannot crystallise, unless the nations of the world cease to exploit one another. Exploitation must go ... that is the essential pre-condition for the establishment of a world free from blood-spilling and destruction.

Gandhi advocated Satyagraha as the sure and potent weapon of combating Inter-state aggression/s. Satyagraha is universally acceptable. Non-violence, according to him, excludes war and ushers in peace. Gandhi's ideas about peace suggest that the solution he offered for effecting world peace transcended the frontiers of international diplomacy. The chief limitation of international diplomacy is that it is based upon recognition of the power-system. The Gandhian way claims to stand for non-violent and non-exploitative social order which alone can ensure just and enduring peace. It may be argued that the Gandhian declarations on peace bristle with some practical difficulties. But Gandhi would ask that if an individual could practice non-violence why whole nations could not do so. He believed that one must make a beginning and the rest would follow. The Gandhian concept of world peace should be viewed within the universal framework of his philosophy of ahimsa. A proper appreciation of his doctrine of ahimsa would facilitate comprehension of the logical application of that doctrine.

Sceptics consider Gandhian plea for disarmament Utopian. In fact, it is not so. Its success depends on the nature of human-beings. Gandhi has great faith in the godliness of human nature. Human nature is essentially peace-loving. Even when man fights violently, he does so out of a desire to live in peace. The way of world peace lies in cultivating the spirit of non-violence and peace in the hearts of men. As the individuals are built, so the nations are built. And as the nations are built, so the world is built. Gandhi says: "there is not one law for the atom and another for the universe."

The life-style of Mahatma Gandhi is quite enough to prove that he was able to reduce himself virtually to "the level of the poorest of the poor." As for an ordinary human being, it would be too much to expect what would have been possible for a great man like Gandhi. We must however, have to learn a lesson from Gandhi's style of living, for as an effective means to achieve Socialism there is no alternative to simple living and noble thinking and this is more so for a developing country like ours.

It goes without saying that a world of peace and prosperity can never be achieved by the use of force. It was Mahatma Gandhi who invented a new weapon that alone could save mankind from a war of total annihilation. Gandhi and the atom bomb were in fact "the two originalities of our time and one would defeat the other before it ended."

Jayaprakash Narayan has very aptly said about Mahatma Gandhi that "He was specifically a prophet of the atomic age in which the engines of violence which man has invented for the first time in history threaten to destroy the whole of mankind. Gandhi not only preached non-violence as a Philosophy and an ideal but practised it on a very colossal scale and did it, if not with complete success, with very great success. As long as there is violence which threatens the very future of the human race, the relevance of Gandhi would continue. Gandhi will remain relevant till the change of total annihilation of the human race is removed."

Peace is a relationship between people and between people. Peace begins with a harmony between individuals. Gandhi lived and worked for the establishment of such relationship among individuals and groups. This is a unique contribution to peace in the modern context. Gandhi's style of life and the techniques he propounded deserved to be studied and applied so that the world may be and remain a safe place to live.

Gautama Buddha preached the message of Ahimsa and Compassion. Asoka, one of the greatest emperors had followed the Buddha's teachings in giving up wars and to tread the path of peace though only after being vexed with the carnage which the Kalinga war had brought about. Jesus Christ whom the Christians worship as the Saviour and Lord is described as the prince of peace. He has lived and preached the message of love, forgiveness and peace. In contemporary times Gandhi has relentlessly voiced the efficacy of non-violence as against violence. Therefore, it will not be an exaggeration to deduce that Gandhi truly carries the legacy of The Buddha and Jesus Christ as far as the ways and means to achieve a peaceful world is concern

H.G. Wells in one of his last writings had predicted that man is unfit to live in this world as he knows what is good but does not know how to do 'good'. Man wants peace but does not know how to achieve it. Hence he being incapable of doing what he knows to be the right would destroy himself. The future would show whether H.G. Wells is right or wrong. However, a survey of the contemporary world is ominous. Since has perfected the weapons of war and nations have manufactured and stored them in enough numbers to such an extent that an outbreak of war would not only destroy the living and the products of civilisation, but also would make the surface and atmosphere of the earth uninhabitable for hundreds of years if not for ever. Leaders of nations and man in general are aware of this fact and they dread another war. War is an international nightmare. Man would like to avoid or escape wars if possible. Although the million Dollar question is that how to achieve the peaceful world and avoid war, everybody just want to know those means.

It is known that Gandhi is opposed to violence and wars. Gandhi is an advocate of non-violence and peace. Though non-violence is "as old as the hills", Gandhi's exposition, clarification and forceful advocacy of non-violence is unique. The Gandhian way of peace springs from the basic concept of non-violence.

War is said to be a way of ending wars. As a matter of fact, the Second World War was fought by the allies with a view to end all wars. Gandhi is of the firm opinion that war can never end wars. And here Gandhi follows the legacy of Buddha who has said in Dhammapada that "Hatred cannot be eliminated by hatred. Hatred can be eliminated by friendliness alone and nothing else." So we can deduce that the violence cannot be finished by violence. It can only be removed by non-violence. Violence breeds only violence but can never end violence. War is destructive whereas peace is constructive. They are two opposite processes. Further violence, being destructive, is a negative process, whereas peace, being constructive is a positive process. Peace is a positive force of cementing people. War which is a destroying and divisive force can never contribute to the establishment of peace. Hence, the search for peace should be in the way of non-violence alone.

Napoleon had sent this appeal for peace at the height of his glory and success. He saw the futility of war to end hostilities and appealed for peace. Napoleon subscribed to the Gandhian view when he said, "There are only two powers in the world, and those powers are the spirit and the sword. In the long-run, the Sword will always be conquered by the Spirit."

Gandhi writes, "There will be international league only when all the nations, big or small, composing it would fully independent." An International league based on non-violence leads to the establishment of world peace. Such a league implies and it is possible only when it consists of independent nations. As long as any nation is not independent, there would not be world peace. It is necessary that all nations should be independent to be equal partners in the League of Nations in order to have peace.

Gandhi in adopting non-violent means to get Swaraj for India aimed at achieving international peace by doing so. Gandhi said, suggest to the friends of peace for the world, that the Congress in 1920 took a tremendous step towards peace when it declared that it would attain her own, namely Swaraj by non-violent and truthful means. And I am positive that if we unflinchingly adhere to these means in the prosecution of our goal, we shall have made the largest contribution to the world peace.

According to Gandhi there are certain conditions which are conducive for international peace. They are:

(i) All nations should be independent;
(ii) The equality of all nations should be recognised; and
(iii) Disarmament should be accepted by the nations both in principle and their practice.

Wars are the result of lust for power. In some way or other some nations want to establish supremacy over at least some of the other nations. They derive to create and perpetuate inequalities so as to maintain their superiority. Self-aggrandisement gives rise to inequality and inequality in return affords scope for self-aggrandisement. It is a vicious circle which can be broken only by an international law by which all nations are treated as equal. The spirit of self-aggrandisement is killed to some extent, though it requires to be more nullified by education, by the proclamation of equality of all nations by an international law. Such a law in the course of time would become a convention and *de-facto* accomplishment. Equality of nations would go a long way to establish peace in this world.

In the present day world all nations have become independent. Political independence of nations which looked like a mirage and dream has become an actuality. There is still ideological imperialism and also economic domination of one nation over others. Such dependencies also would disappear in course of time. Independence is bound to pave the way for the complete independence and equality of nations.

Is peace the real answer to solve conflicts and violence? The problem arises as to how man can realise peace. According to Toynbee, "The source of peace and war is the interior of life of each individual human spirit." We should not forget that man is the source the centre and purpose of all life. Peace begins in our own hearts. The universality of spirit lies not in knowing much, but in loving extensively. Peace is really the reflection of heaven upon earth. In the Hebrew language, the word "Shalom" means peace with justice. It means inner security and external excess. He will be a man of Peace who has in him the combination of both. Arnold Toynbee espousing the cause of peace observed: "When the pursuit of peace is whole-hearted, it covers every aspect of human affairs.

Today, we live in a violent world. But man fundamentally desires peace; it is recognised by all that no positive civilisation, no just social order or stable peace can flow from violence, war and repression. A true social order must be based, upon persuasion, conviction, and a positive will to co-operation and fellowship among them. These are the only bonds which can hold society together with any permanence and to any real advantage. But because of the differences in world—outlook, thinkers, statesmen and politicians differ as to the effective way of establishing just and lasting peace. Gandhi made singular contribution to the cause of world peace and his views therefore demand close scrutiny.

Gandhi has often been described as an apostle of peace. Certainly he was. He strove and died for peace. Gandhi advocated "peace—but not at any price", for his philosophy was a philosophy of commitment—it was based upon the concept of moral responsibility, as well not that of "peace at any price" which underlay his ethic of intention.

Gandhi's philosophy of peace is to be sharply distinguished from the conservative plea for "Peace at any cost" which is in essence a plea for the maintenance of *status quo*. Peace, Gandhi advocated is integrally related to justice. As Gandhi wrote: "Peace must be just". Peace is not mere cessation of hostilities. Gandhi did not share the diplomatic view of peace. Peace for him connoted a positive state of affairs, the pre-condition being freedom from exploitation. What he advocated was non-violent and just peace which alone in his opinion could ensure lasting peace. Gandhi's ideas about peace suggest that the solution he offered for effecting world peace transcended the frontiers of international diplomacy. The chief limitation of international diplomacy is that it is based upon recognition of the power-system.

The Gandhian way claims to stand for non-violent and non-exploitative social order which alone can ensure just and enduring peace. Non-violence, according to Gandhi, excludes war and ushers in peace.

One may argue that the Gandhian declarations on peace contain some practical difficulties for them to be implemented in the present day world. But Gandhi would not countenance such a "practical" difficulty. He would counterpoise by saying: "If an individual can practise non-violence, why not whole groups of individuals and whole nations? He believed that one must make a beginning and the rest would follow. The Gandhian concept of world peace should be viewed as in integral part of his philosophy of life and one should try to appreciate his attitude within the general framework of philosophy of ahimsa. Good means alone can lead us to ever lasting peace. If peace is established by violence it will be of no use. Now days, quite often we read in the newspapers that police, in some places army, marching into an agitating place and peace being established. But that peace is undoubtedly that of the grave yard." But when the non-violent person wins, he wins the heart of the foe.

Gandhi's concept of peace on earth and goodwill among mankind lead to the development of Sarvodaya Social order which India's distinctive contribution to world of thought. The application of moral truth to the facts of social life is the essence of Gandhian and Valluvar's way of life. Their dynamic Philosophy can make possible the advent of a radically transformed society. They serve as a system of norms and moral values that can guide our conduct and action in society and state. The truth of a few will count; the untruth of millions will vanish even like chaff before a whiff of wind. The message of Gandhi and Tiruvalluvar will remain permanent in the hearts of one and all. Tiruvalluvar really transcends Jesus who only wants to forgive them. In advising to forget the trespasses Tiruvalluvar is only in the positive degree. Mahatma Gandhi and Tiruvalluvar have become the symbols of peace, truth, non-violence and dharma. If an individual can practise non-violence why not whole groups of individuals and again why not whole nations? Gandhi believed that one must make a beginning and the rest would follow. Gandhian concept of world peace should be viewed as an integral part of his philosophy of life and one should learn to appreciate his attitude within the general framework of his philosophy of ahimsa.

Human nature is essentially peace loving. Even when man fights making use of violence he does so, to be able to live in peace. The way of world peace lies in cultivating the spirit of non-violence and peace in the hearts of men.

The end of the Cold War and the simultaneous beginning of the process of globalization brought about changes both in the structural and operational dynamics of the world. These developments have both positive and negative implications for the world in general and for developing countries in particular.

Positively, the era of competitive influence building in a bipolar ideologically divided world is over. Even the unipolar hegemony of the only surviving superpower could not be established in the form predicated in terms of the 'end of ideology' or a 'triumph of capitalism.' Gradually, a 'non-polar' world order is becoming the reality in which multiple groups of states are enjoying predominance in a limited area, leaving space for the workings of other states as well. Besides, with the collapse of centripetal forces in terms of global institutional structures, some regional economic realignment of force can be witnessed. In this process, new regional economic forums are enhancing their strength not to compete with other such groupings felt to strengthen the position of their member-states. Regional free trade is consolidating and enhancing interaction between the member-states. Simultaneously, inter-group cooperation in terms of trade, FDI and joint ventures is being witnessed. However, negative competition among these groups is not being witnessed to a greater degree.

Despite the twin positive fallouts, the negative dimensions of such developments are also strong and visible. Politically, the end of bipolarity has on the one hand created an unstable condition in the world system and on the other an edge towards the hegemony of only a hyper power. The latter has not only created the problem of an interventionist role on the part of the USA but also motivated it for war against non-compliant states in the name of 'preventive attacks.' Besides, the very structure of international organization has crumbled due to the enhanced role of the only available military alliance system "NATO" under the leadership of the USA. Simultaneously, developing countries are being marginalized by the weakening of their forums like NAM. Hence, the global system is passing through a phase in which the developing countries are finding it difficult to protect their autonomy or find space in the global system.

Economically, the beginning of the process of liberalization, privatization and globalization (LPG) led to the crumbling of the tariff barriers of developing economies against developed states on the one hand but on the other also consolidated the capitalist mode of production and distribution. This globalization of the economy is not contributing to the growth of an equalitarian and just global order. Rather, the demand of the developing countries for the establishment of a new international economic order (NIEO) has been pushed further back. Besides, it has led to the consolidation of the Bretton Woods model with the establishment of the third institutional arrangement in the form of the World Trade Organization (WTO) despite the presence of other twin institutions in the form of the IMF and World Bank. The 'South' opening up its markets to the countries of the 'North' in the form of large scale trade, FDI or Joint Ventures has failed to ameliorate the economic conditions of the recipient states, instead creating glaring disparities in society. The rising gap between rich and poor in these states has resulted in social tensions, political upheavals and other such problems.

The Humanitarian concern, in the form of arms race, terrorism and environmental degradation has reached an alarming stage with the onset of a new world scenario in the wake of the end of the Cold War.

- Though the problem of the arms race has existed for numerous decades, today the issue has potential consequences of serious magnitude given the increasing threat of the use of WMDs. Besides, the approval of extending the NPT for an indefinite period has not been able to stop the process of nuclear proliferation. The CTBT has not only been rejected by some of the countries outside the purview of the NPT but has also not been approved by the Senate of the USA, the very country that proposed the Treaty. Rather, the addition of three new members (South Korea, India and Pakistan) to the nuclear club of P-5 has made the club of P-8. Whatever be the justification and counter-arguments for and against such an increase, one thing is certain. The arms race has acquired serious proportions. Though efforts are being made to control the new entrants by engaging them through coercive diplomacy, uncertainty still looms large about the dangerous consequences of such developments.
- Terrorism, especially its increasing high-tech nature is another serious problem faced by the present day international system. This has acquired all the more significance since the event of 9/11 in the States, because it has exposed the susceptibility of even the mightiest power of the world. Consequently, many parts of the world have been demolished to finish Al Qaeda. But the latter cannot be wiped out despite the use of heavy bombing in Afghanistan and similar such actions taken in other parts of the world. Terrorism is, in fact, post-modern warfare illusive, amorphous, personal, emotive, enduring and scattered. Hence, it has moved beyond the competence of

the state. International organizations have not only failed to curb the menace of terrorism but have also failed to define the very term. Hence, in this situation of gross anarchy and chaos, nations are finding it difficult to find their way and are groping in the dark.

- Finally, the swift pace of industrial development has created a severe problem of ecological degradation. Despite the organization of four international UN conferences at Stockholm (1972), Nairobi (1982), Rio de Janeiro (1992) and Johannesburg (2002) the problem of environmental degradation has not been solved. Rather, the last conference seems to have been influenced by the wave of globalization. The role of corrective measures was left solely to be handled by NGOs and MNCs, and states have been bereft of their accountability towards people at large. Some important protocols like Kyoto have not been implemented so far. Nor have effective steps been taken to deal with the issue of global wanning. Even the pertinent policy directive to make efforts towards 'sustainable development' could not been operational. The greed of the advanced industrial nations has dominated the global agenda. They are pressing the lesser developed world to adhere to the norms and principles of preserving the environment while they themselves are busy destroying the same.

Solutions to the above problems can be found in the Gandhian ethos. Strategies based on the core values of Gandhism can resolve these issues, if these values are extended in the following manner:

Most of the political problems seem to be based on a lack of trust between the states. Consequently, there is urgency to restore faith among nation-states. Such conflict can be resolved through the use of non-violent techniques propagated by Gandhi. This can be achieved either through the evolution of new institutional arrangements or by altering the behaviour of the concerned states. In this context, the initiation of CBMs (confidence building measures) among the states involved can be a step in the right direction. This mechanism is likely to restore faith among the states by way of building goodwill in the concerned parties. It can be further strengthened with the use of Track-11 diplomacy in the form of people-to-people contacts. This process would not only resolve the immediate problem but is also likely to open new vistas for durable peace.

Economic disparities exist in the present world order either due to concentration of wealth or due to non-equalitarian distribution of the same. The demand for a just and equalitarian order raised by the poor countries is not addressed. Rather, this issue has been marginalized on the sidelines of the core global economic agenda. Even in the post-Cold War era, the process of globalization has created more problems for the developing states than it has ameliorated their conditions. This calls for the trusteeship system envisaged by Gandhi wherein the rich should contribute for the well-being of deprived sections of humanity. Under such a system, any kind of exploitation would be done away with and people treated at par whether they become rich or poor. It is the moral duty of the rich to take care of their deprived fellow brothers. This is also likely to meet the old demand for NIEO by the developing states and simultaneously strengthen global development with a human face.

Similarly, humanitarian problems involving the arms race, terrorism and environmental decay can be solved through the application of Gandhian values. The problem of the arms race is more a problem related to misperception than the growth of arms. This stems mainly from a lack of trust between states. Hence, the most important question is how to inculcate trust among neighbouring states. This can be achieved through a change in the states' behaviour and attitude. When one state exhibits this through its actions, the other will follow suit. Hence, it is the moral force of a fellow nation-state which can do away with prevailing tensions in regions. In this context, Gandhi always favoured unilateral disarmament by states irrespective of the policy followed by others.

The problem of terrorism is more a political and social issue, rather a war-like development. The roots of terrorism are attached to socio-psychological factors. Hence, the individual's behaviour is a pertinent factor. Consequently, any solution that does not call for changing the psychology of the terrorist is not going to be successful. This is where Gandhian values come in. Gandhism believes in the potential for a change in the heart of the man involved in such activities. Gandhi believed that without a transformation of the individual's soul, society cannot be reformed. Hence, reform in the behaviour of the individual is a must for durable peace and a complete resolution of the problem of terrorism.

Similarly, today's environmental problem is largely caused by the technological advanced states and their lust for more wealth by all means as they desire to accumulate all the wealth and resources of nature to strengthen their country's strength and economic position. This exploitative nature of the few states is causing problems for a large stratum of the world society. Gandhism believes in limiting one's demand and sharing the fruits of nature with humanity at large since nature has provided everything in abundance to meet the needs of everyone but not the greed of all. Therefore, the Gandhian percept allows the sustainable development to continue in order to meet the needs of humanity.

The parameters of defining peace vary from the traditional approach to Gandhian approach. In traditional approach, peace was defined just as the absence of violence and an acceptance of unbalanced power relationships, inequalities and lack of access to resources which may be associated with such a condition. In such condition, major concerns are early detection of conflict, prevention of conflict turning into violence, limiting the spread of violence if it does occur, or to avoid reoccurrence of violence. Early warning system and troop deployment are used in this mechanism. Even though the traditional approach acknowledges socio-economic 'and political reasons of conflict, the priority goes to prevent the outbreak of violence or contain its intensity rather than eliminating the root causes of conflict. Absence of violence does not indicate peace if its root causes are remaining unhealed. Violence may erupt at any time in this situation, if early warning mechanism or troops fail to fulfil their entrusted responsibility. Unfortunately, state's leaders have always been guided by this negative notion of peace. Physical force has been largely deployed to curb communal or ethnic violence at the state level to international level. For instance, the United Nations Organization was formed to prevent another World War and maintain peace across the globe. Major mechanism to maintain international peace is its peace-keeping forces.

Chapter six and seven of the UN Charter lay down the provision of deploying peace-keeping force to halt violence. Here peace-keeping is considered as a surveillance mechanism to monitor developments in the violent-torn area or limit the intensity of violence through light military intervention. The definition of peace-keeping in its traditional sense also reflects the requirement of military intervention to maintain peace.

Peacemaking process in the traditional approach is participated by the heads of the states or governments and the top brass in the military and bureaucracy (primary parties). For instance, war between two nation-states is normally ended with the conclusion of peace agreement. Even though the common people are the victims of war, they are treated only as the secondary parties to the conflict. They do not have any role in peace process other than accepting provisions laid down in the agreement.

A major flaw of this approach is its weakness to resolve protracted, intractable, and deep-rooted conflicts. For instance, India-Pakistan conflict is protracted, intractable, and deep-rooted in nature. India-Pakistan conflict is protracted because it has been continuing for sixty-four years. It is intractable in the sense that the conflict is an obstacle to make any positive change in relations between the two countries. Moreover, the conflict is primarily between the two governments but it is also deep-rooted in the thinking and attitudes of people in all walks of society across two sides. In such cases deployment of multi-track approach is inevitable to have an amicable solution to the conflict. Multi-track approach opens up various channels of interaction between the parties to conflict. This approach accommodates the initiatives of people from all walks of life; therefore, it involves common people, academic community, etc. in the peace process.

The end of the Cold-War necessitated a new approach to analyse conflict and peace initiatives. The disintegration of Soviet Union challenged the top-down approach in determining the state of affairs in a political society. Rather it proved that the mandate of citizens is also important in shaping the programmes and policies of state. Dismemberment of Soviet Union also confirmed that heavy military build-up will not be the sole element in strengthening the national integration process and state security. Emergence of civil society groups into international peace initiatives is a new development in the Post-Cold War period. The 1993 Oslo Accords in the West Asia is a prime example. The civil society initiatives, especially a series of problem-solving workshops and dialogues between Israeli and Palestinian academics could bring Oslo Accords into reality. Such developments are enhancing the scope of peace-building and involving more actors in the process.

Neo-liberal policies, rolling back of welfare measures and growing number unemployment, environmental issues followed by health issues and displacement of people are some of the major sources of conflict today. These elements compel the policy-makers to develop a human-centred approach to resolve conflicts. Having conceived by the changed global scenario, the UN also redefined the role of its Peace-keeping Force from a narrow view of surveillance and light use of force to larger and more complex UN peace-keeping missions. Now peace-keeping forces are assigned to help in implementing comprehensive peace agreements between the parties to intra-state conflicts and civil wars. In addition to that, the UN Peace-keeping Forces are involving non-military functions to promote peace in the violent-torn areas. The UN Department of Peace-keeping Operations was established in 1992 to fulfil this mission.

The concept of peace has been changed from its earlier notion of 'absence of violence' to a positive one. Today, peace is conceived as an environment where people strive to transform society and communities into fairer and more just places to live. In such environment, concern is not limited to tackle direct experience of violence, but also focused on the structural elements in society (socio-economic and political components) which perpetuate potential sources of conflict. In this broad concept, peace-building means empowering people to become involved in non-violent change process themselves, to build sustainable conditions for peace and justice. Peace-building process includes providing humanitarian relief, protecting human rights, ensuring security, establishing non-violent modes of resolving conflicts, fostering reconciliation, providing trauma healing services, repatriating refugees and resettling internally displaced persons, supporting broad-based education, and economic reconstruction.

Peace-building is an all encompassing approach that includes conflict prevention in the sense of preventing the recurrence of violence, conflict management (efforts to prevent, limit, contain, or resolve conflicts), and conflict transformation (addressing structural roots of violence through applying non-violent means). Peace-building is aimed at creating an environment of peaceful relationships and governance structures, a mechanism to address the root causes and effects of conflicts, as well as building institutions that can manage conflict without resort to violence. Apart from the traditional peace process, peace-building is a participatory approach involving all the parties to conflict. Peace-building is much broader notion than that of peace-making, whereas the latter is focused only on the activities to halt ongoing conflicts and bring hostile parties to partial agreements or broader negotiated settlements. It is necessary, in this context, to understand the contributions of Mahatma Gandhi in the arena of peace-building.

Even though Gandhi did not use the term peace-building, he is acknowledged as its mentor. He has transformed the concept of peace from its negative sense to a constructive one. Gandhi developed a distinct framework to understand conflict and bring sustainable peace. This was integrally related to his conception of human nature. It is pertinent to compare the traditional paradigm that conceived human nature, conflict and peace with that of Mahatma Gandhi. Thomas Hobbes is considered as the precursor of traditional realist approach, who set forth a paradigm to resolve conflicts in accordance with his understanding of human nature. For Hobbes, human-beings were motivated by self-interests and often contradictory in nature. Therefore, the period before the birth of political authority, human-beings were in constant conflict with one another. In such a condition life was "solitary, poor, nasty, brutish and short." Upon realizing the danger of the anarchy, human-beings became aware about the need of a mechanism to protect them. As far as Hobbes was concerned, rationality and self-interests persuaded human-beings to combine in agreement, to surrender sovereignty to a common power. Hobbes called this common power, state, as Leviathan. According to the view of Thomas Hobbes, human nature itself was the source of conflict. Since it is a condition of all against all, it was impossible to evolve a mechanism for conflict resolution within society. Rather, a political authority was inevitable to prevent conflict. His view supported a unilateral state action instead of voluntary initiatives for conflict resolution. There was no room for consensus among people, but the application of armed forces was the only way to maintain peace. These notions have largely influenced in shaping traditional approach to conflict but proved to be inadequate in the present period.

Gandhi believed in the inherent goodness of human-beings. He held that all human-beings had the capacity to develop their full potential of non-violence. He believed that all human-beings belonged to God. Since God and human-beings were interdependent and interrelated, non-violence was the inseparable quality of the latter. For him, the path to non-violence was none other than the path to God. Having belief in the inherent goodness of human-beings, Gandhi developed a human-centred approach for peace-building. Apart from physical force deployed by the political authority, Gandhi held that human-beings had the potential to resolve conflicts through non-violent means. Non-violence remained as the most fundamental principle of his philosophy of peace. According to Gandhi, the universal human value of non-violence ought to be cultivated not only at the individual level, but also at village, national and global levels. This was the effective approach to bring sustainable peace in the world. In its ostensible sense non-violence is the absence of violence, or the absence of mental intention of injuring, harming, disturbing and agonizing opponent. But Gandhi imparted a positive meaning to non-violence by inculcating an altruistic approach.

Bibliography

Primary Sources

Collected Works of Mahatma Gandhi, Hundred Volumes (New Delhi; Publications Division, Ministry of Information and Broadcasting, Government of India), 1958-83.

Desai, Mahadev, Gandhiji in Indian Village (Madras: S. Ganesan), 1927.

Devadoss, T.S., Hindu Family and Marriage (Madras: University of Madras), 1979.

Gandhi, M.K., From Yervada Mandir (Ahmedabad: Navajivan Publishing House), 1932.

Gandhi, M.K., Key to Health (Ahmedabad: Navajivan Publishing House), 1948.

Gandhi, M.K., Non-violence in Peace of War (Ahmedabad: Navajivan Publishing Press), n.d.

Gandhi, M.K., Towards Lasting Peace (Ahmedabad: Navajivan Publishing House), 1999.

Gandhi, M.K., Constructive Programme: Its Meaning and Place (Ahmedabad: Navajivan Press), 1945.

Gandhi, M.K., Delhi Diary (Prayer Speeches from 10-9-47 to 30-1-48), (Ahmedabad: Navajivan Press), 1948 (Written in third person and corrected by Gandhi).

Gandhi, M.K., Economic and Industrial Life and Reflection (Ahmedabad: Navjivan Publishing House), Vol. III.

Gandhi, M.K., Ethical Religion: Neethi Dharma, Tr. by A. Rama Iyer from Hindi (Madras: S. Ganesan), 1930.

Gandhi, M.K., Satyagraha in South Africa (Ahmedabad: Navajivan Press), 1972.

Gandhi, M.K., Story of My Experiments with Truth, Vol. 1 (Tr. By Mahadev Desai from Gujarati) and Vol. II Tr. (By Mahadev Desai and Pyarelal Nair (sic) from Gujarati) (Ahmedabad; Navajivan Press), 1927-29.

Gandhi, M.K., The Bhagvadgita (Delhi: Orient Paperbacks), 1998.

Gandhi, Mahatma, *Hind Swaraj* (Ahmedabad: Navajivan Publishing House), 1962.

Gandhi, Mohandas, K. *Hind Swaraj* or Indian Home Rule (Ahmedabad: Navajivan Press), 1931.

Secondary Sources

Abdalid, Hammudhah, Islam in Focus (Delhi: Crescent Publishing Co.), 1988.

Abi-Saab, G., The United Nations Operation in the Congo, 1960-64 (Oxford: Oxford University Press), 1978.

Ackerman Peter and Jack Duvall, A Force More Powerful: A Century of Non-violent Conflict (New York: Palgrave), 2000.

Alagappa, Muthiah and Inoguchi, Takashi (eds.), International Security Management and The United Nations (New York: United Nations University Press), 1999.

Alexseev, Mikhail A., Without Warning: Threat Assessment, Intelligence, and Global Struggle (New York: St. Martin's Press), 1997.

Alfred Alfanso, Glimpses of World Religion (Madras: Jaico Publishing House), 1995.

Alfred, Alfanso, (*et. al.*), Moral Science, Holy Faith International (New Delhi: Oxford University Press), 1990.

Alien Devere, Pacifism in the Modern World (New York: New York Press), 1929.

Andreski, Stanistav (ed.), West European Pacifism and Strategy for Peace (New York: The Macmillan Press Ltd.), 1985.

Andrews, C.F., Mahatma Gandhi's Ideas (London: George Allen & Unwin Ltd.), 1949.

Aram, M., The Future of Mankind (Coimbatore: Shanti Ashram), 1989.

Armstrong, David, The Rise of the International Organisation: A Short History (London: Macmillan), 1982.

Auerswald, Philip, E., Lewis M. Branscomb, Todd M. La Porte, and Erwann,. Michel-Kerjan (eds.), Seeds of Disaster, Roots of Response: How Private Action can Reduce Public Vulnerability (Cambridge: Cambridge University Press), 2006.

Augsburger, David, Conflict Mediation Across Cultures: Pathways and Patterns (Lousville, KT: Westminster/John Knox Press), 1992.

Bailey, Sidney D. and Sam, Daws, The Procedure of the UN Security Council (Oxford: Clarendon Press), 1988.

Bains, Margarita, India Today and Tomorrow (London: OUP), 1937.

Baird, Robert, D. (ed.), Religion in Modern India (New Delhi: Manohar Publication), 1981.

Bandyopadhyaya, Jayantanuja, Social and Political Thought of Gandhi (Bombay: Allied Publishers Ltd.), 1969.

Bardalai, A.K., Changing Security Scenario: Implications for UN Peace-keeping (New Delhi: Knowledge World), 2006.

Barker, Rodney, Making Enemies (New York: Palgrave Macmillan), 2007.

Barsh, David, P. (ed.), Approaches to Peace: a Reader in Peace Studies (New York: Oxford, U.P.), 2000.

Basic Facts about the United Nations (New York, UN Department of Public Information), 2004.

Baylis, John and Steve Smith, The Globalisation of World Politics (New York: Oxford University Press), 2008.

Beales, A.C.F., The History of Peace (London: London Press), 1931.

Beitz, Charles, R. & Herman, Theodore (eds.), Peace and War (San Francisco: Freeman), 1973.

Bernhardt, Friederich, On War of Today (London: London Press), 1911.

Betty Reardon and Eva Nordland (eds.), Learning Peace: The Promise of Ecological and Cooperative Education (Albany, NY: The State University of New York Press), 1994.

Bhattacharya, Buddhadeva, Evolution of the Political Philosophy of Gandhi (Calcutta: Calcutta Book House), 1969.

Bhutani, Surendra, The United Nations and the Israel Conflict (Gurgaon: Academic Press), 1977.

Biddle, Stephen, Military Power (New Delhi: Manas Publications), 2005.

Bilgrani, S.J.R., International Organization (New Delhi: Vikas Publishing), 1977.

Bloom, William, Personal Identity, National Identity and International Relations (Cambridge: Cambridge University Press), 1959.

Bondurant, J., Conquest of Violence: The Gandhian Philosophy of Conflict Resolution (Bombay: Oxford, U.P), 1959.

Bose, Anima, Dimensions of Peace and Non-Violence: The Gandhian Perspective (New Delhi: Gian Publishing House), 1987.

Bose, Anima, Mahatma Gandhi—A Contemporary Perspective (Delhi: B.R. Publishing Corporation), 1977.

Bose, Anima, Peace and Conflict Resolution in the Community (New Delhi: Vikas Publishing House Pvt. Ltd.), 1977.

Bose, N.K., Selections from Gandhi (Ahmedabad: Navajivan Publishing House), 1957.

Boulding, Elise, Cultures of Peace: The Hidden Side of History (Syracuse, NY: Syracuse University Press), 2000.

Boulding, K.E., Conflict and Defence: A General Theory (New York: Harper and Row Publishers) 1963.

Boulding, K.E., Stable Peace (Austin: Texas University Press), 1978.

Boyer, Paul, By the Bomb's Early Light (New York: Pantheon), 1985.

Brennan, Donald, Arms Control and Disarmament (London: Jonathan Cape), 1961.

Bright, Brocke, Utne, Educating for Peace (New York: Pergamon Press), 1985.

Broader, James F., Risk Analysis and the Security Survey (Boston: Butterworth Publishers), 1984.

Brown, F.J., Charles Hodges and I.R. Roucek, Contemporary World Politics (New York: John Wiley and Sons), 1940.

Brown, Judith, Gandhi's Rise to Power (Cambridge: Cambridge University Press), 1972.

Bruce, Franklin, H., Countdown to Midnight (New York: DAW), 1984.

Bunker, Robert J. (ed.), Non-State Threats and Future Wars (Portland: Frank Cass Publishers), 2003.

Burton, J.W., International Relations (Cambridge: Cambridge University Press), 1965.

Buzan, Barry, People States and Fear: An Agenda for International Security Studies in the Post-Cold War Era (Boulder: Lynne Rienner Publishers), 1991.

Caldwell, Dan and Robert E. Williams, Jr., Seeking Security in an Insecure World (Lanham: Rowman N. Littlefield), 2006.

Carr, E.H., Twenty Years Crisis (New York: Harvard University Press), 1986.

Catlin George, In the Path of the Mahatma (London: MacDonald), 1998.

Centre for Strategic and International Studies, Panel Report: Professional Military Education: An Asset for Peace and Progress (Washington, D.C.), 1997.

Chabra, H.K., Relations of Nations (Delhi: Surjeet Publications), 1980.

Chakraborty, Bimal, The United Nations and The Third World: Shifting Paradigms (New Delhi: Tata McGraw Hill Publishing Co.), 1996.

Chakraborty, Mohit, Fire Sans Ire: A Critical Study of Gandhian Non-violence (New Delhi: Concept Publishing Company), 2005.

Chander, J.C. (ed.), Teachings of Mahatma Gandhi (Lahore: Lahore Press), 1945.

Chandra, Satish and Chandra, Mala, International Conflicts and Peace-making Process: Role of United Nations (New Delhi: Mittal Publications), 2006.

Charbonneau, Louis, "UN Probes Allegations of Corruption, Fraud," *Reuters*, January 10, 2008.

Chattopadhyay, Santi Nath (ed.), World Peace: Problems of Global Understanding and Prospect of Harmony (Kolkata: Punthi Pustak), 2005.

Chauhan, Sandip, GATT to WTO, Gandhian Alternative to NIEO (New Delhi: Deep and Deep), 2001.

Cirinone, Joseph, John B. Wolfsthal, and Miriam Rajkumar, Deadly Arsenals—Nuclear, Biological, and Chemical Threats (Washington, DC: Carnegie Endowment for International Peace), 2005.

Clark, G. and L. Sohan, World Peace Through World Law (New York: Harvard University Press), 1960.

Cobban, Helena, The Moral Architecture of World Peace: Noble Laureates Discuss Our Global Future (Charlottesville: University of Virginia Press), 2000.

Cohen, Raymond, Threat Perception in International Crisis (Madison: University of Wisconsin, Press), 1979.

Comay, Joan, The United Nations in Action (New York: Macmillan), 1965.

Constantine, G. Ted, Intelligence Support to Humanitarian-Disaster Relief Operations (Washington, DC: Central Intelligence Agency Center for the Study for Intelligence), 1995.

Coomaraswamy, Anand K. and I.B. Homer, The Living Thoughts of Gautama, the Buddha (London: Oxford University Press), 1948.

Cordesman, Anthony H., Strategic Threats and National Missile Defenses: Defending the U.S. Homeland (Westport, CT: Praeger Publishers), 2001.

Creveld, Martin Van, The Transformation of War (New York: The Free Press), 1991.

Crile, George, M., A Mechanistic View of War and Peace (Cambridge Mass: Cambridge University Press), 1927

Csaky, Corinna, "No One to Turn to: The Under-Reporting of Child Sexual Exploitation and Abuse by Aid Workers and Peace-keepers", Save the Children, 2008.

Dalton, Dennis, Mahatma Gandhi: Non-Violent Power in Action (New York: Coloumbia University Press), 1993.

Dasgupta, Arunachandra, Non-violence and Invisible Power (Calcutta: Calcutta Khadi Prathisthan), 1956.

David, Alexander, Natural Disasters (London: UCL Press), 1993.

David, Armstrong, The Rise of the International Organisation: A Short History (London: Macmillan), 1982.

De, W.T., The Liberal Tradition in China (New York: Columbia University Press), 1983.

Desai, Vaiji Govindji (ed.), The Diary of Mahadev Desai (Ahmedabad: Navajivan Publishing House), 1953.

Desai, Vaiji Govindji (ed.). Unto This Last: A Parapharase (Ahmedabad: Navajivan Publishing House), 1956.

Deshpande, P.O., Gandhiana: A Bibliography of Gandhian Literature (Ahmedabad: Navajivan Publishing House), 1948.

Deustch, Merton, The Analysis of International Relations (Englewood Cliff, NJ: Prentice Hall), 1998.

Devadoss, T.S., Sarvodaya and the Problem of Political Sovereignty (Madras: University of Madras), 1974.

Devanesen, Chandran, D.S., The Making of the Mahatma (New Delhi: Orient Longmans Ltd.), 1969.

Devere, Allen, Pacifism in the Modern World (New York: New York Press), 1929.

Dhawan, Gopinath, The Political Philosophy of Mahatma Gandhi (Ahmedabad: Navajivan Publishing House), 1949.

Doctor, H. Adi, International Relations (Delhi: Vikas Publications), 1969.

Eichelberger, M. Clark, UN: The First Twenty Years (Delhi: Sterling Publishers), 1966.

Elliott, Charles F. & Carl A. Liden (eds.), Marxism in the Contemporary West (Boulden, Colodaro: West View Press), 1981.

Ellwood, Robert, S., Words of the Worlds Religion: An Anthology (New York: Prentice Hall), 1977.

Erikson, Erik, Gandhi's Truth: On the Origins of Militant Non-violence (London: Faber & Faber), 1970.

Ervin, Clark Kent, Open Target: Where America is Vulnerable to Attack (New York: Palgrave, Macmillan), 2006.

Evans, Gareth, Co-operating For Peace: The Global Agenda for the 1990 and Beyond (Atchison: Alien and Unwin), 1993.

Falk, Richard A., Robert C. Johansen, and Samuel S. Kim (eds.), Constitutional Foundations of World Peace (Albany, NY: State University New York Press), 1993.

Falk, Richard, A., Samuel S. Kim, and Saul H. Mendlovitz (eds.), United Nations and a Just World Order (Boulder, CO: Westview Press), 1991.

Fang, T.H., Chinese Philosophy: Its Spirit And Its Development (Taipei: Linking), 1981.

Ferguson, J., War and Peace in the World's Religions (Sheldon: Sheldon Press), 1977.

Fien, Robert A. and Bryan Vossekuil, Protective Intelligence and Threat Assessment Investigations: A Guide for State and Local Law Enforcement Officials (Washington, DC: United States Department of Justice, Office of Justice Programs, National Institute of Justice), 1998.

Fischer, Frederick B., That Strange Little Brown Man Gandhi (New York: The Macmillan Co.), 1932.

Fischer, Louis (ed.), The Essential Gandhi (New York: The Macmillan Co.), 1963.

Fischer, Louis, A Week with Gandhi (London: Jonathan Cape Thirty Bedford Square), 1951.

Fischer, Louis, Gandhi: His Life and Message for the World (London: George Allen and Unwin), 1962.

Frank, Jerome, D., Sanity and Survival in the Nuclear Age (New York: Random House), 1982.

Frankel, Joseph, International Relations in a Changing World (Delhi: Oxford University Press), 1990.

Frick, Marie-Luisa and Andreas Oberprantacher, Power and Justice in International Relations Interdisciplinary Approaches to Global Challenges (New York: Routledge), 2009.

Friedman, Milton, Capitalism and Freedom (Chicago: University of Chicago), 1970.

Friedmann, Wolfgang, An Introduction to World's Politics (New York: St. Martin's Press), 1956.

Fumer, J.F.C., The Reformation of War (New York: New York Press), 1923.

Galtung, Johan and Carl G. Jacobsen, Searching for Peace: The Road to Transcend (London: Pluto Press), 2000

Galtung, Johan, Essays in Peace Research (Copenhagen: Christian Ejlers), 1975.

Galtung, Johan, Peace by Peaceful Means (London: Sage Publications), 1996.

Galtung, Johan, Peace Research for Peace Action (New Delhi: Sat Sahitya Kendra Press), 1974.

Galtung, Johan, The Struggle for Peace (New Delhi: Sage Publications), 1996.

Galtung, Johan, The Way is the Goal: Gandhi Today (Ahmedabad: Navajivan Publishers), 1992.

Ghanshyam (ed.), Contemporary Peace Research (New Delhi: Radiant Publishers), 1982.

Gibbs, D., 'The United Nations, International Peace-keeping and the

Question of 'Impartiality': Revisiting the Congo Operation of 1960', *Journal of Modern African Studies*, 2000.

Gilpin, Robert, War and Change in World Politics (Cambridge: Cambridge University Press), 1981.

Goeggrey, Blainey, The Causes of War (London: London Press), 1973.

Goldstein, E., War and Peace Treaties 1816-1991 (New York: Routledge), 1992.

Goodrich, Leland, M. Korea, Collective Measures Against Aggression, International Conciliation No. 495, 1953.

Graham, David T., and Nana K. Poku (eds.), Migration, Globalization and Human Security (London: Routledge Research in Population and Migration), 2000.

Gray, Cox, The Ways of Peace: A Philosophy of Peace as Action (New York: Paulist Press), 1986.

Greenfeld, L., Nationalism: Five Roads to Modernity (Cambridge: Cambridge University Press), 1992.

Gregg Richard B., The Power of Non-violence (Canton, ME: Greenleaf Books), 1959.

Guehenno, Jean-Marie, Key Challenges in Today's UN Peace-keeping Operations (Washington, DC: Council on Foreign Relations), 2006.

Guha, Ramachandra, India After Gandhi: The History of World's Largest Democracy (London: Macmillan), 2007.

Haaveisurd, M., Approaching Disarmament Education (Guildford: Westbury House), 1981.

Hammes, Colonel Thomas X., The Sling and the Stone: On War in the 21st Century (St. Paul, MN: Zenith Press), 2004.

Harper, Malcolm, Empowerment Through Enterprise: A Training Mannual for NGOs (New Delhi: Oxford and IBH Publishing Co.), 1973.

Harvey, Robert, Global Disorder: America and The Threat of World Conflict (New York: Carroll & Graf Publishers), 2003.

Hatcher, W.S., Martin J.D., The Bahá'ís Faith: The Emerging Global Religion (California: Harper and Row), 1984.

Helton, Arthyr L., Forced Displacement and Human Security in the Former Soviet Union: Law and Policy (New York: Transnational Publishers), 2000.

Hilderbrand, Robert C., Dumbarton Oaks: The Origins of the United Nations and the Search for Post-war Security (Chapel Hill: University of North Carolina Press), 1990.

Hindmarsh, A.E., Force in Peace (Cambridge: Cambridge University Press), 1933.

Hinsley, P.H., Power and the Pursuit of Peace (Cambridge: Cambridge University Press), 1963.

Hirshleifer, Jack, Theorizing Adult Conflict (Amsterdam: North Holland), 1995.

Hirst, F.W., The Political Economy of War (London: London Press), 1915.

Hirst, M.E., The Quakers in Peace and War (London: London Press), 1923.

Hobbes, Thomas, Leviathan (New York: Penguin), 1977.

Holcombe, Arthur N., Strategy of Peace in Changing World (Cambridge: H.U.P.), 1967.

Holt, Kate and Sarah Hughes, UN Staff Accused of Raping Children in Sudan, *The Telegraph*, January 4, 2007.

Horowitz, Irving Louis, War and Peace in Contemporary Social and Philosophical Theory (London: A Condor Book Souvenir Press (Educational & Academic) Ltd.), 1974.

Horwitz, Irwing Louis, War and Peace in Contemporary Social and Philosophical Theory (Cambridge: Cambridge University Press), 1978.

Howard, Russell D. and Reid L. Sawyer (eds.), Defeating Terrorism: Shaping the New Security Environment (New York: McGraw-Hill), 2003.

Huddleston, J., Achieving Peace by the Year 2000: A Twelve Point Proposal (Oxford: One World Publications Ltd.), 1992.

Ibrace, L.P., Religion in Various Cultures (New York: Henry Hult), 2000.

Immannuel Kant, Perpetual Peace (New York: Wiley), 1957.

Immannuel, G., Peace Development and Religion (Ahmedabad: Kamavati Publications), 1998

Independent Commission on Disarmament and Security Issues (Palme Commission), Common Security: A Blueprint or Survival (New York: Simon and Schuster), 1982.

Inozemstev, N., War and Peace in the World Today (New Delhi: Soviet Land, Bookland), 1963.

Inozemtsev, N.N. (ed.), Global Problems of Our Age (Moscow: Progress), 1984.

Islam, Nazrul, Reforming the United Nations (New Delhi: Viva Books Private Ltd.), 2005.

Issac, T. Tambyah, A Comparative Study of Hinduism, Buddhism and Christianity (New Delhi: Indian Book Gallery), 1925.

Issac, Harold R., India's Ek-Untouchables (Bombay: Asia Publishing House) 1965.

Jack, H.A. (ed.), World Religion and World Peace (Boston: Beacon Press), 1968.

Jackson, Robert, The Global Covenant, Human Conduct in a World of States (Oxford: Oxford University Press), 1973.

Jacow, P.E. Atherton, L., The Dynamics of International Organization (Illinois: Dorsey), 1965.

James, A., Peace-keeping in International Politics (Basingstoke: Macmillan), 1990.

James, Alan, Peace-keeping in International Politics (New York: St. Martin Press), 1990.

James, Alan, Politics of Peace-keeping (London: Chatto and Windus), 1969.

Jenkins, R., Social Identity (London: Routledge), 1996.

John Paul Lederach: Preparing for Peace (Syracuse: Syracuse University Press), 1996.

Johnson, L. Gunnar, Conflicting Concepts of Peace in Contemporary Peace Studies (Beverly Hills: Sage Publications), 1976.

Jurgen, Albert, Iraq War: The History Behind the Conflict (Kolkata: Sparrow), 2004.

Kaplan, Morton, System and Process in International Politics (New York: Wiley), 1957.

Kaul Inge, Marc Stem and Isabelle Grunberg (eds.), Global Public Goods: International Cooperation in the 21st Century (New York: Oxford University Press), 1999.

Kaur, Balvinder, Teaching of Peace and Conflict Resolution (New Delhi: Deep and Deep Publications), 2007.

Kay, Cristobal (ed.), Globalisation, Competitiveness and Human Security (London: Frank Cass and Company Limited), 2000.

Kay, Sean, Global Security in the Twenty-first Century: The Quest for Power and the Search for Peace (Lanham, MD: Rowman and Littlefield), 2006.

Kelman, Herbert C. (ed.), International Behaviour: A Social-Psychological Analysis (New York: Holt, Rinehart and Winston), 1965.

Kennedy, J.F., The Strategy of Peace (New York: Popular Library), 1961.

Keshwani, Khemchand B., International Relations in Modern World (1900-1995) (New Delhi: Himalaya Publishing House), 1996.

Khanna, V. N., Interntional Relations (Delhi: Vikas Publishing House Pvt. Ltd.). 1997

King, Martin Luther, Strike Towards Freedom (New York: Harper and Brothers), 1958.

Kinger, Kamal, National Security: Theoretical and Practical Aspects (Nabha: Urvashi Printers), 2008.

Kirdar, Uner and Leonard Silk (eds.), People: From Impoverishment to Empowerment (New York: NYU Press), 1995.

Klineberg, Tensions, Affecting International Understanding (New York: Roultedge), 1964.

Knorr, Knorr (ed.), Historical Dimensions of National Security Problems (Lawrence: University Press of Kansas), 1976.

Korb, Lawrence J. and Robert, Boorstin, Integrated Power: A National Security Strategy for the 21st Century (Washington, DC: Center for American Progress), 2005.

Kothari, Rajani, Footsteps into the Future: Diagnosis of the Present World and Design for an Alternative (New York: The Free Press), 1974.

Kothari, Rajni, Transformation and Survival (Delhi: Ajanta Publications), 1990.

Krahmann, Eike (ed.), New Threats and New Actors in International Security (New York: Palgrave Macmillan), 2005.

Krishnakripala (ed.), All Men are Brothers (Ahmedabad: Navajivan Publishing House), 1950.

Krsmse, Keinth and Michael C. Williams (ed.), Critical Security Studies, Concepts and Cases (London: UCL Press), 1997.

Kumar, Mahendra, Current Peace Research and India (New Delhi: Indra Prustha Press), 1968.

Kumar, Rajendra, World Famous Religions: Doctrines and Sects (Delhi: Pustak Mahal), 1993.

Kumar, Rajendra, World Famous Religions: Doctrines and Sects (Delhi: Pustak Mahal), 1993.

Kumarappa, B., Gandhi: For Pacifists (Ahmedabad: Navajivan Publishers), 1949.

Lake, Anthony, Nightmares: Real Threats in a Dangerous World and How America Can Meet Them (New York: Little, Brown & Company), 2000.

Lederach, John Paul, Preparing for Peace: Conflict Transformation Across Cultures (Syracuse, NY: Syracuse University Press), 1995.

Lee, Mark, The United States and World Relations (New York: OUP), 1965.

Lenin, V.I., The National Liberation Movement in the East (Moscow: Foreign Languages Publishing House), 1964.

Lentz, Theodore, Towards a Science of Peace (Varanasi: Navachetna), 1970.

Lider, J., Problems of War and Peace (Moscow: Progress), 1972.

Lider, J., Marxism-Leninism on War and Army (Moscow: Progress), 1972.

Lider, J., On the Nature of War (Farnborough: Saxon House), 1983.

Linus, Pauling, Science and World Peace (New Delhi: Indian Council of Cultural Relations), 1967.

Lowie, R.H., Primitive Religion (London: British Commonwealth), 1960.

Luard, Evan, War in International Society: A Study in International Sociology (London: Tauris), 1986.

lyer, Raghavan, N., The Moral and Political Writings of Mahatma Gandhi, Three Volumes (Delhi: Oxford University Press), 1987.

Lynch, Colum, Audit of UN's Sudan Mission Finds Tens of Millions in Waste, *The Washington Post*, February 10, 2008.

Lynn-Jones, Sean M. and Steven E. Miller (ed.), Global Dangers: Changing Dimensions of International Security (Cambridg, MA: MIT Press), 1995.

MacDonald, Scott B., Dancing on a Volcano: The Latin American Drug Trade (Westport, CT: Praeger Publishers), 1988.

Macquarrie, John, The Concept of Peace (London: S.C.M. Press), 1973.

Malhotra, A.R., Philosophy of Religion – An Analysis to World Religions (Jalandhar: Sterling Publishers Pvt. Ltd.), 1985.

Malhotra, A.R., Philosophy of Religion (New Delhi: Sterling Publishers Limited), 1983.

Mandel, Deadly Transfers and the Global Playground (Westport, CT: Praeger), 1999.

Mandel, Robert, The Changing Face of National Security: A Conceptual Analysis (Westport, CT: Greenwood), 1994.

Manwaring, Max G. (ed.), Gray Area Phenomena: Confronting the New World Disorder (Boulder, CO: Westview Press), 1993.

Martin, Debra, L., and Frayer, David, W. (ed.), Troubled Times Violence and Warfare in the Past (Amsterdam: Gordon and Breach Publishers), 1977.

Martin, Laurence W. (ed.), Neutralism and Non-Alignment (New York: New York Press), 1962.

Mary, Kan, Capital (in 3 Vol), (Moscow: Progress Publishers), 1977.

Mathews, M. Alice (ed.), Peace Projects (Washington: Washington Press), 1940.

Mathur, D.B., Prefacing Gandhi (Jaipur: RBSA Publishers), 1988.

Mathur, J.S. (ed.), Economic Thought of Mahatma Gandhi (Allahabad: Kitab Mahal), 1971.

Matsumue, Tatsyro and Lincoln C. Chen (ed.), Common Security in Asia: A New Concepts in Human Security (Tokyo: Tokai University Press), 1995.

McDowall, David, Palestine and Israel: The Uprising and Beyond (London: I.B. Tauris), 1989.

McDowell, Josh and Stewart, Don, Concise Guide to Today's Religions (England: Scripture Press), 1990.

McDowell, Josh and Stewart, Don, Concise Guide to Today's Religions (England: Scripture Press), 1990.

McNeil, Elton B. (ed.), The Nature of Human Conflict (Englewood Cliffs, NJ: Prentice Hall), 1965.

McSweeney, Bill, Security, Identity and Interests: A Sociology of International Relations (London: Cambridge University Press), 1999.

Mehrish, B.N., Restructuring the United Nations and Global Governance (Delhi: Maadhyam Books Services), 2003.

Meisler, Stanley, United Nations: The First Fifty Years (New York: Atlantic Monthly Press), 1995.

Michael, Mousseau, Market Civilization and Its Clash with Terror, *International Security*, Vol. 27, No. 3, Winter 2003-04.

Michael, Mousseau, The Social Market Roots of Democratic Peace, *International Security*, Vol. 33, No. 4, Spring 2009.

Michael, Sheehan, International Security: An Analytical Survey (USA: Lyne Rienner Publishers), 2007.

Milburn, A. and H. Warman, On the Nature of Threat (Cambridge: Cambridge University Press), 1999.

Mische, Patricia and Gerald, Towards a Human World Order Beyond the National Security Stratyacket (New York: Paulist Press), 1977.

Mishra, R.P. (ed.), Gandhian Model of Development and World Peace (New Delhi: Concept Publishers), 1988.

Moller, Bjorh, Common Security and Non-Offensive Defense: A Neorealist Perspective (Boulder: Lynne Rienner), 1992.

Moore, Raymond, A., United Nations Reconsidered (Columbia: University of South Corolina Press), 1963.

Morgenthau, Hans, Politics Among Nations: The Struggle for Power and Peace (New York: Alfred A. Knopf), 1948.

Morphet, S., 'UN Peace-keeping and Election-Monitoring' in A. Roberts and B. Kingsbury (eds.), *United Nations, Divided World* (Oxford: Oxford University Press), 2000.

Mousseau, Michael, 2003, "The Nexus of Market Society, Liberal Preferences, and Democratic Peace: Interdisciplinary Theory and Evidence", *International Studies Quarterly*.

Mroz, John, E., Beyond Security: Private Perception Among Arab and Israil (New York: Harper & Collins), 1980.

Nagler, Micheal N., Is There No Other Way?: The Search for a Non-violent Future (Berkeley: Hills Books), 2011.

Nathan, O., Norden, H., Einstein on Peace (New York: Simon and Schuster), 1960.

National Security Strategy of the United States of America (Washington, DC: White House), 2002.

Nicholas, H.G., The United Nations as a Political Institution (Oxford: Oxford University Press), 1974.

Nolan, Janne, E., Global Engagement: Cooperation and Security in the 21st Century (Washington, DC: The Brookings Institution), 1994.

Norman Lowe, Mastering Modern World History (New Delhi: Macmillan), 1997.

Noss, John, B., Man's Religions (New York: Macmillan Company), 1969.

Oddie, G.A., Religion in South Asia (New Delhi: Dhawan Publications), 1977.

Overt, R., How Effective are Peace Movements? (London: Housmans), 1983.

Palmer, Norman, D. and Howard C. Perkings, International Relations (Boston: Houghton Miffin Company), 1969.

Pana, S. (ed.), Obstacles to Disarmament and Ways of Overcoming Them (Paris: UNESCO Press), 1981.

Pasricha, Ashu, Peace Studies: The Discipline and Dimension (Delhi: Abhijeet Publishers), 2003.

Pasricha, Ashu, WTO, Self-Reliance and Globalistion (New Delhi: Deep and Deep), 2005.

Patil, Anjali, V., The UN Veto in World Affairs, 1946-90 (Monsell: UNIFO), 1992.

Paul, Battersby, Joseph M. Siraccija, Globalisation and Human Security (USA: Roman and Littlefield Publishers), 2009.

"Peace-keeping Procurement Audit Found Mismanagement, Risk of Financial Loss, Security Council Told in Briefing by Chief of Staff," UN Security Council, February 22, 2006, http://www.un.org/News/Press/docs/2006/sc8645.doc.htm

Peri, Raphael E., International Terrorism: Threat, Policy, and Response (Washington, DC: Congressional Research Service Report for Congress), 2007.

Porritt, Arthur (ed.), The Causes of War (London: London Press), 1932.

Posnet, Richard A., Catastrophe: Risk and Response (Oxford: Oxford University Press), 2004.

Prasad, D., Peace Education or Education for Peace (New Delhi: Gandhi Peace Foundation), 1984.

Prins, Gwyn, Threats without Enemies: Facing Environmental Insecurity (London: Earthscan), 1993.

Puri, Rashmi Sudha, Gandhi on War and Peace (New York: Prager Publishers), 1987.

Pyarelal, Mahatma Gandhi, The Last Phase, Vol. I (Ahmedabad: Navajivan Press), 1956.

Quincy, Wright, "Changes in the Conception of War", *American Journal of International Law*, Vol. XVIII, 1926.

Radhakrishnan, N. and Vasudevan, N. (eds.), Gandhi in the Global Village (New Delhi: Gandhi Medai Centre), 1998.

Radhakrishnan, N., Gandhi Youth and Non-violence: Experiment in Conflict Resolution (New Delhi: Centre for Development and Peace), 1992.

Radhakrishnan, S. (ed.), Mahatma Gandhi: 100 Years (New Delhi: Gandhi Peace Foundation), 1968.

Radhakrishnan, S., Eastern Religions and Western Thought (London: Oxford University), 2000.

Rai, Chhaya, "Gandhi's Role and Relevance in Conflict Resolution", International Seminar on Conflict Resolution, 15-17 February, 2003.

Ram, Gopal, Indian Muslims (Bombay: Asia Publishing House), 1959.

Rand, Ayn, Capitalism: the Unknown Ideal (United States: New American Library), 1996.

Raymond, Aron, On War (London: Seeker and Warburg), 1958.

Raymond, Aron, Peace and War: A Theory of International Relations (London: London Press), 1966.

Read, H., Education for Peace (London: Routledge and Kegan Paul), 1950.

Reardon, B., Comprehensive Peace Education: Educating for Global Responsibility (New York: Teachers' College Press), 1988.

Reardon, B., Militarization, Security and Peace Education: A Guide for Concerned Citizens (Valley Forge: United Ministries in Education), 1982.

Renner, Michael, Fighting for Survival: Environmental Decline, Social Conflicts and the New Age of Security (Washington, DC: Wondwatch Institute), 1966.

"Report of the Office of Internal Oversight Services on the Activities of the Procurement Task Force for the 18-Month Period Ended 30 June 2007, A/62/272, October 5, 2007 at http://www.eyeontheun.org/assets/attachments/documents/5522_report_OIOS_activities_procurement_task_force_30_june_2007.doc

Richardson, A Mathematical Study of the Causes and Origins of War (ed.) by Nicholas Rashevsky and Ernesto Trucco (Pitsburg: Boxwood), 1960.

Richmond, O.P., The Transformation of Peace (London: Palgrave Macmillan), 2005.

Robbins Lionel, The Economic Causes of War (London: London Press), 1939.

Robin, Corey, Fear: The History of a Political Idea (Oxford: Oxford University Press), 2004.

Rogers, Paul, Losing Control: Global Security in the Twenty-first Century (London: Pluto Press), 2002.

Ross, Alf, Constitution of United Nations: Analysis of Structure and Function (New York: Rinehart), 1950.

Rousseau, David L., Identifying Threats and Threatening Identities: The Social Construction of Realism and Liberalism (Stanford, CA: Stanford University Press), 2006.

Rummel, Rudolph Joseph, Peace Endangered: Reality of Détente (London: Sage Publications), 1976..

Russett, Bruce and Haivey Stars, World Politics: The Menu for Choice (Bombay: Vakils, Feffer and Simon Ltd.), 1986.

Ryan, Bryce, F., Social and Cultural Change (New York: The Ronald Press), 1967. Saraswati, Baidyanath (ed.), Culture of Peace: Experience and Experiment (New Delhi: Indira Gandhi National Centre for Arts), 1999.

Saksena, K.P., The United Nations and Collective Security: A Historical Analysis (Delhi: D.K. Publishing), 1974.

Saltmarsh, Mathew, "A Bloated U.N. Bureaucracy Causes Bewilderment," *The New York Times*, January 5, 2011.

Saraswati, Baidyanath (ed.), Culture of Peace: Experience and Experiment (New Delhi: Indira Gandhi National Centre for Arts), 1999.

Schaefer, Brett, D., "A Progress Report on U.N. Reform," Heritage Foundation Backgrounder No. 1937, May 19, 2006.

Schaeter, Brett, D., "Who Leads the United Nations?" Heritage Foundation WebMemo No. 1054, December 4, 2007.

Scott, Andrew M., The Revolution in Statecraft: Informal Penetration (New York: Random House), 1965.

Sen, Gita, Development, Crisis, and Alternative Visions: Third World Women's Perspectives (New Delhi: Dawn), June, 1985.

Sen, K.M., Hinduism (New Delhi: Penguin Books), 2001.

Sethi, J.D., International Economic Disorder (Shimla: Indian Institute for Advanced Study), 1986.

Shakhnazarov, G., The Coming World Order (Moscow: Progress), 1984.

Sharma, Jai Narain, Alternative Economics (New Delhi: Deep and Deep), 2003.

Sharma, Manish, Non-Violence in the 21st Century: Application and Efficacy (New Delhi: Deep and Deep Publications), 2006.

Sharp, Gene, The Politics of Non-violent Action: Part One: Power and Struggle (Boston, MA: Porter Sargeant Publishers), 1973.

Sharp, Gene, Gandhi as a Political Strategist (Boston, MA: Porter Sargeant Publishers), 1979.

Sherif, M. and C. Sherif, Groups in Harmony and Tensions (New York: Harper), 1953.

Shoghi Effeendi, The Advent of Divine Justice (Illinois: Bahá'í Publishing Trust), 1969.

Shu... A.C. and Vandana, A., Military Exploits of Environment (New Delhi: Third Concept), 1993.

Simmel, George, Conflict, Translated by Kurt H. Wolff (New York: Free Press to Glance, Inc.), 1956.

Singh, Ramjee, *et. al.*, Aspects of Gandhian Thought (Madurai: Vanguard Press), 1994.

Smith, P., A Concise Encyclopedia of the Bahá'í Faith (Oxford, UK: Oneworld Publications), 1999.

Smoke, Richard & Andrie Kortunov (eds.), Mutual Security (New York: St. Martin's Press), 1991.

Sondhi, Sunil, International Relations: A Framework for Analysis (New Delhi: Sanjay Prakashan), 2004.

Sood, Vikram, "Clash of Ideas and Convictions", *The Hindustan Times*, Kolkata, 28 March 2005.

Stanford, Barbara (ed.), Peacemaking: A Guide to Conflict Resolution (New York: Bantham Books), 1976.

Stephen, Badsey and Paul Latawaski (eds.), Britain, NATO and the Lessons of the Balkan Conflict, 1991-99 (London: Frank Cass), 2004.

Stockhome International Peace Research Institute, SIPRI, Year Book 2005.

Stoeff, Peter, Human and Global Security: An Exploration of Terms (Toronto: University of Toronto Press), 1999.

Stoessinger, John, G., Might of Nations (New York: Random House), 1973.

Sturzo, D.L., Nationalism and Internationalism (New York: Roy Publishers), 1946.

Syed, Mohammad Aslam (ed.), Islam and Democracy in Pakistan (Karachi: Crystal Printers), 1995.

Tadjbakhsh, S. & Chenoy, Human Security: Concepts and Implications (London: Routledge), 2006.

Tehrariian, Majid & David W. Chappel (eds.). Dialogue of Civilization: A New Face Agenda for a New Millennium (London: I.B. Taurist Publishers), 2002.

Tendulkar, D.G., Mahatma (New Delhi: Publications Division, Ministry of Information and Broadcasting, Government of India), Vol. I, 1990.

Thakur, Ramesh and Edward Newman (ed.), New Millennium, New Perspectives, The United Nations, Security and Governance, UNG Millennium Series (Tokyo: United Nations University Press), 2000.

The Economist, "Call the Blue Helmets: Can the UN Cope with Increasing Demands for its Soldiers?", 4th January 2007.

Thick, Nhat Hanh, Being Peace (Berkeley: Parallax Press), 1996.

Thomas, Caroline, Global Governance, Development and Human Security, The Challenge of Poverty and Inequality (London and Sterling, VA: Pluto Press), 2000.

Thompson W. Scott and Kenneth M. Jensen (eds.), Approaches to Peace: An Intellectual Map (Washington, DC: United States Institute of Peace Press), 1988.

Thornton, Rod, Asymmetric Warfare: Threat and Response in the Twenty-first Century (Cambridge: Polity Press), 2007.

Tinbergin, Jan, "Limit to Growth", *The Economic Times*, 1972.

Titze, Kurt, Jainism: A Pictorial Guide to the Religion of Non-Violence (Delhi: Motilal Banarsidas), 1998.

Tiwari, K.N., Comparative Religion (New Delhi: Motilal Banarsidas), 1993.

Tiwari, K.N., World Religion and Gandhi (New Delhi: Classical Publishing Co.), 1988.

Trager, Frank, N. And Frank, L. Simonie, An Introduction to the Study of National Security (Kansa: Kansas University Press). 1973.

Treverton, Gregory F., Reshaping National Intelligence in an Age of Information (Cambridge: Cambridge University Press), 2001.

Turner, James T. and Michael G. Gelles, Threat Assessment: A Risk Management Approach (New York: Haworth Press), 2003.

Turner, Tell, A., The Causes of War and the New Revolution (Boston: Marshauones Co.), 1927.

U' Thant, Toward World Peace: Addresses and Public Statements, 1957-63 (New York: Yoseloff), 1964.

UN Department of Public Information, Executive Summary, A More Secure World: Our Shared Responsibility, 2004.

UN, The Blue Helmets: A Review of United Nations Peace-keeping (New York: UN Department of Public Information), 1990.

Vatsyayan, Kapila (ed.), Culture and Development (New Delhi: D.K. Printworld Pvt. Ltd.), 1999.

Volkogonov, D.A. (ed.), Problems of War and Peace (Moscow: Progress), 1972.

Vyas, Ramnarayan, Peace, Philosophy and Progress (Delhi: Sterling Publishers), 1966.

Walker, Charles C., World Peace Guard: An Unarmed Agency for Peace-keeping (Hyderabad: Academy of Gandhian Studies), 1981.

Wallace, V.H. (ed.), Nehru, Jawaharlal, Introduction to Path to Peace (Melbourne: Melbourne University Press), 1957.

Wallerstein, Immanuel (ed.). Social Change (New York: John Wiley), 1966.

Walton, Richard, E., Interpersonal Peace-making: Confrontations and Third Party Consultation (London: Addison Wesley), 1969.

Waters, Malcolm, Globalisation (London: Routledge), 1995.

Welch, H., Taoism: The Parting of the Way (Boston: Beacon Press), 1966.

Wesley, Michael, Casualties of the New World Order: The Causes of Failure of UN Missions to Civil Wars (Basingstoke, U.K.: Macmillan), 1997.

Wiener, N., The Human Use of Human-beings (New York: Eyre and Spottiswoode), 1950.

Willis, Harman, Global Mind Change: The Promise of the 21st Century (Sausalito, CA: Institute of Noetic Sciences), 1996.

Wilmerding, John, The Theory of Active Peace (London: Sage Publications), 2006.

Wolfers, Arnold, Discord and Collaboration (Baltimore: John Hopkins University Press), 1962.

Wolfgang Dietrich, Daniela Ingruber, Josefina Echavarría, Gustavo Esteva and Norbert Koppensteiner (eds.), The Palgrave International Handbook of Peace Studies: A Cultural Perspective (London: Palgrave Macmillan), 2011.

Wright, Quincy, Causes of War and Conditions of Peace (New York: Longmans Green and Co.), 1935.

Zacanas, Agostinho, Security and State in Southern Africa, (London: I.B. Tayn's Publishers), 1999.

Zachner, R.C., Hinduisim (Delhi: Oxford University Press), 1962.

Articles

"Clinton Girds, U.S. for Terrorism War," *USA Today*, May 22, 1998

"Issues Before the Twelfth General Assembly," *International Conciliation*, No. 514 (September 1957).

Abramovitz, Janet N., "Unnatural Disasters," *World Watch* (July/August 1999), Vol. 12.

Andreski, StamsXav, "Pacifism and Human Nature" in West European Pacifism and Strategy for Peace (ed.), Andreski, Stanistav (New York: The Macmillan Press Ltd.), 1985.

Bergstrom, Lass, "What is a Conflict of Interests." in *Journal of Peace Research*, 1970.

Bernard, Jessie, "Parties and Issues in Conflict", *Journal of Conflict Resolution*, June 1957.

Bernard, Jessie, "The Sociological Study of Conflict", International Sociological Association, The Nature of Conflict (Paris: UNESCO), 1957.

Branscomb, Lewis M., "Vulnerability of Critical Infrastructure in the Twenty-first Century," in *Seeds of Disaster, Roots of Response*, eds. Auerswald, Branscomb, La Porte, and Michel-Kerjan (Cambridge: Cambridge University Press), 2006.

Dean G. Pruitt, "Definition of the Situation as a Determinant of International Action," in *International Behaviour: A Social-Psychological Analysis*, ed. Herbert C. Kelman (New York: Holt, Rinehart and Winston), 1965.

Flynn, Stephen E., "The Brittle Superpower," in *Seeds of Disaster, Roots of Response: How Private Action Can Reduce Public Vulnerability*, eds. Philip E. Auerswald, Lewis M. Branscomb, Todd M. La Porte, and Erwann O. Michel-Kerjan (Cambridge: Cambridge University Press), 2006.

Galtung, Johan, "On the Meaning of Non-Violence", *Journal of Peace Research*, No. 2, 1965.

Galtung, Johan, "Violence, Peace and Peace Research", *Journal of Peace Research*, Vol. 3, 1969.

George, Alexander, L. Philip, J. Parley & Alexander Dallin (eds.), US-Soviet Security Cooperation: Achievements, Failures and Lessons (New York: Oxford University Press), 1988.

Haash, Michael, "Societal Approaches to The Study of War", *Journal of Peace Research*, 1965, No. 2.

Haglund, David G., "Lies Damned Lies, and Threat Perceptions", *Comparative Strategy*, Vol. 24, January 2005.

Hodges, Charles, "Why War?" in F.J. Brown, Charles Hodges and I.R. Roucek, *Contemporary World Politics* (New York: John Wiley and Sons), 1940.

Jervis, Robert, "Cooperation Under the Security Dilemma", *World Politics*, Vol. 30, No. 2, January 1978.

King, Gary and Christopher Murray, "Rethinking Human Security", *Political Science Quarterly*, Vol. 116, No. 4.

Knickerbocker, Brad, "Could Global Warming Cause War?", *Christian Science Monitor*, April 19, 2007.

Knorr, Knorr, "Threat Perception," in *Historical Dimensions of National Security Problems*, ed. Klaus Knorr (Lawrence: University Press of Kansas), 1976.

Krahmann, Elke, "From State to Non-State Actors: The Emergence of Security Governance," in *New Threats and New Actors in International Security*, ed. Krahmann (New York: Palgrave, Macmillan), 2005.

Laqueur, Walter, "Post-modern Terrorism," *Foreign Affairs* (September/ October 1996), Vol. 75.

Lewis M. Branscomb, "Vulnerability of Critical Infrastructure in the Twenty-first Century," in *Seeds of Disaster, Roots of Response: How Private Action Can Reduce Public Vulnerability*, eds. Philip E. Auerswald, Lewis M. Branscomb, Todd M. La Porte, and Erwann O. Michel-Kerjan (Cambridge: Cambridge University Press), 2006.

Luttwak, Edward N., "The Traditional approaches to Peace", in W. Scott Thompson and Kenneth M. Jensen, (eds.) *Approaches to Peace: An Intellectual Map* (Washington, DC; United States Institute of Peace Press), 1988.

Mack, Andrew and Pauline Kerr, "The Evolving Security Discourse in the Asia-Pacific", *Washington Quarterly*, Vol. 18, No. 1, 1995.

Mandel, Robert, "Fighting Fire with Fire: Privatizing Counterterrorism", in *Defeating Terrorism: Shaping the New Security Environment*, eds. Russell D. Howard and Reid L. Sawyer (New York: McGraw-Hill), 2003.

Mandel, Robert, "Security and Natural Disasters," *Journal of Conflict Studies* (Fall, 2002), Vol. 22.

Manwaring, Max G. and Courtney E. Prisk, "The Umbrella of Legitimacy," in *Gray Area Phenomena: Confronting the New World Disorder*, ed. Max G. Manwaring (Boulder, CO: Westview Press), 1993.

Neal, Marian, "United Nations Technical Assistance Programs in Haiti," *International Conciliation*, No. 468 (February, 1951).

Neil Munro, "The Pentagon's New Nightmare: An Electronic Pearl Harbor," *Washington Post*, July 16, 1995.

Olshansky, S. Jay, Bruce Carnes, Richard G. Rogers, and Len Smith, "Infectious Diseases—New and Ancient Threats to World Health," *Population Bulletin*, (July 1997), Vol. 52.

Paris, Roland, "Human Security: Paradigm Shift or Hot Air?" *International Security*, Vol. 26, No. 2, 2001.

Philip E. Jacob, "The United Nations and the Struggle for World Welfare," *Pennsylvania School Journal*, 1950.

Pitsuwan, Surin, "Regional Cooperation for Human Security", Keynote address to the International Development Studies Conference on Human Security, The Asian Contribution. October 2007.

Sabina, Alkire, "A Conceptual Framework for Human Security", Centre for Research on Inequality, Human Security, and Ethnicity (CRISE), Working Paper 2, (London: University of Oxford. Press), 2003.

Scott B. MacDonald, "The New 'Bad Guys': Exploring the Parameters of the Violent New World Order," in *Gray Area Phenomena: Confronting the New World Disorder*, ed. Max G. Manwaring (Boulder, CO: Westview Press), 1993.

Shelly, Louise L., "Transnational Organized Crime: An Imminent Threat to the Nation-State?," *Journal of International Affairs* (Winter, 1995), Vol. 48,

Stewart, Frances, "Development and Security", Centre for Research on Inequality, Human Security, and Ethnicity (CRISE), Working Paper 3 (London: University of Oxford), 2004.

Sunga, Lyal S., "The Concept of Human Security: Does it Add Anything of Value to International Legal Theory or Practice?" in *Power and Justice in International Relations Interdisciplinary Approaches to Global Challenges,* edited by Marie-Luisa Frick and Andreas Oberprantacher (New York: Routledge) 2009.

Tadjbakhsh, S., "Human Security In International Organizations: Blessing or Scourge?", *The Human Security Journal*, Volume 4, Summer 2007.

Tenet, George J, "Introductory Remarks," National Defense University U-2 Conference, Washington, D.C., September 17, 1998.

Thomas, Caroline, "Global Governance, Development and Human Security: Exploring the Links", *Third World Quarterly*, Vol. 22, No. 2, 2001.

Wijk, Rob de, "The Limits of Military Power," *Washington Quarterly*, No. 25, Wintry, 2002.

Williams, Phil, "New Context, Smart Enemies," in *Non-State Threats and Future Wars*, ed. Robert J. Bunker (Portland, OR: Frank Cass Publishers), 2003.

Reports

General Assembly, Official Records, 11th Session, 1957, Suppl. No. 18, Report of the Special Committee on the Problems of Hungary (A/3592).

U.N. Document S/1510 (1950)

U.N. Document A/3849, July 14, 1958.

UNDP, Human Development Report, 1994, New York and Oxford: Oxford University Press for the UNDP. 1994.

United Nations Charter, 1945.

United Nations Development Programme (1994): Human Development Report.

United Nations Press Release SG/ISM/110, July 16, 1964.

United Nations, Human Development Report UNDP, 2004.

United Nations, Human Development Report UNDP, 2005.

Encyclopaedia

Encyclopaedia Britanica World Atlas (Chicago: Encyclopaedia Britanicalnca), 1959.

Encyclopaedia of Violence, Peace and Conflict (San Diego: Academics Press), 1992, 3 Volumes.

Microsoft Encarta Encyclopaedia Delux, 2000, Compact Disc.

The Encyclopaedia of Social Sciences, Vol. 13 (New York: Macmillan Free Press).

The World Book Encyclopaedia, Vol. 3, 1992

World Wide Encyclopaedia of the Nations (ed.) by Moshe Y. Sachs, 5 Volumes (New York: Harper and Row), 1967.

Dictionary

Webster Dictionary.

English Dictionary.

Periodicals/Journals.

Alternative (Boulder: Lynne Rienner Publishers).

Asian Review, London.

Asian Survey, Berkeley, California.

Development and Change (London: Sage Publications).

Disarmament and Arms Control, New York.

Eastern World, London.

Gandhi Marg (New Delhi: Gandhi Peace Foundation).

Gandhi Prasang (Allahabad: Basant Behari Jairani Shanti Adhyayan Sansthan).

Harijan—A Journal of Applied Gandhism, 1933-55 (New York: Garland Publishing), 1973.

India Quarterly, New Delhi.

Indian Opinion, 1 April 1905.

International Development Review, Washington.

International Journal on World Peace, A Monthly Journal of UN (New York: Paragon House).

International Social Science Journal (Oxford: Blackwell Publishers Ltd.)

Journal of Asia Studies, Ann Arbor, Mich.

Journal of Conflict Resolution, Ann Arbor, Mich.

Journal of Gandhian Studies (New Delhi: Gandhi Smriti and Darshan Samiti).

Journal of Peace Research, Oslo: International Peace Research Institute.

Mainstream (New Delhi: Perspective Publication Pvt. Ltd.).

Perspective (Atlanta: The Perspective).

Young India, 1919-31 (Ahmedabad: Navajivan Publishing House).

Newspapers

"Membership of Principal United Nations Organs in 2005", United Nations, 15 March 2005. http://www.un.org/News/Press/docs/2005/org 1436.doc.htm.

"Milestones in United Nations History", Department of Public Information, United Nations. http://www.un.org/aboutnn/milestones.htm

Abdul Wadood Shalabi, Islam: Religion of Life; Imam al-Ghezali, The Inner Dimension of Islamic Worship, Website-Islam City.

Abdul Wadood Shalabi, Islam: Religion of Life, http://www.Islamworld.net/nawawi.html.

Financial Times, 24 December 1994

http://www.wordorigins.org/index. php/site/comments/u nited_nation/

Human Security Centre. "What is Human Security." http://www.humansecurityreport.info/index.php?option= content&task=view&id=24&itemid=59

Morning News (Karachi), June 26, 1957.

New York Times, 15 July 1996

Wilton, Wilton, "United Nations", Etymologies & Word Origins: Letter U., WordOrigins.org.

Websites

www. Peacemakers.ca/bibliography

www.globalpolicy.org

www.hugepeace.org

www.non-violence.org

www.questia.com

www.shalomctr.org/html/peace

www.un.org/aboutun/charter

www.un.org/millenium/sg/report

www.unac.org

Index